Philosophy of Religion

A2 Revision Guide for Edexcel

Brian Poxon & Laura Mears

Published by Inducit Learning Ltd trading as PushMe Press

Mid Somerset House, Southover, Wells

Somerset BA5 1UH, United Kingdom

www.pushmepress.com

First published in 2014

ISBN: 978-1-909618-57-2

Contents

How to Get an A Grade

Effective learning involves reducing difficult topics into smaller, "bite-sized" chunks.

Every revision guide, card or coursebook from PushMe Press comes with its own website consisting of summaries, handouts, games, model essays, revision notes and more. Each website community is supported by the best teachers in the country.

At the end of each chapter you will see an `i-pu-sh` web link that you can type into your web browser along with a QR code that can be scanned by our free app.

These links will give you immediate access to the additional resources you need to "Get an A Grade" by providing you with the relevant information needed.

Getting an A Grade has never been easier.

Download our FREE How to Get an A Grade in Ethics App for your phone or tablet and get up-to-date information that accompanies this book and the whole PushMe Press range.

http://philosophy.pushmepress.com/download

Introduction to Philosophy of Religion

At AS level we introduced **EMPIRICISM** and **RATIONALISM**, and considered two empirical arguments for the existence of God - the argument from design (teleological) and the cosmological argument. They are **A POSTERIORI** because they start from looking at the world's features and processes, and conclude (eventually) from these observations, that God exists.

The A2 (Edexcel) course continues to explore empirical arguments, by kicking off with the argument from **RELIGIOUS EXPERIENCE,** which considers whether claims to encounters with the divine constitute solid grounds for belief in God. It will be helpful to utilise some general assessment of the strengths and weaknesses of empirical arguments gained from AS studies for this enterprise. For example, Descartes' contention that we can never be certain whether a malicious demon has duped us into believing something that is not the case may undermine our sense-based assertions. Such problems have led philosophers to seek a non-empirical argument for the existence of God.

RATIONALISM is a theory of knowledge which holds that the most reliable forms of knowledge are gained independently of sensory experience. An **A PRIORI** argument is something true by definition, from reason and before (prior to) empirical evidence. It uses **DEDUCTIVE** reasoning, which means that the conclusion necessarily follows from the premises. Such reasoning will always be expressed in terms of an **ANALYTIC STATEMENT** - a statement where the predicate is contained within the subject, eg married men are husbands.

The only rational argument for the existence of God is the **ONTOLOGICAL ARGUMENT**, and that is our second topic. It attempts to establish that God must necessarily exist, and hence it is a fascinating one, whether you believe it works or not.

Non-existence of God and Critiques of Religious Belief

Traditionally, the onus has been on religion to set out good grounds for belief in God. However, in the twentieth century, a number of sociological and psychological doctrines, which seek to positively assert the non-existence of God, gained momentum. Many are still in popular use today, but to what extent do they succeed in providing adequate grounds for the non-existence of God?

The main challenges come from the areas of **SOCIOLOGY** and **PSYCHOLOGY** but you could also refer to the problem of evil here, provided you focus your material on the question (see AS Philosophy Revision Guide).

KEY TERMS

- **AGNOSTIC** - A person who is undecided about whether God exists or not, or believes there is insufficient evidence to make an assertion either way.

- **ATHEIST** - A person who does not believe in God, or has no knowledge or understanding of the concept (in the Greek: a - without/theos - God).

- **FALSIFICATION** - The means of proving a statement untrue.

- **HUMANISM** - The belief that the highest authority is human reason, and hence that God does not exist. Progress will come from us looking to ourselves to solve problems, not waiting for God to act.

- **MATERIALISM** - The belief that everything that exists is material, and every sensation and experience can be understood through the interaction of matter. This obviously therefore rules out God, angels and demons who are thought to be mainly spiritual beings.

- **NATURALISM** - The belief that knowledge can only be gleaned from the physical, observable world, and not from any supernatural sources. Religion can therefore be understood as a merely social phenomenon.

- **REDUCTIONISM** - Over-simplifying or over-generalising an idea, to the exclusion of certain elements within its scope. For example (one might argue), seeing love as a series of chemical reactions in the brain, and not as a decision to grow a relationship through conversation, mutual service and shared interests.

- **SCEPTICISM** - An attitude of doubt and questioning. This is different to cynicism (tending to be negative about any truth-claim) and gullibility (tending to believe everything one is told).

- **SECULARISM** - The strict separation of the state from religious institutions. The term is used of ideas that are non-religious.

- **UNBELIEF** - The state of not believing; lack of belief or faith.

SOCIOLOGICAL CHALLENGES

Sociology is the study of human interaction, which focuses on ideas and creativity as a product of the society in which they have emerged. The two main thinkers we will consider here are **DURKHEIM** (who held a consensus view), and **MARX** (who held a conflict view).

Emile Durkheim (1858-1917)

As a **FUNCTIONALIST**, Durkheim believed that religion can be best understood as a function of society, or a way of explaining the interaction between people within a particular community. Religion represents, or can be seen as, a **SYMBOL** of certain things which are important to members of society, such as codes of behaviour (ethics). Religious experiences, or feelings of transcendence, can be understood as recognitions of the power of social unity, which emphasises an individual's dependence on the community in which they live.

For example, consider the way you feel at a music festival or sports event. There is a united sense of purpose (in supporting the same team or band), as well as practice (singing the same songs, swaying in time, waving your mobile phone, etc). What you feel may be close to those of a religious experience, yet we do not need to look outside of the realms of material and social phenomena to find the causes.

Hence Durkheim believed that although religion has had a cohesive effect on societies thus far, **WE DO NOT NEED GOD** to explain religious phenomena. In Moral Education, he wrote that man must "discover the rational substitutes for these religious notions that for a long time have served as the vehicle for the most essential moral ideas". (The Free Press, 1961)

Strengths

1. Durkheim's view makes sense of aspects of **PRIMITIVE SOCIETIES** and ancient religions where spiritual belief is caught up with earthly things, such as ancestral worship, or revering a mountain or river.

2. His view recognises the **POSITIVE CONTRIBUTION** of religion, in unifying and giving commonality to groups, families and clans within society.

3. It also seems to account for instances where the **SAME RELIGION MANIFESTS ITSELF IN DIFFERENT WAYS**, depending on the society in which it is functioning. For example, ladies in the Plymouth Brethren will be expected to wear a hat to church, in recognition that they are under the authority of their husband, the Church leader and God. Other Churches, however, such as the Anglican Communion, have women teaching and leading, on a par with men. How else can these differences be understood but by analysing social phenomena, such as the feminist movement?

Weaknesses

1. The challenge within: In seeing religion as a reflection and unifying factor of the views held in a society, Durkheim's view does not leave room for instances where religion has **CHALLENGED THE PREVAILING CULTURE**. For example, Jesus, the Jew, stood up to the Pharisees within the Jewish religion, calling them "whitewashed tombs".

2. The challenge without: **HH Farmer** has pointed to the **UNIVERSAL**, rather than community-based, thrust that religion often brings with it. Rather than sticking within a community, religious believers often feel called to expound their message to other cultural, social and ethical groups. This is much more outward-looking than Durkheim's ideas suggest.

3. Durkheim's ideas seem to assume the non-existence of God, rather than make a case for it. Religious beliefs and practices can reflect and shape some aspects of their communities and bring unity, without ruling out the existence of an external reality. In seeing religious belief as merely a function of society, Durkheim may be laying himself open to a charge of **REDUCTIONISM** (see key terms).

KARL MARX (1818-1883)

Karl Marx held a **CONFLICT VIEW**. He was writing at a time when there was a clear division between rich and poor. He saw society in a state of tension between the "owners of the means of production", and the workers.

As a **HEGELIAN**, (follower of the philosopher Hegel), Marx believed that through conflict and the resulting synthesis, mankind is heading toward what he called the "Absolute Spirit", which is a supernatural standard of peace and justice. Marx's version of this is called **DIALECTICAL MATERIALISM**, because of his focus on material goods as central to the human condition.

He believed that as the poor recognise their power to control the means of production, they will no longer have need of the **MAN-MADE CONSTRUCTS** that have kept their aspirations in check. Marx believed that a major construct, that keeps the poor in submission, is religion. Through sermons and Bible teachings which focus on their reward in heaven, the poor will be deterred from striving for justice, giving the rich free rein over the means of production.

"Blessed are the meek, for they will inherit the earth." (Matthew 5:5)

In calling religion the "opium of the people", Marx was saying that belief in God acts as a **SEDATIVE OR ANTIDOTE TO PRESENT SUFFERING**. In rejecting their condition and improving themselves materially, the poor will realise their error and reject religion as "illusory".

Strengths

1. Marx's view of religion, as a way of keeping the poor oppressed, tallies with the **HISTORICAL RECORD**; many church-going politicians tried to block the abolition of slavery in the 19th C.
2. In arguing for a society where the community collectively owned the means of production, Marx was emphasising **EQUALITY OVER HIERARCHY** and privilege. With the Church manifesting the latter with its magnificent buildings, ownership of land, and layers of authority from archbishops to laity, it seemed sensible to conceive that a **SECULAR PHILOSOPHY** could bring about the desired parity, where the Church had failed.

Weaknesses

1. **MATERIALISM IS UNFULFILLING** - Marx held that the poor are dependent on religion because their lives are unfulfilled by material objectives, but many thinkers and commentators would challenge whether materialism can work in this way; consider for example, the high incidence of depression and suicide amongst the rich.
2. **RELIGION IS TRANSFORMING** - Max Weber argued that religion is a force for social change. Religious people have been at the forefront of movements, such as the abolition of slavery, which was spear-headed by Christians including Methodists and Quakers.
3. **RELIGION IS ENDURING** - In Marx's day, as in the present time, it is not just the poor who believe that religion is an important part of life. In all societies and ages where spirituality has been squeezed out, it has popped back up. Communist China has seen an explosion in the number of underground churches, which include members of all economic groups.

PSYCHOLOGICAL CHALLENGES

Many psychologists would look for the causes of religious phenomena in the interactions of the human mind, rather than in some objective spiritual reality.

Sigmund Freud (1856-1939)

Freud popularised the belief that the mind is made up of **THREE LAYERS**; the conscious self (**EGO**) of which we are all aware; the unconscious self (**ID**), which is made up of repressed thoughts and memories, and the conscience (**SUPER-EGO**), which is entirely a product of our environment and upbringing.

Freud believed that at the heart of the psychological need for religion was **GUILT**. This drew on a popular anthropological idea of the time, known as the **PRIMAL HORDE**. At some point in our ancestry, the young men in the tribe, frustrated by the control of the women exerted by the dominant male, rose up and killed their father. Afterwards, they felt guilt, which fed their need to reinstate the father figure. For Freud, religion is a **PROJECTION OF UNCONSCIOUS NEEDS** in the id. We need a father figure; one isn't to hand, so we employ a substitute in the Father God. These needs are then reinforced through the super-ego, which insists on rituals and behaviours which keep our primitive, unconscious desires in check.

Freud is careful to emphasise that he is **NOT CONCLUDING THAT RELIGION IS A LIE**.

> *"Illusions need not necessarily be false - that is to say, unrealisable or in contradiction to reality." (The Future of an Illusion)*

Freud considers his approach to be a scientific one, which assumes that the only knowledge that can be gained is derived from the scientific method. Since we can never scientifically prove God's existence, religion must be **NO MORE THAN WISH-FULFILMENT**.

Strengths

1. The parallels between the theory of the primal horde and the **GENESIS ACCOUNT** are startling. Christians would agree with Freud that at the heart of the human condition is guilt, induced by the violation of a law: Adam and Eve rebelled against God by eating fruit from the tree he had commanded them not to eat.
2. Freud's view has drawn largely on Darwinistic evolution, which is still alive and thriving today. It has also been influenced by respected thinkers such as Rousseau and Hume, who believed that religion was a distortion of human reason.

Weaknesses

1. Karl **POPPER** questions whether Freud's method really is as scientific as he asserts. His ideas are largely based on theory, rather than on hard evidence, and any challenge is met by an alternative explanation, preventing **FALSIFICATION.**
2. Hans **KÜNG** criticises Freud's theory for being a **CIRCULAR ARGUMENT**. Drawing on Feuerbach's ideas, he begins from the assumption that religion is a projection, so it is not surprising that he arrives at the conclusion that religion is wish-fulfilment.
3. **KÜNG** also makes the point that although one's religious views can be heavily influenced by their relationship with their earthly father, this does not mean that God is purely a projection. You may also like to consider religious believers who seem to have excellent relationships with their fathers.

Confusions to avoid

- **BE CAREFUL** how you write about these scholars' views of religion. It would be wrong to speak of Durkheim, Marx or Freud as "anti-religion". They all see the benefits of religion to society. Freud, for example, believes it can provide a means of protection, hope and dignity to the individual. Yet neither are they pro-religion. They all share in common the belief that in a more progressive society, we will have no need of religion.

- **SEE THE DISTINCTIVENESS** of each of their views of religion. Although they commonly share a rejection of religion as an important element of a progressive society, consider what is different about the words each use to describe religion; "symbol" (Durkheim); "opium" (Marx); "illusion" (Freud).

- **AVOID THE ASSUMPTION** that sociology or psychology will inevitably lead to atheism. Many are religious believers because they do not limit knowledge to their particular scientific remit.

Key quotes

1. *"Of all choices, atheism requires the greatest faith, as it demands that one's limited store of human knowledge is sufficient to exclude the possibility of God." Francis Collins of the Human Genome Project*

2. *"I do believe. Help me overcome my unbelief." Mark 9:24*

3. *"Religion is the sigh of the oppressed creature, the heart of a heartless world, the soul of the soulless environment. It is the opium of the people." Karl Marx in the Introduction to the Critique of the Hegelian Philosophy of Right*

4. *"Those who cling to [illusions] do so because of the comfort they bring, God taking the place of a benevolent father, needed later in life, where threats remain but an actual father is not there to help." Sigmund Freud in The Future of an Illusion*

GET MORE HELP

Get more help with non-existence of God and critiques of religious belief by using the links below:

http://i-pu.sh/C3J60W45

Religious Language

KEY TERMS

- **ANALOGY** - When two things are compared as similar because they share common features, eg the brain is like a computer.

- **ANALYTIC STATEMENT** - The internal logic of the sentence gives it its meaning.

- **BLIK** - A way of looking at the world. (Hare)

- **COGNITIVE** - Language that carries meaning, and puts forward a proposition, provable true or false.

- **EQUIVOCAL** - Where the same word is used in two different and unrelated ways, eg someone is at the sink, and someone is starting to sink.

- **FALSIFICATION PRINCIPLE** - A statement is putting forward a genuine scientific proposition if there are conditions under which that proposition can be falsified.

- **LANGUAGE GAME** - Individual terms have meaning because of the way they are used within a group. (Wittgenstein) A form of life is the activities that the group performs using this language.

- **MYTH** - A story which conveys a religious belief or truth.

- **NON-COGNITIVE** - Does not carry meaning in a factual manner, and is not putting forward a proposition provable true or false.

- **REALIST** - Claims that refer to something that objectively exists, not something that exists just within the community of believers (anti-realist).

- **STRONG VERIFICATION PRINCIPLE** - A statement carries meaning only if it is either analytic or empirically verifiable.

- **UNIVOCAL** - Where the same word is used in two different contexts but means the same thing: a black cat and a cat on the mat. The word cat has the one meaning in both sentences.

- **VIA NEGATIVA** (the Apophatic Way) - The way of talking about God by saying what He is not.

- **VIA POSITIVA** (the Cataphatic Way) - The way of talking about God by saying what He is.

- **WEAK VERIFICATION PRINCIPLE** - A statement carries meaning only if it is "either analytic or can be shown by experience to be probably true". (**BURNS** and **LAW**)

THE VIA NEGATIVA (VN)

The **VN** is also known as **THE APOPHATIC WAY**, taken from the Greek verb apophēmi, which means "to deny". The **VN** is an attempt to speak of God using **NEGATION** and stems from the mystical religious tradition, which emphasises the quest to find unity with God. However, God lies **BEYOND** ordinary perception and cannot be described in the same way in which we describe other objects: for example, this teapot is green or that sweatshirt is large. God cannot be described adequately using "the positive", because He is **INEFFABLE**; He defies expression or description.

When we attempt to use the affirmative and use words such as "powerful" about a strong person, we mean something completely different when we say God is powerful. This is called **EQUIVOCAL LANGUAGE**.

We can get some knowledge of God, by the way of the negative - by saying what **GOD IS NOT** - and joining such "not" statements together to arrive at a closer idea of **WHAT GOD IS**. In this sense, language for the person who advocates the **VN** is not descriptive or containing knowledge (**COGNITIVE**), but, as Cole notes, being used in a "functional and evocative" way.

For example, I could get directions to Fraser Street by a series of negatives (don't turn right at the junction). **MAIMONIDES** (12th C), used the example of a ship; by about the time of the 10th negative answer to questions concerning what a ship is, the enquirer had almost arrived at an accurate idea of a ship.

The illustration of the man asking directions works when there are only three or four options. He knew where Fraser Street was because we discounted every other option for him. But can we use this way for a description of God? No, but with a series of questions, and by joining the answers together, we should get closer to what God is via the negative.

The VN has a long history. You may recognise some Platonic tones, where there is an ultimate good beyond the cave world we inhabit, and of which we only see shadows. In the 3rd C **PLOTINUS**, a neo-Platonist (a movement which built on the work of Plato but also altered/adapted Platonism), argued that it was impossible to know the good as it is entirely separate from the world.

ST AUGUSTINE (4th C) and **DIONYSIUS** (also known as **PSEUDO-DIONYSIUS**, 6th C), both wrote about the use of the VN as part of the mystical tradition. Dionysius noted three stages, or "states of knowledge" (**JORDAN**) when talking about God:

1. VIA NEGATIVA

States what God is not, because God is beyond all human categories of knowledge and being. He is "not" anything which we would try to describe such as "life" or "oneness" or "good". "There is no speaking of it, nor name, nor knowledge of it. Darkness and light, error and truth ... [God] is none of these." (**HICK**) So God is beyond any positive assertion.

2. STATE OF AFFIRMATION

Affirm what we know God is: we do know God has been revealed in the Bible as good and just. But these terms can only be taken symbolically.

3. **QUALIFICATION**

When we say God is loving, He is utterly beyond loving as affirmed in the mystical tradition, which is always looking "beyond" descriptions which are limited by human language. Maimonides also argues that the **INEFFABILITY** of God cannot be expressed by positive assertions about God.

Strengths

1. The **VN** avoids **ANTHROPOMORPHISM** (describing God in human terms). It can stop people getting the wrong idea about God as being "warrior like", and taking this literally as saying that God is some kind of Divine Warrior. The **VN** argues that God is entirely "not" like us.

2. **LIMITATIONS OF LANGUAGE** as a vessel to adequately describe God. Reason, logic and arguments are blunt tools when it comes to the spiritual mystery that is God. **AHLUWALIA** points out that anything other than the idea that God is mystery makes God too small.

3. **INEFFABILITY** - The **VN** goes beyond our everyday experience, and allows for recognition that God is not "over there" or, indeed, located anywhere, or "like this". God is entirely ineffable.

Weaknesses

1. **CONTRADICTION** between God's ineffability and the revelation of the Bible of the physical person Jesus Christ. Dionysius may in fact have accepted Christ as "God revealed", ie, a manifestation of God, but this is not "God hidden", who remains ineffable.

2. **REALIST** affirmations made by believers seem to go further. God has certain positive characteristics, for example, a warrior or a mighty king. Within many of the world's religions, **TRUTH CLAIMS ARE NOT NEGATIVELY EXPRESSED**. Judaism, Christianity and Islam believe that God has in fact revealed his nature and affirms that nature in their respective scriptures. Christian theologians argue that at the heart of the Christian faith is the affirmation that God is involved in the world, rather than beyond matter, life, humanity and any description.

3. **DAVIES** does not think negatives can get us closer to the actual thing we are trying to describe.

4. **BEGS THE QUESTION**, as every time we give a negative answer, we are showing that we already know what God is, and so the VN only works for those who already know who and what God is, which seems self-contradictory.

5. **DEATH BY A THOUSAND QUALIFICATIONS** by continually saying God is not this, and God is not that, **FLEW** contends that there is little difference between saying that "God is anything we can affirm" and "God does not exist" - by saying that God is invisible, soundless, incorporeal and so on, there is very little difference between our definition of God and our definition of nothingness; we argue God out of existence by "a thousand qualifications". (**AHLUWALIA**)

Key quotes

1. *"We do not know what God is. God Himself does not know what He is because He is not anything. Literally God is not, because He transcends being." John Scot Erigena (9th C).*

2. *"God is utterly transcendent, totally ineffable, indescribable and incapable of being conceptualised by the human mind." Hick on Dionysius*

3. *"Perhaps a more balanced approach [than complete reliance on the VN] would be to argue that we need both the via negativa and the via positiva." Wilkinson and Campbell*

4. *"The negative way is the way of darkness, suffering, silence, letting go, and even nothingness." Sheldrake and Fox*

Confusions to avoid

People who take the VN approach do think it is possible to talk about God, but God is beyond what we say in human language. To say God is loving does not have any frame of reference as we only know what loving is in human understanding. God is "beyond assertion". (**DIONYSIUS**) But anything we say about God, even the negative, does not tell us about God, so also "beyond denial" as language is **EQUIVOCAL**. So the experience of God is real, and is what the mystics seek by union with Him, and although the "infinite can penetrate the finite" there can be "no corresponding language statements made" and hence God is ineffable.

THE USE OF ANALOGY

AQUINAS was very familiar with the work of both Dionysius and Maimonides. Aquinas rejected the via negativa because he thought that it is possible to speak positively of God in non-literal and analogical terms. Hence he rejected **EQUIVOCAL LANGUAGE** as it has no link between what we say using our language to describe things available to us (ie something is beautiful or good) and how we use the same language when referring to God.

Does this mean that when we talk about beautiful and good in our language, this means exactly the same when applied to God? This sort of use of language is known as **UNIVOCAL** and Aquinas went on to reject this also, as things do not mean exactly the same when they are used in description of a thing in this world and when used to describe God. "God is strong" and "I am strong" do not mean the same thing.

Aquinas' alternative was to make use of **ANALOGICAL LANGUAGE**. which carries some kind of shared understanding between what it means when describing an object and when that same term is used to describe God. There is some **COMPARISON** that can be made between two different things when using analogy. **WE CAN SAY SOMETHING.** For example, to say a computer is like a brain is to note similarities between those two things, like they both have a kind of electrical circuit, they both receive input and produce output and they both process data, without saying they are the same.

Aquinas goes on to define two types of analogy that can be used. The first is the **ANALOGY OF ATTRIBUTION**. This is when there is a **CAUSAL RELATIONSHIP** that can be described by the terms being used. For example, if someone says that the piece of furniture is good, we can say that the carpenter must be good. Now, we do not mean that the carpenter has a polished finish and finely shaped handles (that would be univocal language); neither do we say that there is no connection between how we are using good to describe the piece of furniture and good to describe the carpenter (that would be equivocal language). We see that there is some causal link between saying that the furniture is good, and that the carpenter is good. **BECAUSE** the carpenter is good, the furniture is good. The example that Aquinas gave is that of a bull's urine. If one sees a sample of the bull's urine and it is healthy (not cloudy etc), then we can **ATTRIBUTE THIS TO THE HEALTH OF THE BULL**. There is a causal link between the two.

Aquinas argued that this meant we can, by the analogy of attribution, begin to **AFFIRM SOME THINGS OF GOD**. As God is the creator of the world, **WE CAN ATTRIBUTE THE GOODNESS OF THE WORLD TO THE GOODNESS OF GOD** in the same way we can say that the good quality of the urine is due to the good quality of the bull.

Aquinas' second use of analogy is the **ANALOGY OF PROPORTION**. This simply means when we use a word like "good", and we say God is good, what we are saying is that **THERE IS A WAY TO BE GOOD THAT BELONGS TO GOD**, just like there is a way for a person to be good that is appropriate for a person. There is an understanding between the use of the words, but there is also a difference, as **EACH IS USED PROPORTIONATELY TO THE SUBJECT**. So, when we say humans are powerful and God is powerful, we are saying that God is powerful in a greater way than humans could ever be.

We are saying that good is what it means for something to act well according to its **NATURE** - for a computer to be good is very different from what it means for an umbrella to be good, but both have their way of being good. This is the way in which Aquinas is using these terms (such as good or powerful), and it has links back to Aristotle's function argument.

SO BY ANALOGY THERE ARE FORMS OF LANGUAGE THAT CAN PROVIDE SOME WAYS OF TALKING ABOUT GOD THAT CARRY MEANING AND UNDERSTANDING - there is something in common in the terms being used - which is more than there is in equivocal use of language, and affirmative in a way that the via negativa could never be.

RAMSEY also made use of analogy to argue that it is possible to speak meaningfully about God. Ramsey noted that we can use **MODELS** when talking about God. If we say that God is loving, we have a model of loving because we know what loving is in human terms; the example of it we see in human interactions acts as some kind of model and gives us understanding of what loving means.

However, because we are talking about **GOD'S LOVE**, we have to **QUALIFY** our model. The models are useful, but they do not paint the whole picture - they are limited. Whilst humans model love, God is **INFINITELY LOVING**; without this qualification, we are just left with our model of what human love looks like.

This model and qualifier idea can lead to an insight into the quality being spoken about, in this case, the love of God, and Ramsey called such insight a **DISCLOSURE**. At this point, the qualified model has helped take us "beyond" to some disclosure about God. He used this argument to criticise the narrowness of the **VERIFICATION PRINCIPLE**, which, with its focus on empirical facts, did not take account of the empirical meaning found through personal "disclosure experiences".

Strengths

1. Analogy avoids **ANTHROPOMORPHISM**, where God is given human qualities, because both Aquinas' analogy of proportion and Ramsey's models and qualifiers, avoid saying that "this describes God". They both qualify their use of language when applying things found in human experience to God.

2. **POSITIVE** - Analogy enables a person to say something positive of God which might be more appropriate to the experience of most believers than that of the **VN**. At the same time, both Aquinas and Ramsey acknowledge the limited nature of language when used to try to describe God.

3. **COMPLEXITY** - By taking human experience as a starting reference point, Aquinas and Ramsey think that analogy can give insight into complex ideas such as God as all-loving and all-powerful.

Weaknesses

1. **ATTRIBUTING EVIL** - Should we not also attribute the evil of the world to God? This would then weaken Aquinas' idea of what type of God he is wishing to put forward by the use of analogy. **HUME** argues that we tend to use whatever analogy supports our existing belief. In looking at the world as it is, what qualities would we attribute to its maker? **DAWKINS** argues that it is the world that would indicate a fight for survival rather than a world which can be attributed to a loving God.

2. **ASSUMES SOMETHING** - To use the analogy of attribution

assumes we know something of nature of God in order for us to say that "a good world" is indicative of "a good God", so this may be confirming what a person already believes. Analogy also "assumes some similarity between the humans and God" (**EYRE**); the opposite conclusion might be equally valid, that God and humans share no similarities.

3. **SWINBURNE** has argued that we do not need to use analogy at all, as univocal language is sufficient when talking of God. When we call humans good and God good, we are using the word univocally, which is sufficient, carries meaning and can be understood.

4. **BARTH** has criticised analogy because knowledge of God cannot be gained from creation. Knowledge of God by its very nature, argues Barth, is only given by revelation from God.

Key quotes

1. *"It seems that no word can be used literally of God." Aquinas in Summa Theologiae*

2. *"Analogy enables language drawn from the spatio-temporal universe to be applied to a timeless and spaceless God and for this language to be held to be true, but the content of this language is extremely limited." Vardy*

3. *"The most we can say is that: Under the analogy of attribution, God has whatever it takes to create goodness (for instance) in human beings - but we don't know what it is. Under the analogy of proportion, it is true that God is good in whatever way it is appropriate for God to be good. We do not, however, know in what way it is appropriate for God to be good." Vardy*

4. *"Religious language consists of 'disclosure models' that are made up of both analogy and existential depth." Jackson on Ramsey*

Confusions to avoid

Both Aquinas and Ramsey are very clear that the use of analogy is still limited by human language. It would be wrong to say that they think they have found a way in which God can be adequately described. If you said that the way Usain Bolt runs is similar to the way in which an arrow leaves the bow and reaches its target, you are not saying that Bolt is a thin aluminium alloy shaft attached to an arrowhead fired from a 60 pound bow. What you are saying is that the speed with which he is released from the blocks has similarities to the way in which the arrow is fired from the bow, as is the way in which he runs straight and true, and with speed, towards a final target. The archery analogy "points towards"; it helps provide a comparison which highlights similar features between one thing and another.

THE USE OF MYTH

A **MYTH** is a story which conveys a religious belief or truth, or which points to a deeper reality, but is not factually true. A myth can include the use of symbols or metaphors or other literary devices, which are used to convey important truth(s) or unfold a worldview. Myths often deal with issues of ultimate significance such as the creation of the world, human identity, suffering, evil, morality and purpose.

Many Christians think that the **CREATION STORIES** are not meant to be read in a factual manner, but as myth, and are attempts by the writer(s) to point the reader towards things like structure within the universe, rhythm and order within creation, a creator who desires a relationship with humanity and the idea of work being part of the purpose of mankind. To ask whether a myth is "true" in a historical or scientific sense is the wrong question, just as one would not ask if poetry is "true".

As creation stories convey 'truths' about the worldview of that community, it could be argued that there is **COGNITIVE MEANING** contained within them and this will be important when we come to study the **VERIFICATION PRINCIPLE** and how that principle seeks to measure how meaning is carried in language.

In the 20th C **BULTMANN** argued that the New Testament must be **DEMYTHOLOGISED** if truth is to be discovered in it. Scientific understanding will not allow us to read scripture, and accounts such as a literal virgin birth, as previous generations did, which was in a very simplistic, "supernatural" and non-scientific way. The writers of the Gospels who weave their stories around the life of Jesus did so because they wanted to portray Jesus as having miraculous powers and draw the reader towards that conclusion, which would then require a response to Jesus. They would also attach details to the stories about Jesus to emphasise the message they were trying to convey, such as when they describe Jesus as conversing with a prostitute, or when they place Pharisees (religious rulers of the day) together with "sinners", both of which would never have occurred. Bultmann argues that these little stories, created for emphasis of the message of Christ, are not essential for the message; there is a need for these accounts to be demythologised in order to return to the message of Christ.

WILKINSON and **CAMPBELL** note that, "perhaps Bultmann's approach is mistaken. Rather than stripping out the myths from Scripture, perhaps the task of the believer might not be to deny that the myths are myth, but rather to accept that they are myths and to try to discern what truths they might contain".

Strengths

1. **TRUE MEANING** - The use of myth utilises story and a more flowing, lively and memorable narrative when trying to convey truths that might not fit other mediums. This might broaden our understanding of truths which could not be outlined in a factual manner but which nonetheless carry meaning.

2. **STORY** - There is a recent move to retell history such as the events of the Tudor Court as story, and, in these stories, factual truth is used where it suits the story, but the fabrication of other details adds to the overall message the historian is trying to get across. However, it could be argued that the use of the word "myth" is inappropriate here, as there is still enough factual history in the retelling of the Tudor period for example, unlike the creation myths, which for many readers contain very little, or even no, factual truth at all.

3. **MORAL IMPETUS** - Religious language, **Braithwaite** argues, is meant to assert moral claims which express the desire to act in a certain way. In this way, they carry meaning in a wider way than can be measured by the **VERIFICATION OR FALSIFICATION THEORIES**. Braithwaite claims that the stories in which the truth is outlined give **MORAL IMPETUS** for how people should live towards one another, and do not need to be true for the "religious person to … resolve to live a certain way of life" (**JORDAN** et al) after listening to the truths contained within them.

Weaknesses

1. **CHALLENGE OF SCIENCE** - The stories may have fitted a world in which the beginning of the universe was mystery, but now we have the theory of the Big Bang, it is questionable if the use of myth is still needed to convey truths or, in the words of **WILKINSON** and **CAMPBELL**, "fill gaps" which now no longer need filling.

2. **CULTURALLY DETERMINED** - "Mythological imagery has a tendency to be culturally determined", **AHLUWALIA**. Many religious believers want to say that there are central truths, or even a central Truth, that their sacred text is conveying, and these core elements might get missed or misinterpreted if myth is the medium in which those truths are told. "If a myth is just a made-up story like a fable, then it does not communicate any truths about God". (**TAYLOR**)

3. **COMPETING MYTHS** "There is no agreed criteria for judging which myth communicates truth." (**TAYLOR**) Napoleon once

noted that history is the lies of the winner; how do we know that the myths that have survived are not those from the dominant worldview? Do such stories still contain truths or are they more like propaganda? Myths may change over time to respond to current concerns so that it is difficult to assess if they contain eternal truths. Taylor notes that an example of this is how in recent years Christians have interpreted the "dominion over nature" idea portrayed in the creation myth as containing the instruction to "steward" (caretake) creation, which has a very different connotation than that of dominion.

4. **FLEW** might argue that it is convenient how stories in the Bible that were once held to be factually true, such as the creation story or that of Noah's ark, are now viewed as mythological, and carrying "deeper-than-literal" truth. If this is the case, have Christians who take this line shifted the goalposts as it were, and maintained the truth of holy scripture but by a disingenuous re-reading of text; is this "death by a thousand qualifications"? Christians might reply that this is now a significantly better way of reading the text, which is more true to the writer's intentions. But in doing so have they reduced sacred text to a series of nice pieces of advice, rather than the giving of Truth (with a capital, realist T)? Yet many Christians do not read the creation story or that of Noah and other stories, as myth, but as literally true.

Key quotes

1. *"The more real things get, the more like myths they become."*
   Fassbinder

2. *"Myths are stories that express meaning, morality or motivation. Whether they are true or not is irrelevant."* *Shermer*

3. *"Through myth, believers are able to communicate something positive about God, without having to resort to the via negativa."* *Ahluwalia*

4. *"Myths and creeds are heroic struggles to comprehend the truth in the world."* *Adams*

5. *"It is a sure sign that a culture has reached a dead end when it is no longer intrigued by its myths."* *Marcus*

Confusions to avoid

A clear definition of myth needs to be used when writing about this use of religious language. Myth as "old wives' tales" is not the way in which the term is understood in theology and by religious believers.

Different parts of sacred text are interpreted in different ways, so that when a believer says that the creation story is myth, this does not mean that a) it is less important than other parts of scripture or that b) the rest of the text is myth. Many Christians argue that there are different genres in scripture, such as myth, history and poetry, and the reading of each in a particular way is respectful of literary interpretation.

THE USE OF SYMBOL

20th C philosopher **PAUL TILLICH** wrote extensively about the use of **SYMBOL** in religious language, and how such could carry meaning.

Tillich argued that God is the **GROUND OF ALL BEING**, or **BEING ITSELF**. A crude illustration might help explain what Tillich meant by this: If you imagine a number of things on a shopping list, such as carrots, milk and tea bags, God is not one more thing on the list like any other object, which could or could not exist (many theologians have criticised **DAWKINS** for his description of God as one more thing on the list of contingent things). God is the list itself - God is the ground of all other things, being itself. For Tillich, God is the **ULTIMATE CONCERN**. If this is so, how is it possible to speak of, or journey towards, such Being (not "a being")?

For Tillich, **SYMBOLS** help us in this journey as they point **BEYOND THEMSELVES** and, "open up new levels of reality". Just as a flag of a country can no longer be viewed by the winning athlete who sees it raised at the Olympics as a piece of coloured cloth but something that seems to take them on a journey of pride in themselves, their country and all that the flag means and represents, so a symbol such as bread and wine takes a person beyond the elements of bread and wine to ultimate reality, to being itself.

An example of a symbol is water, which is used in many religions. When water is used in a religious ritual, it is a symbol that enables those who are immersed in it to have the experience of purity or spiritual cleansing, perhaps even a sense of a fresh beginning. Now the water does not and cannot actually provide those things, but rather symbolises or points towards Being itself, which can be accessed through this participatory symbol. The way in which religious language is understood, and being used here, is both **EVOCATIVE** and **POETIC**, but Tillich is clearly claiming that it also carries some **COGNITIVE, IF NOT LITERAL, MEANING**.

Tillich used examples such as music and painting to help us understand how symbols move us towards a deeper reality, releasing in the observer something which only that symbol could do. However, to really understand Tillich it is necessary to realise that **STATEMENTS** about God, such as God is love, are symbolic too; it is not just physical objects that act as symbols but language has to be symbolic when talking of God as he is Being Itself (not just another being).

EYRE et al explain this idea when they write that whilst "we are familiar with religious symbols such as the cross or the bread and wine ... " what Tillich is suggesting is that even statements such as "God is good" are symbolic rather than literal ... Tillich refers to God as "the ground of being", and suggests that this is "the only non-symbolic statement that can be made about God". Here Tillich is meaning that statements about God are symbolic and participate in the reality of God, without meaning that language has ever captured what God is in a literal way.

To summarise Tillich and religious language - a symbol:

1. **ELICITS A RESPONSE**.

2. **EVOKES PARTICIPATION** in the intended meaning (be careful here - look at the third quotation below).

3. **POINTS TO SOMETHING** beyond itself.

4. **MAY BE UNDERSTOOD** on a number of levels.

Strengths

1. **UNIVERSAL** - We use symbols widely in art, poetry or music to point us to something which is difficult to express, and this "beyond" to which it points does carry meaning for us.

2. **AVOIDS ANTHROPOMORPHISM** - The symbols of God's power and other attributes are not interpreted in ways which "describe" God or bring Him down to a human level; the opposite happens as symbols point towards Being itself rather than a being who is like a person.

3. **METAPHORIC** - It could be argued that we do use language in a symbolic or metaphoric way all the time. When we say that we could murder a cup of tea, we are not meaning that literally, but symbolically pointing towards the fact of our thirst.

Weaknesses

1. **NON-COGNITIVE** - Symbols enable us to delve deeper into human experience rather than act as something that point us to any ultimate reality in which they participate. **EYRE** et al note that this is how **RANDALL** interprets symbol: it does not point to any external reality.

2. **AMBIGUOUS** - Hick has questioned what Tillich means when he argues that a symbol "participates" in the thing towards which it points and "somehow represents the event and gives access to a deeper level of understanding of the event". **(TAYLOR)** Tillich argues that music takes us to a reality beyond the actual notes to communicate feelings and emotions and evokes beliefs. How?

3. **MEANINGLESS** - What meaning does religious language have if it is symbolic and not literal? Is it actually saying anything of meaning? And even if such might carry meaning, who is to know if that meaning is correct, as what the symbol points towards is not available to us through experience?

Key quotes

1. *"Symbolic language alone is able to express the ultimate because it transcends the capacity of any finite reality to express it directly."* Tillich

2. *"When the Bible speaks of the kingdom of God, the symbol of a kingdom is concerned with the ultimate reality of God's power and rule."* Jordan et al

3. *"Symbols are meaningful on account of their relationship to the ultimate. There is an idolatrous tendency to confuse the symbol (eg a holy person, book, doctrine, or ritual) with the ultimate."* Tillich

Confusions to avoid

Signs do not participate in the reality of that to which they point, and can be replaced "for reasons of convention or expediency". Symbols do participate and also "cannot be replaced except after an historic catastrophe that changes the reality of the nation which it symbolises". (Tillich)

THE VERIFICATION PRINCIPLE (VP)

Having studied ways in which it is proposed that religious language carries meaning, the **VP** puts forward a test to see if in fact that is the case.

From 1907 onwards a group of philosophers who had a scientific background attempted to define how meaning is carried in language and, according to **PHELAN**, "to eliminate metaphysics from philosophy". This group, known as the **VIENNA CIRCLE**, was influenced by **WITTGENSTEIN'S** proposal that the meaning of a proposition being put forward lay in knowing what is pictured by those words. The circle also built on the work of **HUME**, who had argued that statements only contain meaning if they are **ANALYTIC, APRIORI AND NECESSARY** or **SYNTHETIC, A POSTERIORI AND CONTINGENT**. This distinction became known as **HUME'S FORK**. The Vienna Circle saw themselves as guardians of language in judging what statements carried meaning; the metaphysical did not, as it did not meet the criteria outlined by either Wittgenstein or Hume.

AJ AYER, who, I am sure, impressed his first wife by visiting the Vienna Circle whilst on honeymoon in 1932, approved of the rigorous test that the VP put towards language, and he felt that it helped philosophy to have clear guidelines concerning what language carries meaning and what doesn't. Building on the work of the Vienna Circle, Ayer published Language, Logic and Truth at the age of 25, and this became enormously popular as a classical definition of the Circle's **LOGICAL POSITIVISM**, whereby meaning is established in language.

Within this work, Ayer stated that a statement only carried meaning if it was: a **TAUTOLOGY** - true by definition (bachelors are unmarried men, which is an apriori statement), or **VERIFIABLE IN PRINCIPLE** by evidence (there is life on at least one other planet - there might not be, but, in principle with the development of technology, we could one day find out, ie verify it using our senses; this is an a posteriori statement).

Ayer's addition of the words **IN PRINCIPLE** to the verification criteria is often seen as progression from the very strict definition of meaning that was arrived at by the VP. The verification demanded by the Vienna Circle required direct observation of an event for it to have any meaning, which automatically ruled out any historical events. Ayer's **VERIFICATION IN PRINCIPLE** meant that historical and future events could in principle be verified. Ayer used an illustration from **SCHLICK**, a member of the Vienna Circle, to make this point when he suggested that one day we may be able to verify if "there are mountains on the far side of the moon". As such a statement was verifiable in principle it carried meaning.

In his first edition of Language, Logic and Truth, Ayer also wrote of a type of verification called **WEAK VERIFICATION**, in which he argued that there are general laws which cover many individual cases. To check that "a body tends to expand when heated" is impossible on a case-by-case basis, ie, impossible to verify; however, this is most probably the case, and the principle of weak verification accepts that there is meaning in such statements. This was different to **STRONG VERIFICATION**, which was when a statement was conclusively verified by sense-experience and observation.

Later, following much criticism of these criteria, Ayer would reject the strong and weak verification distinction, suggesting that the latter allowed for too many statements to carry meaning, whilst strong verification was too difficult a demand for most statements. He went on to develop a different distinction by arguing for **DIRECTLY AND INDIRECTLY VERIFIABLE OBSERVATION STATEMENTS**. Direct verification was possible where a person could check that, for example, "the tide is out at Weston-super-Mare", or that "exit signs are green" - these are verifiable by observation. Indirect observations are statements about things which cannot be directly observed. **TAYLOR**, in interpreting Ayer's criteria, describes these statements as those that "could be verified if other directly verifiable evidence could support it". This would be the case, for example, with the observation of quarks, where all the evidence of other observable things points to their existence, even though quarks themselves are not directly observable.

Ayer makes clear that any religious or metaphysical statements fail the test as they a) are not tautological in nature or b) ever verifiable, observable, or supported by other direct observation statements. Thus, for Ayer, **METAPHYSICAL** language is **MEANINGLESS**. While disciplines such as history and science put forward either tautologies or propositions that are verifiable, metaphysical language (which includes religious language claims for God) does not meet such a standard. They are "factual non-sense", as there is actually no way of verifying such claims.

Strengths

1. **RIGOROUS** - The attempt to define what is meaningful and meaningless could be seen as useful in helping to filter out statements that seem to be philosophically valid but in fact do not actually say anything. As **COLE** notes, Ayer felt that "through the misuse of language people assumed that because a word existed there must be some corresponding reality". Ayer has provided a useful check to counter absurd claims.

2. **REVISED** Ayer's revision of the verification principle so that a

statement can carry meaning if its claim can be verified in principle can be seen as both a strength and a weakness. It shows a philosopher who is willing to revise his theory, but this change might critically weaken what the verification principle.

Weaknesses

1. **FAILS ITS OWN TEST** - The Verification Principle does not carry any meaning according to its own criteria. The VP itself is not analytical, and nor could any empirical evidence be provided to verify it. By its own standards therefore, the VP is itself meaningless. So how can its own claims can be true?

2. **VERIFICATION IS POSSIBLE** - The VP's rejection of any meaning in religious and metaphysical language is countered by **HICK**, who suggests it may be possible to verify the claims of religion at the end of our lives. He uses the parable in which two people journey along a road, one believing that it leads to a celestial city and the other that it is leading nowhere. One of these two will be correct, but the verification of which view is correct is not possible until after death. This is known as **ESCHATALOGICAL VERIFICATION** and meets the "verifiable in principle" condition.

3. **EVIDENCE** - It is difficult to know what sort of evidence counts when trying to meet the weak verification principle. What evidence is admissible? What if many people claim to have had a religious experience - does this provide empirical evidence?

4. **ASSUMES** - That the scientific method is the only way of assessing meaning in language. This is not argued for, and thus is an assertion which there is no obligation to accept.

Key quotes

1. *"No statement which refers to a 'reality' transcending the limits of all possible sense-experience can possibly have any literal significance."* Ayer

2. *"A sentence is factually significant ... if, and only if [a person] knows ... what observations would lead him, under certain conditions, to accept the proposition as being true, or reject it as being false."* Ayer

3. *"A proposition is ... verifiable in the strong sense of the term if, and only if, its truth could be conclusively established ... But it is verifiable in the weak sense if it is possible for experience to render it probable."* Ayer

4. *"We ... define a metaphysical sentence as a sentence which purports to express a genuine proposition, but does, in fact, express neither a tautology nor an empirical hypothesis."* Ayer

5. *"If we take in our hand any volume; of divinity or school metaphysics, for instance, let us ask, Does it contain any abstract reasoning containing quantity or number? No. Does it contain any experimental reasoning, concerning matter of fact or existence? No. Commit it to the flames: for it can contain nothing but sophistry and illusion."* Hume

6. *"The Verification Principle eventually died the death of a thousand cuts."* Phelan

Confusions to avoid

Ayer is not saying that the statement "God exists" is false. He is saying that any statements about God are statements that cannot be **VERIFIED** (even the agnostic who says "I don't know if God exists" is putting forward his lack of knowledge about God as a meaningful question, when such a question could never be meaningful for Ayer).

The purpose of the Logical Positivists is to create a method of verification which decides if a statement carries meaning, not if that statement is true or false - that requires secondary research to go and see if the statement is true (eg giraffes have six legs). To make this assessment Ayer argues that the VP is the necessary tool. Statements about God "fail" the test proposed by the VP.

THE FALSIFICATION PRINCIPLE

POPPER rejected the findings of the Logical Positivists and argued that the VP was bad science. He proposed that science should not be looking for continual verifications of its propositions, but rather **FALSIFICATIONS**. He used the example of Freudian psychology to explain this; when Freud argues that difficulties in adult life stem from our traumatic experiences in childhood, this is easy to verify as it is so wide a proposition, and Freud does exactly this when he suggests that every person requires psychiatric counselling. However, what marks real science out from what Popper calls pseudo-science is that a proposition should be able to be falsified. The VP might suggest "there will be sunshine somewhere tomorrow" whereas the FP will suggest "there will be thunder over Birmingham at 2pm tomorrow" - the latter is better because it puts forward something specific that can be falsified; the former can hardly fail and is irrefutable, but this is bad science, not good.

FLEW built on the FP to criticise religious language as non-falsifiable, and because it is, statements such as "God exists" carry no meaning. Flew uses the parable provided by **WISDOM**, in which he describes two people who come across a clearing in the jungle, where there are both flowers and weeds. One person argues that it is tended by a gardener while the other argues that there is no such gardener. The latter suggests that they watch for the gardener's appearance and even sets up elaborate traps and bloodhounds who would smell the gardener if he came in the night. No gardener appears, but the person who believes a gardener comes is not convinced that this has shown there is not a gardener. He suggests that the gardener is invisible, intangible, soundless and even scentless. The unbelieving explorer asks his friend who believes in such a gardener how his gardener differs from there being no gardener at all.

If a believer claims that God is love and someone responds by saying that a loving God would not allow children to die of cancer, the believer might reply that this is because of "God's bigger plan for us", or something along those lines.

Flew argues therefore that there is little difference between their belief in God and the belief the traveller had about the invisible gardener, and thus no difference between what they are claiming about God and there being no God at all. Belief must **ASSERT** something, and if it asserts something it must **DENY** or **RULE OUT** something too. If it does not, and keeps making exceptions, then it "dies the death of a thousand qualifications". (**FLEW**) As **PHELAN** writes, Flew is asking for "details of a situation in which belief in God would be untenable; the situation need not be real but simply hypothetical". Without providing such, religious language is **UNFALSIFIABLE** and thus is not putting forward a genuine assertion which is of any significant factual importance.

HARE devised the parable about a man who is convinced that his university teachers are out to kill him, despite evidence against this, such as his teachers' kindness towards him. His entire life, behaviour and reading of events around him are shaped by this conviction, which Hare calls a **BLIK**. Hare argues that such bliks carry deep meaning and they are widespread in the human community, similar to some kind of psychological conditioning. No one is without some kind of unfalsifiable blik which makes deep sense to us and through which we interpret the world. Hare argues that religious language does not make factual claims but imparts knowledge nonetheless, through the way it influences people's view of the world.

Flew responded to Hare by saying that religious believers are claiming more than he thinks, and are not just saying that their blik is one of many. What believers are claiming is something about the cosmos, in a

REALIST sense; they claim to be making assertions, which is what Hare fails to realise. If they are making assertions, Flew argues that these must be open to falsification (which they aren't).

A further response to Hare was provided by both **EVANS** and **HICK**, who argued that Hare makes a mistake in writing about bliks being right or wrong or sane or insane; if there is no way of falsifying them, then there is no way of judging what is a right or wrong, sane or insane blik.

A further parable in response to Flew was provided by **MITCHELL**. A French resistance fighter in **WWII** meets a Stranger who says that he is on the side of the resistance, and who convinces the resistance fighter so much that he trusts him. However, the Stranger insists that at times his behaviour will look at though he is on the side of the German Gestapo. Despite this, the fighter, who represents the religious believer, maintains his faith in the Stranger, who represents God. Mitchell maintains that the person's belief in the personal character of the Stranger (obtained at the first meeting) is sufficient to enable the believer to sustain faith; religious belief has a quality, depth and reason to it that a believer will not simply abandon when difficult times come, and he argues that Flew has not correctly understood how religious belief operates.

In summary:

- **FLEW** - Argues that statements about God are not genuine scientific assertions as they cannot be falsified.

- **HARE** - Argues that religious beliefs, like bliks, are unfalsifiable but carry meaning.

- **MITCHELL** - Argues that the believer is aware of problems that would count against his belief, but these do not provide sufficient reasons to discard faith.

Strengths

1. **TRUE TO SCIENCE** - Many have argued that **POPPER'S** criteria for marking science from pseudo-science was a much more useful and valid move than looking for continual verification of a proposition, which actually does not move scientific understanding on.

2. **EVALUATIVE** - Flew challenges the believer to evaluate what is being claimed in such statements such as "God is love" or "God has a plan"; are such factual claims?

Weaknesses

1. **AHLUWALIA** - Writes that Flew's "confidence in empirical evidence as the final test of meaning is, in itself, unfalsifiable".

2. **PHELAN** - Writes that the evidence required by Flew's falsifying test would have to be a) unambiguous, b) identifiable by everyone and c) non-jargonistic, and it is not clear if religious language works like that, or whether such is possible. He notes that it would be possible to falsify the belief that there is a loving God if it could be proved that the world works ultimately against our welfare, but that is a difficult challenge.

Key quotes

1. *"Hare is echoing Wittgenstein's point that religious beliefs are used to evaluate reality, rather than something that one checks against reality."* Phelan

2. *"Metaphysical claims about the existence and nature of God are obviously not open to empirical verification or falsification since God is not an empirically observable object."* Brummer

3. *"To say that religious sentences are not reducible to scientific assertions is a wholly separate question from whether they are true or false."* Wilkinson and Campbell

4. *"By saying that God is invisible, soundless, incorporeal and so on, there is very little difference between our definition of God and our definition of nothingness; we argue God out of existence by 'a thousand qualifications'."* Ahluwalia

Confusions to avoid

- Do not just list the many scholars who have contributed to the debate concerning the VP and the FP. The parables given by the different philosophers were illustrative of major criticisms and you must use them in this way; if you do not draw out the meaning and expand this, then retelling the parable itself will not gain you marks.

- Flew is not talking about the meaningfulness of religious language; he is arguing that the FP is a test of whether something is making a scientific assertion or not. Religious language does not make a scientific assertion because it cannot be falsified, which genuine assertions can be. Religious language may have meaning in other ways.

- Note that Hick's eschatological verification might meet the qualification of the weak verification principle, in that it is possible to suggest that the existence of God is verifiable in principle, post death. However it is impossible to falsify such a claim. Hick was actually pointing out the limitations of the falsification theory, that whilst some things can be verified, such as the eschatological celestial city, they cannot necessarily be falsified.

WITTGENSTEIN'S LANGUAGE GAMES

WITTGENSTEIN did not so much look at meaning of language but how language is used. Words, when used within their "game", do not simply describe an object, but have a **FUNCTION** or **USE**, like **TOOLS**, which is how Wittgenstein described and viewed words. There are many "language games", such as rugby or music, and Wittgenstein's own example is that of chess, where language such as "move pawn to E4" makes sense, carries meaning and performs a function within the rules of the chess language game. Within that language game, if someone gave an instruction to move the pawn three spaces to the left, then that would be "nonsense", literally of no sense, as the instruction does not follow the rules of that particular language game. Similarly, if someone said, "pick up the ball and run 10 metres", that language is not appropriate or used in the chess game.

If you are reading this in class, there will be many language games going on in the school, such as in the Physics classroom, or in PE. Even individual words such as "mass" will have different understandings within the different games in which they are used - if mass is being taught in Physics it will have a very different meaning when taught in an RE lesson about Roman Catholic practice. To understand the meaning of the language, you must look at the activity that it refers to within its game.

These language games are part of life; when we joke or give thanks, we participate in a game that has particular rules. Language games are the way in which we enter into understanding of the world. Wittgenstein developed this idea further when outlining how speaking is a **FORM OF LIFE** shared with others; **BURNS** and **LAW** describe a form of life as "the activity with which a language game is associated" so that "talk of the love of God must be understood not only in the context of other things that are said about God, but also by looking at what it means in practice".

Because these games are forms of life, language is never private as it takes place and has the meaning and function within its game, and develops within that setting. Wittgenstein would therefore reject any ideas that we can use language in a private capacity, such as carried out by Descartes and his claim, "I think therefore I am". It would appear that Descartes thinks such a claim is formed by the private use of language whereas language is always a public discourse for Wittgenstein, and it is from such use in its form of life that it gains its meaning.

In outlining this philosophy, Wittgenstein deliberately moved away from his earlier support of the Logical Positivist's definition of meaning in language. Later Wittgensteinian philosophy allows for religious language to have meaning within its game, although it is followers of Wittgenstein, such as **PHILLIPS**, rather than Wittgenstein himself, who have developed his theory with reference to religious language. The statement "God is love" is very meaningful within the group or game in which that sort of language is used, whilst not understood by those outside that particular game. Therefore, it is not possible to offer simple verification or falsification tests to religious language, or indeed, any other language; these sorts of tests may be more relevant to the physical world, as **TAYLOR** notes, but cannot assess meaning in language. Language carries significance and meaning within the game through its use.

Wittgenstein argued that philosophical problems arise when "language goes on holiday". For example, if we take the word "soul" and think that we are talking about some physical object, then we are applying the wrong rules to it, and the "physical" game rules do not apply in this instance.

Strengths

1. **TRUE TO LANGUAGE** - The VP and The FP have limited use in explaining how the metaphysical is deeply meaningful, which is what religious language purports to do.

2. **TRUE TO RELIGIOUS LIFE** - As **TAYLOR** notes, "for many religious believers, religion is not a philosophical enquiry into the nature of belief, but a shared community life, culture, identity and practices".

Weaknesses

1. **ANTI-REALISM** - Wittgenstein has removed any **REALIST** claims that religious believers would want to make. "Jesus died for the salvation of everyone" Christians might want to assert as **TRUE**, as such statements **CORRESPOND** to an actual truth, they are not just assertions that make sense within the community of believers in a way which **COHERES** with other language that is used within the game.

2. **DIALOGUE IMPOSSIBLE** between people on two sides of an argument: the believer and the atheist. Language does not make sense just within its own game, but has universal meaning.

3. **CIRCULAR** - Wittgenstein's proposal is circular. Words take their meaning from the language game which they are in, and the game gets its meaning from the words from which it is constructed.

Key quotes

1. *"The limits of my language mean the limits of my world."*
   Wittgenstein

2. *"Don't ask for the meaning, ask for the use."* *Wittgenstein*

3. *"We cannot get 'outside' the games to ask the 'real' meaning of
   words. We can only play another game."* *Wilkinson and Campbell*

4. *"The philosopher's task is to describe the way we use language,
   not to ask questions about whether or not things exist."* *Burns and
   Law*

Confusions to avoid

- The meaning of language is found through its use in its form of
  life rather than its description of any reality. The issue here is if
  this anti-realist understanding is an accurate representation of
  what believers are saying when they make such statements as
  "God is love".

- Do not say that Wittgenstein thinks each language game
  describes reality, even a reality that makes sense within that
  game; instead, each language game is using words in a
  particular and internally coherent way. No language is either
  "true" or "false" for Wittgenstein.

GET MORE HELP

Get more help with religious language by using the links below:

http://i-pu.sh/N5R30K06

The Argument from Religious Experience

KEY TERMS

- **CORPORATE RELIGIOUS EXPERIENCE** - Religious experience that happens to a number of people at the same time.

- **INEFFABLE** - Something that cannot be described in normal language.

- **NOETIC** - Knowledge revealed during a religious experience which is not available through other means such as study.

- **NON-PROPOSITIONAL REVELATION** - God reveals himself through the experience of the believer, accepted by faith.

- **NUMINOUS EXPERIENCE** - Awareness or direct experience of the presence of something "wholly other".

- **PASSIVITY** - The recipient is not in control and is being acted upon rather than initiating the experience themselves.

- **PRINCIPLE OF CREDULITY** - Unless we have good reasons to think otherwise we should accept that how things seem to be is how they are.

- **PRINCIPLE OF TESTIMONY** - Unless we have good reasons to think otherwise we should accept other people's testimony, including their account of their experiences.

- **PROPOSITIONAL REVELATION** - God reveals facts or truths about himself either through natural revelation or through Holy Scripture.

- **TRANSIENT** - A brief and temporary experience as far as time is concerned.

RELIGIOUS EXPERIENCE

A **RELIGIOUS EXPERIENCE** is sometimes used as an **A POSTERIORI** argument for the existence of God and provides unique challenges to the philosopher of religion. Careful definition has to be in place, and rigorous **ANALYSIS** and **EVALUATION** have to be offered, using specific examples (eg visions and voices).

SWINBURNE classifies religious experiences into **PUBLIC** and **PRIVATE** categories, though **JACKSON** notes these are not always as clear-cut as this distinction suggests:

1. **PUBLIC RELIGIOUS EXPERIENCES** are:
   a. Where people perceive the action of God through an ordinary event, for example, in the beauty of a sunset.
   b. Those which are observable but unusual, such as Jesus walking on water or healing a leper, in which natural laws are violated.

2. **PRIVATE RELIGIOUS EXPERIENCES**:

   a. Happen to a person who then describes them in ordinary language. For example, Moses' experience at the burning bush (Exodus 3) or an angel appearing to Joseph to announce the birth of Christ (Matthew 1:20).

   b. Happen but cannot be explained to others, for example, mystical experiences such as those of Teresa of Ávila.

   c. Involve someone becoming aware more generally of the presence of God which is interpreted from a religious perspective.

Religious experiences can also be divided into **DIRECT** and **INDIRECT** experiences. Direct experiences refer to where a person feels that they directly encounter God or the divine. This could be:

1. **SEEING A VISION** - Such as described by the young girl Bernadette at Lourdes.

2. **HEARING A VOICE** - Such as described by Samuel in the Old Testament. (1 Samuel 3:1-21)

3. **AN ENCOUNTER** - Or a distinct awareness of a presence. **OTTO** describes this as the **NUMINOUS** or "apprehension of the wholly other", suggesting that God is above knowledge and logic. Otto describes it as different to the mystical which seeks unity of all things; a numinous experience is mysterious, tremendum et fascinans - mysterious, awe-inspiring in an overwhelming and almost terrifying way, and fascinating. It draws us towards the divine.

DREAMS that are recorded in the Bible (for example, Jacob, Genesis 28: 10-22 or Peter, Acts 10:1-28) are times when a voice or vision is described as part of a direct experience. But what do we mean by "direct" and "encounter" when a person is asleep?

INDIRECT experiences are when a person is moved or inspired by nature or in prayer and/or worship to think of and reflect upon the divine, which might lead to a response of submission, repentance, confession and/or thanksgiving. **KIRKWOOD** uses an analogy to describe the difference between direct and indirect religious experiences: Imagine a person arriving at their house to find a bear eating the porridge (direct experience), as opposed to arriving after the event to find clues that a bear has been there, such as an empty bowl and droppings on the floor (indirect expereience).

"Some people have suggested that indirect experiences are not necessarily different from ordinary experiences; they are made significant by the person who has the experience and for whom the experience has religious meaning." (**TAYLOR**) The acronym **PIE** raises an important point about whether a person's existing perspective affects what type of interpretation they give.

(**P**) A person's existing **PERSPECTIVE** affects their

(**I**) **INTERPRETATION OF THE EVENT**, which affects their

(**E**) understanding of the **EXPERIENCE**

Would you interpret a sunset as light from a massive ball of energy reflecting on water (through natural laws governing light and reflection), or evidence of the beauty that God has placed within creation? Does this interpretation depend on your existing perspective on the question of God's existence? **JAMES** argued that some people are unlikely ever to have a religious experience because they would not be open to such an event being a possibility.

Sometimes a person's existing perspective is changed through a religious experience, particularly during a direct experience (in which case **PIE** would not be the model to apply). This was particularly the case in the story of **PAUL** when he was not looking for an encounter with Jesus, but was trying to stop people speaking about Christ being the Messiah. This is an example of a **CONVERSION EXPERIENCE**; a more recent example would be the conversion to Christianity of CS Lewis, author of The Lion, the Witch and the Wardrobe.

A useful question to ask is if any change in the recipient of the experience is far more likely to happen during a direct as opposed to an indirect religious experience. The question of how much our existing perspective affects our experience, or whether such can be changed and overcome in a dramatic religious experience, is also worth pursuing in an essay, and it can open links to whether a religious experience is "simply" a psychological experience, (see James later) a "feeling" or a combination of these, and possibly more. Furthermore, it can be asked if all of the above experiences are simply events which make people view the world in a different way when a person has reached a particular stage in life; the person might be influenced by a specific occasion that then shapes their life and subsequent worldview and psychology. This does not mean necessarily that the event was a "religious" experience, but that the event was interpreted that way. **HICK** regards this as "experiencing as" - where two people will view the same event differently and such viewing will affect the way the event and the wider world is perceived.

Religious experiences may be both the strongest proof that God exists for a person who has had one, and the weakest argument for the onlooker, as it is difficult to assess the evidence second-hand. Keep in mind therefore the question of whether religious experiences are **VERIDICAL**, and, if so, how; can they be shown to be what the recipient believes them to be, that is "experiences of God rather than delusions"? **(TAYLOR)**

The Varieties of Religious Experiences (William James)

James found that there were four distinguishing features of a mystical religious experience:

- **PASSIVE** - The person who has this type of religious experience is not in control of what is happening; it is not willed by the person but they feel that they are in the grip of a superior power during it.

- **INEFFABLE** - It is not possible to describe the experience in normal language (see Swinburne's private experiences, point b above).

- **NOETIC** - The person receives some significant and authoritative knowledge and illumination, **REVEALED** through intuition rather than to the intellect, that could not be gained without this experience.

- **TRANSIENT** - The actual experience is short, (though time may seem to be suspended for the recipient having the experience), but the effects of it are long-lasting.

As well as identifying what he felt was going on during a mystical experience, (which is an existential judgement) **JAMES** studied what such religious experiences meant for the recipient (which is a value judgement), and concluded that:

1. Religious experiences have a significant impact upon a person's life in that they:

   a. have great **AUTHORITY** for the person

   b. are understood by the recipient to be **VERY REAL** (James was impressed by the **CERTAINTY** of the experiences he studied) and

   c. can bring about real and **LONG-LASTING CHANGE** in the person's life. In fact, James said that the feelings of reality from a religious experience are more convincing than "results established by logic ever are", and that the results of the experience demonstrate that something of great value has taken place.

2. The view of the world, and our place within it, alters following the event, for example peacefulness, hope and love of others. The religious aims, following a person's conversion, become the "habitual centre of his energy". Whether induced or spontaneous, these experiences ("states of consciousness" - **JORDAN** et al) have long lasting effects.

3. Religious experiences are part of a person's psyche, yet James concludes that there might be a supernatural element also. Neither was he concerned that they could be a product of neurosis, as **FREUD** would argue, suggesting that it was not necessary to have a "whole mind" to have a religious experience, marked by great certainty about the event. "For James, saying that religious experiences are psychological phenomena is a statement that a religious experience is natural to a person, just like other psychological experiences such as

self-awareness or thinking." (**TAYLOR**) James takes an **EMPIRICAL** approach to religious experience suggesting that these events, "point with reasonable probability to the continuity of our consciousness with a wider, spiritual environment". (**JAMES**)

However, this does lead to the problem of whether a religious experience is just "real for them" and of no worth when used as an argument for a God who is objective, really "out there" (rather than in the mind).

What James was very careful to conclude was that the religious experiences he studied **DID NOT ACT AS PROOF FOR GOD** but that the individual had encountered what they perceived to be the divine, the effects of which were very real. Religious experience "cannot be cited as unequivocally supporting the infinitist belief ... but that we can experience union with something larger than ourselves and in that union find our greatest peace". (**JAMES**)

Strengths

1. **OBJECTIVE** - James is someone trained in the medical profession studying similar experiences and effects experienced by a range of people. James is not out to prove the existence of God from his studies but to take an objective approach to what he finds.

2. **NOETIC** - We expect to find noetic elements if an encounter with a divine being has taken place. Whilst this leaves the onlooker no wiser as to what happened, it may be the case that description of it in ordinary language is not possible.

3. **EXPERIENTIAL** - James does not suggest that religious experiences bypass the human psyche, but includes emotions and feelings as part of the evidence for a religious experience.

Weaknesses

1. **TOO BROAD** - James' conclusions about religious experiences are so broad that religious experience could include drug-induced hallucinations. The lack of regard for how doctrine and creeds work to move the believer away from too much emphasis on subjective experience could be seen as a weakness in James' understanding of religion.

2. **PRE-DETERMINED** - If religious experiences are real it begs the question why people in different religions experience very different revelations. The doctrine of the religion seems to determine the type of experience (for example, the Cross and **STIGMATA**).

3. **LACK OF AUTHORITY** - James's conclusion that mystical religious experiences could be psychological in origin has been criticised, as, if this is the case, notes **MACKIE**, they lack any real authority, and are no different to other psychological experiences. However, God may have put that desire for him into people's psyche and therefore religious experiences are a natural part of personhood.

4. **ASSUMES REALISM** - James concluded that an undoubtedly real event has to be caused by a reality. Thus, God as a real being could be the cause of the real event, if that is what a person believes. Is this a strong or valid argument?

SWINBURNE, in his analysis of a number of arguments for God, put forward two principles when assessing religious experiences:

1. The **PRINCIPLE OF CREDULITY** states that "if it seems to a subject that X is present, then probably X is present; what one seems to perceive probably is so".

   It is entirely up to the person who is listening to the account of the religious experience to prove that the person who had the experience did not do so; the burden of proof does not lie with the person who is describing the account.

2. The **PRINCIPLE OF TESTIMONY** states that people usually tell the truth. Swinburne argues that in everyday life, our default position is to believe that people have told us what they have actually perceived to have happened. The burden rests on the person who does not believe that we have told the truth to prove that is the case.

Swinburne recognises situations which would challenge the principle of credulity:

1. A person could be drunk or hallucinating or an unreliable witness.

2. Similar perceptions have been proved to be false.

3. It can be shown that whoever/whatever the recipient was claiming to have experienced was not actually present during the experience.

4. It is possible to show that "whatever/whoever the recipient is claiming to have experienced was there, but was not involved in/ responsible for the experience". (**JORDAN** et al)

The principle of testimony suggests that we should accept the statement about what has happened during a religious experience unless further proof is provided (as above) which suggests that the person is not telling the truth.

The most significant challenge relates to points 3 and 4. James has already suggested that the impairments suggested in point 1 need not necessarily bar a person from having a religious experience; however, how one disproves or proves that it was God involved in the religious experience seems a very great challenge as we are not talking here about the experience we have when we encounter another human being.

MACKIE also suggests that it is perfectly conceivable that a normally reliable person could be either mistaken or give a false account, and thus Swinburne's principle of testimony does not hold. The balance of probability "suggests that the mistake is more likely than the supernatural explanation, however sincere they might be" (in **AHLUWALIA**). Do the normal rules about how we recount sensory experiences apply in the case of religious experiences? **RUSSELL** also suggests that there are cases which meet Swinburne's criteria in which people have said that they have encountered Satan rather than God.

CORPORATE RELIGIOUS EXPERIENCE

A corporate religious experience is when many people seem to undergo the same experience and demonstrate similar responses, for example, "All of the disciples were filled with the Holy Spirit and began to speak in other languages, as the Spirit gave them ability." (**ACTS 2**) The annual Hajj pilgrimage by Muslims is another example of corporate religious experience.

THE TORONTO BLESSING (20 January 1994). Following a message to the Toronto Airport Church from visiting preacher Randy Clark, people began to laugh, cry, fall to the floor, roar like lions, speak in tongues and claim healings. The blessing spread to Christian churches around the world.

WILKINSON and **CAMPBELL'S** note that it would still be necessary to evaluate each person's experience as some might be carried along with the atmosphere, whilst others might fake an experience. Social psychologists also point to group hysteria.

What does Toronto show of a God who is love, which is a central Christian belief? Would all the events described above be consistent with existing belief? Does God take away human reason, and is it reasonable to think that God would visit "a small group in Toronto while doing nothing for the starving of Somalia or the persecuted [Christians] in China?" Wilkinson and Campbell have strayed into the dangerous territory of trying to guess the mind of God here, but critical analysis of corporate religious experiences is essential. We could apply the tests that James and Swinburne suggest to these unusual events.

RESPONSES TO THE IDEA OF RELIGIOUS EXPERIENCES

1. **COLE** - How is it possible to say that we have had an encounter with God if we have no previous knowledge of what God is? How could we recognise and identify the "other" as God? To say that the experience is one in which we "just know" it is God is philosophically dubious because, as Cole notes, it is based on a conviction rather than reasons.

2. **STARBUCK** - Carried out a study of **CONVERSION**, and noted that most religious conversions happen in late teens/early twenties when people speak of finding a peace through beginning to follow God. However, he found that, at that same stage in life, many non-religious young people also went through a stage of psychological angst and unease before finding their own identity in early adult life, and this process did not involve a religious conversion event. However, **EYRE** et al write that, in response to Starbuck, "some theists recognise that there are psychological aspects of conversion experiences but argue that to reduce conversion to just a psychological phenomenon fails to address the question of the cause of the experience".

3. **FREUD** - Argued that religious experiences are reactions to a hostile world, in which we seek help from a father figure. Human identity is marked by repressed sexuality, deeply embedded into us from childhood experiences, which leads to psychological unease and unrest. Religion and religious experiences, argues Freud, are ways in which we attempt to deal with our psychological needs, but are simply childlike desires for a good relationship with a father figure (God), and they actually avoid us coming to terms, and dealing properly, with our needs.

4. **MARX** - Suggested that religion acts like an opiate to dull the pain people feel in daily life caused by lack of economic power.

5. **JAMES** - Argued that such a dismissal of religious experiences arose from those who were already deeply hostile to religion. Furthermore, many who have been committed to the cause of their religion, strengthened by their religious experiences, have found religion to be far from an opiate but something that has led to them being persecuted and even martyred.

6. **FLEW** - Suggests that it is not possible to give any credence to statements such as "I saw the risen Christ", due to the fact that there is no test by which we can assess if such a statement is true or not; verification and falsification are both impossible and therefore the statement is meaningless.

7. **KANT** - Argued that it is simply not possible to experience things beyond the phenomenal realm as we do not have any senses that can access a noumenal realm. Such may exist, but "given that human senses are finite and limited, it is impossible for humans to experience an unlimited God", **EYRE** et al.

Key quotes

1. *"Religious experience seems to the subject to be an experience of God or of some other supernatural being."* Richard Swinburne

2. *"In the natural sciences and industrial arts, it never occurs to anyone to try to refute opinions by showing up their author's neurotic constitution."* William James

3. *"From a scientific point of view, we can make no distinction between the man who eats little and sees heaven and the man who drinks much and sees snakes."* Bertrand Russell

4. *"To say that God spoke to him in a dream, is no more than to say that he dreamed God spoke to him."* Hobbes

5. *"Religion is the feelings, acts, and experiences of individual men in their solitude in relation to whatever they many consider the divine."* William James

6. *"God establishes himself in the interior of this soul in such a way it is wholly impossible for me to doubt that I have been in God, and God in me."* Teresa of Ávila

7. *"The fact that a belief has a good moral effect upon a man is no evidence whatsoever in its favour."* Bertrand Russell

8. *"How things seem to be is good grounds for a belief about how things are."* Richard Swinburne

Confusions to avoid

- **WRONG CONCLUSION** - James did not state that religious experiences proved the existence of God. He did state that the experience was "real" (you can discuss what "real" means), and he did say more than the fact that religious experiences are passive, ineffable, noetic and transient. I have read many essays that outline **P.I.N.T.** as this was all that James said about religious experiences. His conclusions are far more wide-ranging.

- **PSYCHOLOGICAL QUESTIONS** - This particular topic has many links with psychology, and things such as how accurate our memory of events are, (see brilliant treatment of this in "The Invisible Gorilla and Other Ways Our Intuitions Deceive Us", Chabris and Simons), how we can access other minds and what it means to have a psychological experience. The challenge for the philosophy student is to see if religious experience stands up to **PHILOSOPHICAL** scrutiny. The examiner will not expect, or want you, to produce a psychological critique of religious experiences.

- **FALLACY** - Students can be prone to commit the "fallacy of the excluded middle" in this topic: a religious experience is either real or an illusion (ie false). There might be another sort of **MIDDLE** experience going on, so that it is not entirely illusory that "something" happened. How one argues this **EXCLUDED MIDDLE** presents difficulties, but that goes right to the core of this particular subject.

- **TRUTH CONDITIONS** - A reasonable way in which to assess visions and voices and other types of religious experience is to see if they:

  - fit in with the general teaching of the religion and

  - lead to an outcome that accords with the teaching of that religion.

  - This widens out the analysis from that specific experience; however, whether it says anything about the "truth" of that particular experience might depend on what one thinks of the "truth" of the religion.

- **EYRE ET AL** - They rightly point out that there is a difference in saying: "If there is a God there are likely to be experiences of him" (a claim **SWINBURNE** makes) and "there are religious experiences, therefore there is a God". The former statement is less controversial though not necessarily true. The latter commits the fallacy of affirming the consequent (the consequent is the second half of the statement, or the consequence if the first half of the statement is the case). It is like saying, "I have a wet house, therefore it is raining", whereas there could be many other reasons why I have a wet house, such as my neighbour watering his prize roses. There might be religious experiences, but one cannot conclude from these that there is a God.

GET MORE HELP

Get more help with religious experience by using the links below:

http://i-pu.sh/P9D69P81

The Ontological Argument for God's Existence

KEY TERMS

- **ANALYTIC STATEMENT** - A statement where the predicate is contained within the subject, eg married men are husbands, or, for Anselm, God [subject] necessarily exists [predicate].

- **A POSTERIORI** - Knowledge gained after experience.

- **A PRIORI** - Knowledge gained prior to experience.

- **CONTINGENT EXISTENCE** - Something which, by its nature, does not necessarily have to exist, and could or could not have existence, eg you or me. Once existent, can go out of existence.

- **DEDUCTION** - A type of reasoning whereby it is demonstrated that the conclusion necessarily follows from the premises (as seen in the ontological argument).

- **IMMUTABLE** - Not capable of or susceptible to change; unalterable.

- **INDUCTION** - A type of reasoning that takes specific instances and from them draws a general conclusion (eg as seen in the cosmological argument).

- **NECESSARY BEING** - A being whose non-existence is a contradiction.

- **ONTOLOGICAL** - Words or wisdom (logos) about being (ontos). What it means for something to be.

- **PREDICATE** - A property of a subject, for example tall, round; for Anselm, necessary existence is a predicate of the greatest possible being.

- **REDUCTIO AD ABSURDUM** - An argument that shows that the opposite of what it is claiming cannot be true.

- **SYNTHETIC STATEMENT** - A statement where the predicate is not contained with the subject, eg married men are happy (predicate - happy), and some knowledge of the world is required to assess its validity.

The ontological argument (**OA**) for the existence of God (a title **KANT** gave to this argument) is the only argument studied that does not start from empirical evidence and work back to God (the latter types of arguments are **A POSTERIORI** and inductive in nature). The OA commences with a definition of God given by **ANSELM** which, once understood, entails actual (and then in a later argument) **NECESSARY** existence.

ANSELM'S ONTOLOGICAL ARGUMENT

The first form of the argument is found in the Proslogion (Discourse on the Existence of God) chapter 2:

- God is the greatest possible being that can be thought of.

- If God exists only in the mind (or understanding) then a greater being could be conceived to exist both in the mind and in reality.

- This "greatest possible being" (of premise one) must therefore exist in the mind and in reality.

Therefore God must exist as a being in reality (in re) as well as in the mind (in intellectu).

Anselm was writing with reference to **PSALMS 14** and **53** where it notes that "the fool says in his heart there is no God". He stated that the fool understood that God is "that than which nothing greater can be conceived".

Anselm argued that the fool, once he understood this, logically had to acknowledge that it was not possible for such a being to exist in thought alone as then there would be a greater being who existed in thought and reality.

Anselm noted that it would be **CONTRADICTORY** to state, once the fool has in his mind the greatest possible being, that such a being cannot exist, as existence in reality is an intrinsic quality in the greatest being (by definition). Therefore God exists.

Chapter 3 of the Proslogion developed this argument by stating again that God is the greatest possible being, and that, as such, has

NECESSARY EXISTENCE. God cannot not be, and a necessary state of being is always greater than **CONTINGENT EXISTENCE**, which is dependent on other things for existence (again, think you or me). If the state of necessary existence is greater than contingent existence, and God is the greatest possible being, God must be, uniquely, a **NECESSARY** being, entirely not dependant on anything else for existence, ie intrinsically necessary.

Something having the possibility of not existing or coming in and going out of existence - a **CONTINGENT** being - will always be less than that which cannot not exist. Anselm's claim was that the predicate of existence is an intrinsic part of the concept of God just as a spinster has the predicate of "being unmarried" (this will be important later when **KANT** critiques Anselm), and this type of argument, where the **PREDICATE** (exists necessarily) is contained in the **SUBJECT** (God) is known as an **ANALYTIC STATEMENT**. The idea of God not existing is a logical impossibility and hence Anselm's argument is a **REDUCTIO AD ABSURDUM**. Remember that this is an argument based on the consideration of the very "beingness" or intrinsic nature of God, not on a posteriori evidence from the world that may lead us to conclude there is a God.

GAUNILO'S CHALLENGE TO ANSELM'S ARGUMENT AND ANSELM'S REPLY

GAUNILO, a French monk and contemporary to Anselm, wrote On Behalf of the Fool as a response to Anselm. He argued that someone could imagine something like a beautiful island, and think that this was the most excellent, **PERFECT** island. Using Anselm's reasoning, Gaunilo argued that for the island to really be the greatest island it must exist in reality as well as in the imagination. If it did not exist in reality it would not be the greatest island. You can apply Gaunilo's point here to anything and say because it is perfect it must exist in reality not just in the mind.

Gaunilo said that this island obviously does not exist just because we have imagined it to be so, defined it as the greatest and then said that because it is the greatest that means it must have existence. Gaunilo suggested that those who believe such an island existed because of this reasoning are either joking or foolish, and anyone who believed them would likewise be a **FOOL**. He used this counter-example to challenge Anselm on his argument for God's existence which, as outlined above, goes along similar lines, and, Gaunilo suggests, is as flawed as the argument for the island's existence.

We cannot just define things into existence.

ANSELM'S REPLY TO GAUNILO

Gaunilo's criticism concentrates on the first formulation of **ANSELM'S** argument about things existing in the mind and reality. In Anselm's Reply to Gaunilo he emphasised that the island he used in his example is **CONTINGENT**, and would never have to exist in the way that God as a necessary being has to, as the greatest thing that can be thought. It is logically conceivable to think that the island could not exist, unlike God.

God as the greatest thing that can be thought is, by his very nature, in a category of one, and is something that cannot not exist or be greater or bettered.

The island however could always have one more palm tree, or a bluer sea, and could either not exist, or exist without perfection as that is not something of its intrinsic nature. **PLANTINGA** noted that, unlike the greatest being that can be thought of, God, islands have no **INTRINSIC** maximum. A contingent island and a necessary God cannot be compared.

DESCARTES' ONTOLOGICAL ARGUMENT

In Meditation 5 of Meditations on Philosophy, Descartes built on his previous thought that certain truths are, by their very nature, impossible to be doubted, and that people are innately able to understand that some things cannot be different, ie equality and shape. He thought that one **INNATE IDEA** people had was a concept of God as a perfect being.

Working from this and drawing on his background as a mathematician, Descartes argued that there are certain things that have an unchangeable nature, and we know that this is the case. He used the example of a triangle. Essential to its nature are "three angles equal to two right angles", and the nature of the triangle could not be different; it is **IMMUTABLE**.

God's nature is likewise immutable and part of that **IMMUTABLE NATURE** is having all perfections, of which one is existence. Triangles have essential characteristics, without which they would not be triangles; God has the essential characteristic of existence, without which such a being could not be God.

However, what if it could be argued that we can think of a triangle which has to have certain characteristics for it to be a triangle, but then acknowledge that such a triangle doesn't have to exist in reality? **DESCARTES** noted this but said that existence is a perfection, and as God, by definition and as part of his essence, has all perfections, he has to exist in a way that a triangle has to have internal angles of 180°.

It is a contradiction to claim otherwise, but it is simply that the triangle doesn't have existence as one of its necessary essences, whereas God does.

(Note here that Descartes is claiming that existence is "more perfect" than non-existence, as Anselm said existence was part of the greatest being). An object has to have certain **NECESSARY** things for it to be that object; it cannot be separated from those characteristics. Descartes used a further example of a mountain which cannot exist without a valley; likewise, it is not possible to talk of God (and God alone, not any contingent items) without perfection, and existence is a **PERFECTION**.

KANT'S OBJECTIONS

Kant argued that existence is not a **PREDICATE** like green or tall. The latter helps to describe the object. "Existence" cannot be used in that way, as existence refers to the whole object.

All that Descartes has done is to say, if a triangle exists it has interior angles adding up to 180°; similarly Kant argued that the **ONTOLOGICAL ARGUMENT** says, if God exists he is a necessary being, but this does not mean he does exist in reality.

Kant's argued that "existence is not a predicate". A **PREDICATE** is something that adds to our knowledge of what a subject is like, for example, such a thing is big or brown or flat. **EXISTENCE** doesn't work in this way, as it does not tell us anything about the object that helps us in the identification of that object. Existence is actually the thing and all its characteristics, rather than just another predicate.

For example, if I say that my boat is fast, I give more information about the boat, but if I say the boat exists then I add nothing to the description of it; I am actually saying that there is a real example of this boat, and this is not what the role of a predicate is. Try this in reverse: If I say, "the boat does not exist" then I have not actually just taken away one property (or predicate) of the boat but have taken away the entire boat.

What **KANT** noted was that when we say something exists we are saying that such an object has been **ACTUALISED**, but he argued that we cannot simply add existence to the concept of God and say we have proved or actualised the existence of such a concept. Noting the essential characteristics of a triangle as certain angles only actually gets us as far as saying, "If a triangle existed it would have these characteristics."

Believing that God exists, and, following on from that belief to say that God has necessary existence, is not an argument that God necessarily has to exist in reality, just like triangles do not have to have existence, although if they did they would have certain predicates.

If there is a God, he has necessary existence, but the predicate of necessary existence cannot be declared as intrinsic to God and a claim made that as a consequence God has to exist in reality.

Kant thus argues that it is not contradictory to think of a possible being who has **NECESSARY** existence. To describe something as having characteristics would give us a picture of something if it existed, but by describing something, even by saying something has necessary existence, does not establish the existence of that thing. For Kant, all statements about existence are **SYNTHETIC**, true or false after verification, and not analytic, meaning "true by nature". The existence of God needs to be verified from a position exterior to the concept as it were, not by **ANALYTIC** analysis of the term.

If **ANSELM** and **DESCARTES** think they have overcome this idea by suggesting that God has necessary existence as one of the characteristics of the greatest or perfect being, and only this predicate can be assigned to God, then they are in danger of making a circular argument. Are they suggesting that God exists necessarily on the grounds that God has necessary existence?

Has Descartes convinced you that necessary existence has to entail actual existence? Or, as **CATERUS** argued, is this not enough and Descartes still has to show that the "concept of necessary existence entails actual existence" (in Lacewing)?

A modern-day reply to Kant has come from **NORMAN MALCOLM**. After outlining the idea of an unlimited being as one that does not depend on anything for its existence (meaning God is not contingent), and also that if God does not exist then he cannot come into existence, Malcolm put forward the following formulation:

- The existence of an unlimited being is either logically impossible or logically necessary.

- God's existence is not logically impossible, as there is no logical contradiction in the concept of a God/unlimited being who exists (the idea is not logically absurd or internally contradictory).

- God's existence is therefore logically necessary.

But again, has Malcolm answered the key problem of whether the concept of God as necessary entails existence in reality? Does it mean that if the existence of God is not impossible, it is **NECESSARY**, or just **POSSIBLE**? (It is worth reading the Malcolm extract at the end of the chapter.)

Scholars have noted that Malcolm may have proved the concept of the **LOGICAL NECESSITY** of God's existence (that the non-existence of God is a logical impossibility and self-contradictory), but not the existence of God in reality or factually.

Words and concepts do not always describe realities, even when those concepts have internal and logical consistency.

Strengths

1. There is some attraction to a **DEDUCTIVE** and **ANALYTIC** argument that appeals to logical consistency rather than the mixed evidence for God from a posteriori evidence. It is an argument that has received much attention due to the fact that there does seem something to be wrong with it, but what that something is is not always apparent.

2. Anselm and Descartes both responded to criticism that was levelled at their versions of the OA, and stressed what it means for God to be the **GREATEST POSSIBLE BEING** and necessary by definition. Examples of the greatest or perfect contingent things might therefore not count against what Anselm and Descartes argued. Some have argued that with Malcolm's reformulation of the OA, the argument still holds importance.

3. Does Kant's critique of Descartes' OA hold? It might be that saying that "something exists", for example, Spiderman, does add something new to the description because up until that point the listener would have been thinking of a fictional character. Jackson points out that the atheist may be thinking of God as a fictional character so the addition of "and exists" may actually change the definition of the word God, and thus existence, in that sense, may act as a predicate.

Weaknesses

1. The Proslogion was written by a monk as a prayer - can it be used as an argument for the existence of God? Rather, is it a support to those who already believe? Is it, more properly, **FAITH SEEKING UNDERSTANDING**?

2. Is existence in reality **NECESSARILY** and in all cases greater than existence in the mind only? This is a value judgement. Are there counter-examples to this, with even one counter-example being enough to throw doubt on Anselm's position? The many wonderful qualities you imagine when you think of a future partner may never actually be found to be the case in reality, where you might be disappointed.

3. Many scholars hold that Kant has delivered a fatal blow to Descartes' OA, by his argument that going from the concept of God having **NECESSARY EXISTENCE** to God **EXISTING IN REALITY** is flawed and that existence cannot act as a predicate.

Key quotes

1. *"I do not seek to understand that I believe, but I believe in order to understand."* Anselm

2. *"From the fact that I cannot think of a mountain without a valley, it does not follow that a mountain and valley exist anywhere, but simply that a mountain and a valley, whether they exist or not, are mutually inseparable. But from the fact that I cannot think of God except as existing, it follows that existence is inseparable from God, and hence that he really exists."* Descartes

3. *"Caterus put the point to Descartes that the OA doesn't demonstrate that God really exists. It only shows that the concept of existence is inseparable from the concept of God. Descartes' argument is only convincing for the claim that if God exists, God exists necessarily."* Lacewing

4. *"It would be self-contradictory to posit a triangle and yet reject its three angles, but there is no contradiction in rejecting the triangle together with its three angles."* Kant

5. *"The ontological argument is 'a charming joke'."* Schopenhauer

6. *"If God, a being greater than that which cannot be conceived, does not exist, then He cannot come into existence. For if He did, He would either have been caused to come into existence or have happened to come into existence, and in either case, He would be a limited being, which by our conception of Him, He is not."* Malcolm

Confusions to avoid

- "Gaunilo is an atheist"- not so. He believed in God but did not think Anselm's argument about the greatest possible being existing in reality as well as in the mind worked.

- Be very careful to know the differences between Anselm's first and second formulations, and then the difference between what Anselm is arguing and what Descartes and Malcolm are putting forward in their different ontological arguments.

- This is a topic that calls for **PRECISE DEFINITIONS** and these are perfectly possible if you pay attention to the different arguments that are being put forward. Learn and use technical terms, such as **A PRIORI**, **DEDUCTIVE** and **ANALYTIC** to demonstrate your knowledge of the argument, and then do put forward your response to the various scholars' views you have heard - you are expected to show personal and philosophical engagement with the arguments.

GET MORE HELP

Get more help with the ontological argument by using the links below:

http://i-pu.sh/M6S79M64

Life After Death: The Soul

KEY TERMS

- **AKHIRA** - Islamic belief in the afterlife.

- **ANATTA** - Buddhist belief that the idea of self is an illusion.

- **ATMAN** - Hindu name for the self, or soul.

- **DUALISM** - The belief that humans have a non-physical soul and a physical body.

- **MATERIALISM** - The belief that humans are material only.

- **MONISM** - Any theory that denies the duality of body and mind.

- **REINCARNATION** - The belief that the soul of a person is reincarnated into another person or life form post death.

- **RESURRECTION** - The belief that a person continues to exist after death in a separate realm.

- **SOUL** - The spiritual, non-physical "part" of a human, viewed as the centre of a person's identity.

Syllabus note

For the Edexcel syllabus, three main beliefs about life after death are compared and contrasted. They are **IMMORTALITY OF THE SOUL**, **RESURRECTION** and **REINCARNATION**.

Plato's dualism

Human identity and the question of whether anything of that identity continues after death has long intrigued philosophers. **PLATO** argued that humans have a **SOUL**, which is what enables a person to gain knowledge. Knowledge is gained when the soul remembers ideas from the **REALM OF THE FORMS**. The soul is simple, that is, without parts, and cannot be divided, although it is comprised of reason, spirit or will and desires; it should be led by **REASON**, as desires can lead it astray, and a healthy soul is when the three aspects work in harmony.

The soul, but not the body, is **ETERNAL**. It existed before it came to be imprisoned in a body, and will survive death, as it belongs to the realm of the forms. Plato's argument for dualism is based on two ideas: firstly, the soul recognises beauty and goodness as it remembers these from the realm of the forms - a person has not seen these in this world, but only shadows of them, and therefore the soul must have had existence in the realm where these concepts are; and, secondly, things get their existence in relation to each other - opposites such as light and dark are known in reference to the other. In a similar way, death and life are opposites to each other, so that "life comes from death, and death comes from life, in an endless chain of birth, death and rebirth". (**AHLUWALIA**)

Descartes' substance dualism

DESCARTES, as a **SUBSTANCE DUALIST**, argued that in the process of thinking, and even doubting, it was shown that the "I" existed. This "I" was the soul or mind, which is separate from the body. **RYLE** dismissed this idea as a "category mistake" arguing that to suggest there is a body and a soul is like proposing that a cricket team exists in addition to the batsmen, bowlers and fielders, when in fact the batsmen, bowlers and the fielders are the team in its entirety and it does not need this additional description of "the team". There is no mysterious "ghost in the machine", no soul in addition to the body, as if both could be spoken of as the same "type" of thing.

HH PRICE uses dream worlds to show that disembodied existence is not conceivable. Just as we can have non-bodily experiences whilst asleep, so it is possible that we may have purely mental interactions in the afterlife.

RESPONSES TO IMMORTALITY OF THE SOUL

1. Aristotle's monism

ARISTOTLE rejected Plato's argument that the form of something was separate to the object. Pure concepts like goodness and beauty cannot exist as properties separate to good or beautiful objects. Aristotle's idea of soul is that it is the very life-force of the human, our characteristics, or the **FORMAL CAUSE** of the human being. This is not separate to us, but makes us who we are, just as the form of an object is it characteristics; the axe has the form of chopping. This means that the soul cannot be separated from the body and that it cannot exist without the body it enlivens. This characteristic of the human soul is its ability to **REASON**, which is uniquely a human attribute.

It appears that Aristotle meant that the soul could not survive death, as the soul ceased to exist when what it animated died; Aristotle has explained the soul in "natural" terms. However, Aristotle suggests elsewhere that reason could survive death as a type of "abstract property of intellect or reasoning" (**EYRE** et al), not as someone's identity.

2. Dawkins' materialism

Taking a **HARD MATERIALIST** position, **DAWKINS** completely disagrees with Plato. He argues that:

- We are entirely physical beings, blindly programmed "survival machines", products of evolution and DNA mutation. Genes work to develop self-awareness, which is not due to a soul, but simply present because it has evolutionary advantages.

- To argue for a soul is an evasion which tries to explain consciousness without putting forward any evidence.

- Any reference to soul that Dawkins accepts is not the metaphysical, but the capacity for deep reflection and the feelings of which humans are capable.

- Nothing survives death, as there is no separate soul. Our consciousness is extinguished which was the case before we were born and so there is nothing for us to experience upon death. However, Dawkins suggest that **MEMES** are now replicators - that is, a person's contribution to culture and society continues post death, and has survival in that sense.

Strengths of dualistic immortality of the soul

1. **ACCOUNTS FOR MYSTERY** - We feel that there is a difference between a scientific description of the brain and that which we know as consciousness. Physical explanations of many events do not ever seem to get "inside" the event in a first-person way.

2. **PARANORMAL EVIDENCE** - Accounts of what appears to be the paranormal are well documented: **EXTRA SENSORY PERCEPTION, TELEPATHY** or the claims made by **MEDIUMS**, where information is passed and received in ways that are "beyond normal perception". (**EYRE** et al)

3. **LOCKE'S** story of the Prince and the Cobbler, in which the two characters swap bodies and yet remember who they were before the swap. This questions if a person's real identity is in the mind or the body. Would this make disembodied existence coherent, as the real "you" can survive the death of your body?

4. **PRICE'S** argument that the mind could exist post death in a mental world such as we experience in dreams.

5. **NEAR DEATH EXPERIENCES**, such as that experienced by **PAM REYNOLDS** who was able to recount the words of the surgeons and the instruments used despite her having no sensory capabilities during the surgery.

Weaknesses of the dualistic immortality of the soul

1. **REGRESSION** - If the soul controls us, is there something else controlling it, and so on, and so on? This is the homunculus fallacy.

2. **BEGS THE QUESTION** - How can the non-physical soul or mind interact with the physical brain?

3. **NO NECESSARY LINK** - Plato's arguments can be challenged; there is no opposite for a rose, but a rose exists, and, why would something's opposite bring the other thing about, "or necessitate any kind of cycle"? (**AHLUWALIA**)

4. **HICK** criticises **PRICE** (above) stating that the world we all individually desire in our mental world would not be the same world as that desired by others, so there would be no shared world of mental perception.

RESURRECTION

CHRISTIAN BELIEFS about life after death, as reiterated in the historic creeds, centre on the **RESURRECTION OF JESUS**, who defeats the power of death, so that it is no longer the end for people. Mainstream Christian teaching is that his resurrection was **PHYSICAL**, which acts as an example or "first fruit" of what Christians believe happens post death. Paul writes that "when the body is buried, it is mortal; when raised, it will be immortal". **1 CORINTHIANS 15:35-44** acts as an important outline for Christian belief. Although the resurrected body of Christ seemed to be different in character to a body limited by physicality, it is important for Christians that there will be a **RESURRECTION OF THE BODY** which will be transformed for post-death existence; however, this body is recognisable and identifiable with the person who died, which **GEACH** argues is the only meaningful way one can talk of life after death (in **TAYLOR**). Other Christians suggest that Christ's body after he resurrected and before his ascension was a temporary body and not the type of body that he, and believers, will have in heaven, as this will be a purely **SPIRITUAL BODY** or just the continuation of the soul.

Christianity teaches that a person goes immediately to face **JUDGEMENT** but some believe that the resurrection of all people and a final judgement takes place at the end of time. Other positions include the idea of the soul being judged immediately after death but then being clothed again with its body at the last resurrection. Yet others say this distinction is irrelevant as this all takes place outside of time. As well as different Christian beliefs about the exact nature of the resurrected body, Christians hold different beliefs about what the state of **HEAVEN** and **HELL** mean, with some Christians believing in Hell as a literal place of punishment and separation from God, and Heaven accessed only by those who have accepted Christ in this life. Others believe that God ensures everyone eventually gets to be with him in heaven, whilst some believe some souls (people) are annihilated after death rather than eternally punished.

CATHOLIC teaching stresses that souls go to **PURGATORY** where cleansing of the soul takes place to prepare them for the **BEATIFIC VISION**, ie, the meeting with God. After this cleansing the soul is united with the body.

In **ISLAM**, **AKHIRA**, or the afterlife, where body and soul go, is a place of separation between those Allah judges and rewards, who have passed the test of this life by doing good deeds, and those who have failed to show mercy and do good. Allah judges all people on the **DAY OF JUDGEMENT**. Paradise awaits those who have submitted to the will of Allah; some Muslims believe that punishment in Hell is eternal, whilst others believe that Allah will eventually show mercy to all.

CHRISTIANS, JEWS AND MUSLIMS believe in **RESURRECTION** after one life on Earth.

Strengths of resurrection

1. **JESUS CHRIST** - The Christian claim that Jesus of Nazareth rose from the dead, and appeared in bodily form to his disciples and over 500 witnesses, is widely believed. If he did not, then how can history account for the empty tomb, the transformation in the disciples from feckless cowards to fearless preachers, and the rapid growth of the early Church? This argument draws on the Principle of Sufficient Reason. (Leibniz)

2. Encourages **VIRTUE** - The Parable of the Sheep and the Goats (Matthew 25:31-46) suggests that the consignment to heaven or

hell will depend, at least in part, on how one has lived one's life. Clothing the naked, feeding the hungry and welcoming strangers are all aspects of a caring society, and so it could be argued that, even on pragmatic grounds alone, it is **GOOD FOR SOCIETY** for people to believe in an afterlife.

3. **MORE COMPATIBLE WITH SCIENCE** than immortality of the Soul. In contending that existence in the afterlife requires a body, resurrection avoids the criticism that dualism is logically inconsistent. Modern scientific understanding emphasises the physical nature of thought and memory.

Weaknesses of resurrection

1. If resurrection to heaven is only possible for those who have accepted Christ, or lived a good life, is this merciful? What implications does this view have for the idea of an all-loving God, as well as the problem of evil?

2. In what sense does personal identity continue after resurrection - do people continue to age or grow? Paul addresses some of these questions in 1 Corinthians 15.

3. What happens between physical death and the day of resurrection? **PURGATORY**, an intermediate state, arose as a doctrine in the 10th C with the practice of paying for the dead on All Souls' Day. The idea of a "place of purification for departed souls" became formal Catholic Church doctrine in the 11th C.

HICK'S REPLICA THEORY

HICK also rejects substance dualism. Unusually, he is a **MATERIALIST** who supports the idea of life after death, but does not favour the traditional dual substance of soul and body idea, rather suggesting that human beings are a "psycho-somatic unity". Hick argues that the soul is really a person's character or dispositions, and not something separate to them. Hick did suggest that there might be some evidence for an interaction between the brain and the mind in some forms of extra sensory perception, but this is not really similar to Plato's or Descartes' forms of dualism.

HICK'S REPLICA THEORY is a thought experiment which puts forward the idea that the resurrection of the whole person is possible. Because humans do not have this separate soul which would survive death, for Hick, any post-death existence would have to involve the whole person, which he thinks God could bring about.

- If John Smith disappeared in London and reappeared in New York we would presume it is the same person; there would be ways of proving that this "replica" would be identical to the original.

- Imagine if Smith died in London and reappeared in NY. Again, we could test if the Smith in NY had the same body as the Smith who died.

- The possibility exists that when Smith dies as a physical person in this physical world, an all-powerful God recreates him in another world of resurrected people. This person will have all the characteristics and memories and thus be the same person.

This can be questioned on several points:

1. Is the body really a replica of the original if there has been a break in continuity between one existence and another?

2. How many replicas are possible?

3. Hick presumes the existence of God.

The **CHRISTIAN CONCEPT** of soul is of the **DIVINE SPARK** breathed into humans as the pinnacle of God's creation; humans are made in his image, and the soul is where God is experienced.

REINCARNATION

HINDUS, **BUDDHISTS** and **SIKHS** believe in different forms of **REINCARNATION**:

- In Hinduism, the soul, or **ATMAN, TRANSMIGRATES** from body to body. The soul moves to its next incarnation after death, according to the **LAW OF KARMA**. The soul is clothed in **MAYA** (the unreal - flesh) whilst on Earth, but is seeking release so that it can be united with **BRAHMAN**, who is pure consciousness; ultimate reality. The birth-life-death cycle (samsara) is ended when the soul is released (moksha) back into Brahman after properly following one's duty (dharma).

- Buddhism speaks of **REBIRTH**. The idea of permanence, or "the self", is an illusion; **ANATTA** means "no self", a state into which a soul can be born and of which it is a part. Rebirth is seen as "not a continuation of the person's identity. Rather the consciousness of the person becomes one of the contributory causes in a new group of materials from which new persons are formed". (**EYRE** et al) Buddhist belief therefore is not about "souls" - the "I" is "not the person living his or her current life but the union of all lives lived". (**JORDAN** et al)

Strengths of reincarnation

1. Similarly to resurrection (and unlike Immortality of the Soul), reincarnation recognises the need for **COSMIC JUSTICE**; in rewarding good and punishing bad karma, the concept of reincarnation may encourage **VIRTUE**, more so than resurrection, which has the concept of grace at its' heart.

2. **UNIVERSALITY** - The concept of reincarnation, déjà-vu and a sense of having privileged information (see Ian Stevenson, Twenty Cases Suggestive of Reincarnation, referenced in Ahluwalia).

3. **MOKSHA** (meaning "release") is arguably, an attractive concept. Both Hindu and Buddhist versions of the concept of reincarnation see bodiless existence as the ultimate reality. Unlike bodily resurrection, which affirms individual identity beyond the natural world, reincarnation sees the most meaningful version of existence in bodiless, corporate identity: We are no longer "boundaried" by flesh and blood, but released from bodily bondage into the cosmic whole.

Weaknesses of reincarnation

1. Is the person who is reincarnated "me" in any sense, and, if not, how can I learn lessons from a previous life?

2. Reincarnation might solve the problem of evil as karma dictates that people get to face the consequences of their actions (any post-death existence attempts do this). But this might not explain why there is suffering in the first place.

3. There may be **ANOTHER EXPLANATION** for memories of previous lives. John **HICK** looked for a psychological explanation by suggesting that the examples given by Stevenson might be explained by some sort of extra-sensory perception that can be transported via telepathy (summarised in Ahluwalia).

Key quotes

1. Replica is "the divine creation in another space of an exact psycho-physical 'replica' of the deceased person." Hick

2. "There is no spirit-driven life force, no throbbing, heaving, pulsating, protoplasmic, mystic jelly." Dawkins

3. "To say that someone survived death is to contradict yourself." Flew

4. Buddhism teaches that, "the new person is not identical to the old or completely different. They are simply aspects of the continuing stream of consciousness".

5. "Since we believe that Jesus died and rose again, even so, through Jesus, God will bring with him those who have died." 1 Thessalonians 4:14, St Paul

6. "When I die I rot, and nothing of my ego survives." Bertrand Russell

7. "Man does not have a body, he is a body ... he is flesh-animated-by-soul, the whole conceived a sa psycho-physical entity." Bishop JAT Robinson

8. "If only for this life we have hope in Christ, we are to be pitied more than all men. But Christ has indeed been raised from the dead, the firstfruits fo those who have fallen asleep." 1 Corinthians 15:19-20, St Paul

Confusions to avoid

The best answers will show awareness of differences within the topics discussed. For example, within the area of reincarnation, there are many differences between Buddhist rebirth and Hindu reincarnation, as well as differences within those traditions. Likewise, Islam and Christianity both believe in resurrection, heaven and hell, but how that is attained, and what it looks like, are very different. The differences between beliefs within Christianity differ wildly - Catholicism teaches that a place of refining - "purgatory" is a prelude to heaven for all but saints. Use key terms and succinct phrases to show awareness of these differences, and your answer will be distinctive.

If an answer asks for a compare-and-contrast approach, it is best to structure an answer around the similarities and differences, rather than the strengths and weaknesses. A key area here would be whether the belief (reincarnation, rebirth, resurrection or immortality of the soul), emphasises a bodied or disembodied approach to the afterlife. Be careful here with reincarnation; although it (by definition) would appear to be firmly in the "bodied" camp, consider the moksha and nirvana aspects which break the cycle (samsara).

Identify key themes such as "personal identity", "continuity" and the use of language, especially when considering what the term "life after death" means. Explore these with both clarity and correct reference to scholars and religious beliefs. Monism and dualism should also be referred to, as well as different forms of materialism. Do not use "monism" and "materialism" interchangeably. Materialism is the belief that only matter has any real existence; one can be a monist and believe that the body and mind cannot be separated because they are one and the same thing.

GET MORE HELP

Get more help with life after death by using the links below:

http://i-pu.sh/C6F42H15

Bibliography

- **AHLUWALIA, L** - Understanding Philosophy of Religion OCR, Folens, 2008

- **BOWIE, R** - AS/A2 Philosophy of Religion and Religious Ethics for OCR, Nelson Thornes, 2004

- **COLE, P** - Access to Philosophy: Philosophy of Religion, Hodder & Stoughton, 2005

- **DEWAR, G** - Oxford Revision Guides: AS & A Level Religious Studies: Philosophy and Ethics Through Diagrams, Oxford University Press, 2009

- **JACKSON, R** - The God of Philosophy, The Philosophers' Magazine, 2001

- **JORDAN, A, LOCKYER, N & TATE, E** - Philosophy of Religion for A Level OCR Edition, Nelson Thornes, 2004

- **PHELAN, JW** - Philosophy Themes and Thinkers, Cambridge University Press, 2005

- **POXON, B** - Religious Studies AS Philosophy, PushMe Press, 2012

- **EYRE, C, KNIGHT, R, & ROWE, G** - OCR Religious Studies Philosophy and Ethics A2, Heinemann, 2009

- **TAYLOR, M** - OCR Philosophy of Religion for AS and A2, Routledge, 2009

- **WILKINSON, M, & CAMPBELL, H** - Philosophy of Religion for A2 Level, Continuum, 2009

A modern-day reply to Kant has come from **NORMAN MALCOLM**. After outlining the idea of an unlimited being as one that does not depend on anything for its existence (meaning God is not contingent), and also that if God does not exist then he cannot come into existence, Malcolm put forward the following formulation:

- The existence of an unlimited being is either logically impossible or logically necessary.

- God's existence is not logically impossible, as there is no logical contradiction in the concept of a God/unlimited being who exists (the idea is not logically absurd or internally contradictory).

- God's existence is therefore logically necessary.

But again, has Malcolm answered the key problem of whether the concept of God as necessary entails existence in reality? Does it mean that if the existence of God is not impossible, it is **NECESSARY**, or just **POSSIBLE**? (It is worth reading the Malcolm extract at the end of the chapter.)

Scholars have noted that Malcolm may have proved the concept of the **LOGICAL NECESSITY** of God's existence (that the non-existence of God is a logical impossibility and self-contradictory), but not the existence of God in reality or factually.

Words and concepts do not always describe realities, even when those concepts have internal and logical consistency.

Believing that God exists, and, following on from that belief to say that God has necessary existence, is not an argument that God necessarily has to exist in reality, just like triangles do not have to have existence, although if they did they would have certain predicates.

If there is a God, he has necessary existence, but the predicate of necessary existence cannot be declared as intrinsic to God and a claim made that as a consequence God has to exist in reality.

Kant thus argues that it is not contradictory to think of a possible being who has **NECESSARY** existence. To describe something as having characteristics would give us a picture of something if it existed, but by describing something, even by saying something has necessary existence, does not establish the existence of that thing. For Kant, all statements about existence are **SYNTHETIC**, true or false after verification, and not analytic, meaning "true by nature". The existence of God needs to be verified from a position exterior to the concept as it were, not by **ANALYTIC** analysis of the term.

If **ANSELM** and **DESCARTES** think they have overcome this idea by suggesting that God has necessary existence as one of the characteristics of the greatest or perfect being, and only this predicate can be assigned to God, then they are in danger of making a circular argument. Are they suggesting that God exists necessarily on the grounds that God has necessary existence?

Has Descartes convinced you that necessary existence has to entail actual existence? Or, as **CATERUS** argued, is this not enough and Descartes still has to show that the "concept of necessary existence entails actual existence" (in Lacewing)?

Love

is

War

by

Natassha Gray

Love is War
©Copyright 2021 Natassha Gray

This is a work of fiction. Names, characters, places and incidents are used fictitiously and any resemblance to persons living or dead, business establishments, events, locations or areas, is entirely coincidental.

Published by: Natassha Gray
All rights reserved.

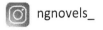 ngnovels_

Dedication:

I dedicate this novel to my wonderful
daughter Georgie - without the maternity
leave that she gave me, this book
would never have happened!

And thanks to all the people
who helped try make it
factually correct –
you know who you are.

Chapter One

June 1940 (present day)

Jack

"What time is it?" I was beginning to feel the nerves now. We had been called up to enter the war zone that was Dunkirk. All the years of preparation and drills had led up to this moment. This is what I was trained for, it was time to go protect our troops, put the Nazi wankers back in their place.

"Twenty to three," Collier replied. Collier was my dear friend and comrade in war, both of us were lucky enough to be part of a trio that flew the Rolls Royce of jets, the Spitfires.

"I'm ready to go! Where's Elvidge?" Collier shouted. Elvidge made up the threesome; these two were my military family.

"I'm here, let's go," Elvidge emerged from the toilet; we were all feeling like the toilet was our best friend at this point. One final hesitant look at each another and we closed our canopies ready to undertake the heroic, yet petrifying journey ahead. That last look was laced with luck.

"How is everyone's fuel looking?" Elvidge asked, we had to monitor it carefully as the journey between Britain and Dunkirk meant we were open to the German fighters.

"69 gallons," Collier replied, "65 gallons," I replied. We were sitting ducks out there over the English Channel, just waiting to be picked off like ants from a garden path. '*SMACK SMACK SMACK*' the sound of bullets from the

Luftwaffe had begun. Collier went left, I split right, and Elvidge zoomed straight on, a tactic we used to try alarm the enemy and get a better vantage point.

"He's above you!" a distressed Elvidge came over the radio, "I'm going down," he urged. His aircraft had been hit already. How can this be happening? The communication went dead. '*SMACK SMACK SMACK*' the bastard was still shooting.

"I've got a clear view, he's mine," Collier shouted. '*FRRRRRRRRRRR,*' the bullets pounded the ME109, the enemy was no more.

"Well done mate!" I chuckled congratulating Collier.

"He had no chance against you and your guns," I smirked. Looking down, I saw the wreckage of a Spitfire bobbing on top of the deep, blue water; Elvidge was gone. I hadn't seen him leave the plane; there had been no parachute or further communication. I managed a choked, "Did ye' see him get out?" to Collier.

"No," was all he could reply. I briefly closed my eyes in disappointment and took a deep breath... and then there were two. Rest in peace my brave friend.

1931

"Afternoon, I'm Jack Watson, from Bath, originally Scotland. I'm 20 years old and into running in my spare time," I didn't really know what else they wanted me to say. I was feeling excited yet nervous about what I was about to undertake. All I ever wanted was to join the Royal Air Force; it had been my passion since I was a wee lad. I had worked so hard to get here, passing the tough exam to get a place, studying my arse off at school. I was fortunate enough to have attended a private school, which meant I had the advantage of being chosen over everyone else. I was always grateful for what my mum and dad had sacrificed for me, in order for me to achieve my dream of becoming a pilot.

I sat back down, looking around at all the young men like myself, signing our life away with great pride, to protect King and country. Everyone looked awkward, like rabbits in headlights, myself included, except one lad, he was sat as bold as brass, just smirking at me from across the room.

"And what is so amusing Collier?" a stern voice boomed across the room. It was the ranking officer, and he was not pleased. Collier was the cool as ice kid that had been grinning at me.

"Nothing Sir," he put his head down, stifling the smile.

"No, we are all dying to know, share it with the group," he became more infuriated. Collier stood, and in an accent I can only imagine placed down at the market selling dodgy clothing, said, "He just reminds me of home." He was referring to me; I was intrigued as my accent was very Scottish, despite only living near Edinburgh until I was seven years old.

When we were dismissed, I ran to keep up with Collier, grateful of finding a friend in this unknown time.

"So, I remind ye' of home, how do ye' explain that, you're more cockney than apples and pears," I laughed. He was a smartly dressed chap with a hard looking exterior. His brown hair sprung across his head, covered in Brylcreem, all dapper and suave. He had a gentleman-like quality about him, which most of the RAF lads tended to have, but Collier possessed this air of calm, like he had

7

his shit together and you just wanted to be his mate.

"My parents were born in Leith, it's just nice to hear some familiarity," he smiled sadly.

"Ah well I'd love to meet 'em, it'd be good to speak to someone from the homeland, most people cannae understand me," I joked.

"Unfortunately, they're long gone, both died many years ago," he smiled nostalgically. What a complete idiot I am.

"Pal I'm so sorry, I didn't realise."

"Don't worry mate, it is what it is, it's why I am here and I intend to give it my all, for them." I shook his hand.

"Well I'm here for ye' pal, if ye' ever need to chat or get drunk, I'm your man," I smirked, and from that day we were inseparable.

His life as he described had been hard, so whatever his future would bring next would surely be a breeze. He lost his parents at just eight years old; his father had been an avid pilot for fun. Ironically, his parents had both died in a plane accident after it was caught in a storm and went down over the English Channel. Even though he had been through the wars, his attitude was strong and positive, and nothing seemed to phase him. He had no siblings, he went to live with his aunt Urma who was anti-children and made that very clear. He spent a lot of his time alone, dreaming of being able to join the RAF and prove to himself that he could be half as good a pilot as his late father. As soon as he was old enough, he left to join. He was two years younger than me, but you would have thought he was ten years older, with the maturity and life experience that oozed out of him. We got into lots of mischief together, but he also pulled me through those hard slogs, the arduous training sessions, and he was the ultimate wingman. I had more memories with him than I did with my mates back home. He had been promoted to Wing Commander ahead of me, but I was happy being Squadron Leader, for now. I felt safe in the knowledge that whatever I did as long as he was by my side, I would be just fine, and I would protect him in return. The brotherhood of the military was true, and I treat him like my own family. He was my brother; we just didn't have the same blood. My parents were like his own too, we spent most Christmases together, and always vowed that one day, when the time came, that we would be best men at each other's weddings. No Nazi berk was about to change that.

Present day

SMACK SMACK SMACK.

"The bastards are back!" I shrieked.

"SPLIT," Collier calmly uttered, we went in separate directions.

"He's got his sights on me," I exclaimed nervously about the fighter jet heading towards me.

"I've got you," Collier replied, but it was too late, my right propeller had been hit and it blew, *shit* I thought.

"I'm going down!" I panicked. I need to stay calm; I have my 'chute I just need to bail. I pulled myself together and looked around at the vast sea below, the water looked steady and the swell looked fair, "I'm going to try land her," I said over the airwaves, I was starting to fall lower, gradually getting closer to the water.

"Take it easy down there," Collier returned calmly, his reassuring voice made me feel at ease but only for a moment before the reality that I was bombing towards the water hit me again. Faster and faster, I fell, my head was spinning, deep breaths, Jack, deep breaths, I said to myself. You didn't go through all that training to die trying to land her... further and further, faster and faster and splashdown! My plane hit the water, and it all went quiet.

I was briefly under water, I knew that much, the plane bobbed up and down on the steady waves, and I realised I had made it down safely - I was alive! I could see, what looked like a small boat in the distance, it grew closer... it was a yacht! Had I travelled that far through the air in my panic that I had somehow landed back near Britain? My thoughts wondered for a moment, inhaling and exhaling at the realisation that I had dodged death, but I was brought drastically back to the present when I saw the most horrific sight of my life. Collier was spiralling down towards the ocean, in a ball of flames. How had this happened, he had just saved me only five minutes before. There was nothing I could do, nothing! I tried to get out but my seatbelt had me fixed in, I couldn't undo it quickly enough, and 'BANG'. His plane hit the water and all I could see was thick black smoke billowing into the sky. I eventually managed to snap my seatbelt clasps open and clambered outside onto the windshield. I sat on the plane, I could see the German wanker had flown off, I could hear his pellets in the distance, no doubt attacking another innocent ship or troop member. We had failed in our mission to not just protect the country, but each other too. I was so near yet so far to Collier and the wreckage, I jumped in the water and began to swim towards the burning wreck.

"Where are you going?" A faint voice shouted from behind me. I ignored it, I was off to save my friend, what did he think I was doing; nothing was more important. I thrashed against the waves and felt like I was getting no closer. My arms grew tired, the harder I swam the further I seemed away from him, the current was stronger than anticipated. Tears welled in my eyes, I was too late, Collier was gone. I battered and whipped against the waves, getting nowhere fast. The smoke billowed from the debris; I could see the orange flames licking the skies, what suffering had he endured? What had I done to try save him? I was a pathetic excuse for a friend and airman.

I decided that I no longer wanted to try, if he was gone, Elvidge was gone, then so was I. I stopped trying to battle against the waves and let them lap over my head. I wanted to give up, I couldn't get my thoughts in order, it all seemed like a dream... no a nightmare. I had a flashback to the day we joined, and the promises we had made to one another - I had let them down. If I couldn't keep my promise to my brothers, if I couldn't protect them or the country, then what was the point in continuing. My mind swirled with dark thoughts, as I felt the water burn into my lungs. I felt a sensation of being pulled, and before I knew it I was being hauled on-board the pleasure yacht from the horizon. I looked up with watery vision, coughing and spluttering, to see an old scruffy looking man and his fisherman friend staring back at me. They passed me a shabby brown blanket. "G-g-go over there...my friend!" I urgently pointed towards the flaming debris – shivering as water dripped down my face, off my clothes and onto the deck. My chest ached with every inhale. The old man looked back at his friend sadly.

"I'm sorry son, but there's no way anyone is getting out of there alive," his gaze rested back on me. I knew this; I just did not want it to be true. I put my head in my hands and sobbed uncontrollably, the old man put his hand on my back and tapped me soothingly, sucking on his pipe and staring into the distance - he understood. We sailed off back towards England, it was the longest, quietest journey home I had ever made. My life changed forever that day. I didn't want to get on to that passing boat. I wanted to sink into the deep blue ocean and be reunited with my pals. I didn't feel like a hero. After being so proud and privileged to be part of it, I now wished I had never joined the Royal Air Force. This was not me, Jack Watson as everyone knew me, this was now a man who didn't want to carry on.

Chapter Two

Two months later (August 1940)

Nina

"Would you like a cup of tea ladies?" She was so softly spoken, so warming, so kind. She was a mother figure to everyone she came across.

"Yes, please Mrs Watson," I replied, even though I had barely finished my last cup, how could I refuse. I sat daydreaming about Mrs Delilah Watson being my own mother, baking cakes and making Sunday lunches together. I had a huge void that needed filling where my maternal figure was concerned, my own mother had been a poor excuse for a parent, and I longed for that bond. Iris, my colleague, quickly snapped me out of my daydream.

"Nina, can you pass me that ticket please?" Iris was a stern Woman Police Constable, WPC for short, and always had my best interests at heart, but often went about it in such a condescending way. She reminded me of a school headmistress, she wore dark, thick framed glasses and her hair was piled upon her head like a grey cloud. She had a musky smell about her and wore lots of cheap looking jewellery on her wrists and fingers. She was widowed and had been alone since her husband had passed fifteen years ago. She lived with many cats, and had no children, I felt sorry for her in a way. Iris was content with her lot though, and even more satisfied with the role we played in the Police Force. She enjoyed counting and documenting the tickets that had been issued to the looters during the riots. I however wanted more, there must be more to being a policewoman, other than administration.

"Sure, here you go," I slid her the ticket exerting a long exhale. Myself and a number of colleagues were in Bath. Avon and Somerset Police Constabulary had called for mutual aid because the riots and looters had got out of hand since the Nazi's had started bombing England, during the Battle of Britain. Myself, Iris and Inspector Harry Ward were staying in Mr and Mrs Watson's home; they had kindly agreed to put us up, as so many other homes had done too, in the local area. Those that hadn't been affected by the war, anyway. The looters were frankly extorting those already suffering and it made me so angry. We were from Lincolnshire, we were miles away from home, the war was in full swing, and all I kept thinking was how scary and dramatic it all was, which strangely filled me with excitement. I felt alive, like I was part of something big, something that I could be stood up and counted for, well, not the admin bits but making sure the women and children were all in order during this god-awful time. Back home, it was just the humdrum of normal life, and I was extremely bored and in need of a new adventure.

"Do you ever wish we could go out and help fight the fight Iris?" I exclaimed. She frowned at me over the top of her glasses.

"Are you joking little one? Have you seen the state of what is happening out there, we'd be no match for those dirty looters, and that is just the tip of the iceberg, they would take advantage of us within minutes. We would be dead quicker than you could shout for help."

"But…," I tried to speak.

"But nothing, stop living in your fantasy land for one minute, keep your mouth shut, your eyes on the tickets and pray we all get home in one piece." The room fell awkwardly silent, Mr Watson looked up at me over his newspaper, Mrs Watson continued to drink her tea, and Iris carried on counting tickets. I sighed, about to retaliate with a snappy comment, when he appeared.

"JACK!" Mrs Watson stood in a flustered panic, Mr Watson put down his newspaper and both approached the front door hastily. There stood the most handsome man I had ever seen. With dark blonde, gingery hair swept across his head in a suave side parting, clean-shaven, tall, broad muscular shoulders and sapphire blue eyes that just pulled you in; I was mesmerised. He was smartly dressed, wearing a light blue chequered shirt and navy chino trousers. His scent wafted across the room, it smelled of pink pepper and lavender, it was desirable. My stomach dipped, what was wrong with me? Firstly, I had a boyfriend, secondly, I had never even spoken to this man, yet I felt like he'd caught me hook, line and sinker. I could not help but stare at his magnificence. I knew who he was immediately; he was Mr and Mrs Watson's son, Jack. There were photographs of him all around the house, I had often seen them as I passed through the living room and had thought he was handsome, but in real life, he was splendid. He was a Pilot in the RAF; there had been plenty of hush hush conversations about him, but all I could gleam from them was that he had lost a friend, and no-one had heard from him since.

"Mother," he was inebriated, swaying slightly. "I'd like ye' to meet Clara..." a monstrosity of a woman walked in wearing a short black skirt, and a low-cut ruby red chemise, with her cleavage on show. Her bleach blonde hair clung to the side of her head in a matted beehive shape, dangly silver hoops hung from her ears, her mascara seeped down her cheek, and her cherry lips were smudged down to her chin. She looked like a common prostitute; Mrs Watson looked on horrified.

"Jack what is going on? Where have you been?" She shrieked upset, tears in her eyes. Jack started looking round the room, he noticed Iris, she stared at him disapprovingly, and then his eyes met mine. I felt sick with excitement. He eyed me up for a short while, and then looked back at Mrs Watson.

"Who are these people?" he asked, in a couldn't care less manner.

"Jack why don't you come in… alone, and we can have a cup of tea and a chat," Mr Watson said in a calm manner, shooting a quick sideways glance at Clara. Mr Watson was someone who you would have loved to have around you in a crisis. Just looking at him immediately made you feel relaxed. He was a traditional gentleman, who wore tweed jackets, suit trousers and a trilby to match; he often smoked a pipe, and sat quietly, taking in everything around him. From what I had gathered, he was a retired newspaper Chief Executive, so was rather wealthy after selling his business. He was softly spoken, and him and Mrs Watson were the perfect couple, and people I would have been proud to call my parents. Mrs Watson was a well-dressed, glamorous woman, with white hair, curled into a bob, her makeup was nothing short of perfect, and she often wore pearls and pantsuits for casual. She was cheerful all the time and made everyone she was around feel welcome. Except Clara, in this instance, which I was secretly rather pleased with.

"I don't think so, we aren't finished..." he looked at Clara and winked. Why her, I asked myself, he could have anyone he wanted looking like he did. I couldn't take my eyes from him, trying to analyse him, trying to work him out; the view was so pretty.

"Jack," Mr Watson said sternly, "that's enough, now say goodbye to your lady friend, and we can have a conversation." Jack was unsteady on his feet, holding onto the door for stability, clear signs that he had been drinking a while. His demeanour was not what I expected at all, his photographs showed him as heroic, proud and happy, this Jack standing in front of me seemed to be hiding a secret, mad at the world and deeply unhappy. Jack kissed Clara on the hand, like she was a lady, and led her outside. I felt a pang of jealousy, jealous of a trollop, that's a first. I overheard a muffled exchange of words, 'I will be out soon,' and he came back in shutting the front door behind him. He stood there, like a helpless boy, his hands tucked into his trouser pockets, looking at Mrs Watson as if he was carrying the world on his shoulders.

"Where have you been my dear boy?" She hugged him tightly. He didn't seem to know how to react, he was emotionless. He said nothing in return, and hugged her back, his eyes remained wide and fixated into the distance.

"How are you?" she continued. Jack suddenly turned his attention to Iris; he then looked at me again. My stomach flipped once more.

"Who are ye'?" he asked, flicking his gaze between me and Iris. I didn't speak, I couldn't, what was wrong with me?

"These are police, Jack, they are here to assist with the riots, they're staying all throughout the city," Mrs Watson interjected.

"Fantastic, ye' have some real heroes under the roof then," he chuckled sarcastically. Was he making fun of us? I felt myself get a little angry, but *he* said it, and although I could feel myself about to snap back at his horrible attempt at humour, I stopped myself; there was more to this.

"Whatever do you mean Jack?" Mrs Watson asked.

"Look mother, I have to go, I don't even know why I came back." He shrugged and turned to open the front door. Mr Watson looked at me, I knew he was trying to hint for us to leave with his gaze, but he was such a polite man, he would never have said it. I nodded in understanding, and finally mustered the courage to speak.

"Iris let's go, we have an early start tomorrow," and I waved Iris towards the door that led upstairs. Jack watched me walk away; I could feel his eyes on me. I felt wobbly legged, as if I could trip at any point. Iris and I closed the door behind us, and went up to our rooms, with thoughts of Jack swimming around my mind.

Five past three in the morning, and I couldn't sleep a wink! Harry still wasn't back. I felt slightly worried but strangely I was more concerned about Jack. Inspector Harry Ward and I were in a relationship and had been together for three months, after meeting through my dad, and we just happened to work for the same police force. Our relationship was very low key and was the ultimate secret. He was a pleasant enough man, got on well with my father and was considerably good-looking, but he lacked emotion, he was short of conversation, and he rarely made me laugh. He was tall, stern looking, rarely smiled, very muscular and had dark brown hair that greased to his head in a side parting. He was what you would envisage when you thought of a typical Alpha Male. He was my first proper relationship and was the only man I had ever slept with, he had that hold over me. Sometimes I felt judged by him, and that maybe I wasn't enough, but I would never say anything to him, after all I didn't know any better, maybe this is just the way it was in grown up relationships. Still, not everyone gets their prince, so I was quite happy seeing how things went. I've never been fussed about relationships, but at twenty-five years old, I figured it was time to start thinking about settling down and having a family of my own. There wasn't love and passion between Harry and me, but it might come in time.

Eurgh, this is no good, I need a glass of water. I walked downstairs, trying my hardest not to creak the wooden floorboards and wake the house. I presumed everyone would be in bed now; it's been a good six hours since the whole 'Jack drama'. I entered the living room, which was open plan and paired with the kitchen and dining room. A small lamp was on in the kitchen on the windowsill, but the living room was in complete darkness, and I couldn't see a thing. The air smelt of lilies, they were placed in a crystal vase on the kitchen table and the streetlight outside the front door hummed. I fumbled through the dark, using the lamp as my guide and tip toed to the kitchen. I helped myself to a glass, gently squeaked the tap on and poured myself a large water. I took a gulp and looked out of the window into the night garden. The house looked out on to a stream that was at the bottom of the lawn, you could hear the trickling water; it was so peaceful. The moon shone down onto the grass and highlighted the midnight dew. I took a moment to gather my thoughts, closing my eyes so I could hear nothing but the running water. It was Zen and I started to feel a little sleepy, finally.

"Did I wake ye'?" A voice boomed out of the darkness behind me.

"HOLY SHIT!" I gasped, turning around in a panic, spilling my water everywhere. I heard a small laugh, and from the darkness of the living room emerged Jack. Still as handsome as ever, but he looked extremely tired, his hair was dishevelled, and he had his top buttons undone on his shirt, he looked like a man with demons. "Erm no, erm I was just thirsty, what are you doing sat in the dark?" I asked, still trying to catch my breath. He sat down at the kitchen table and put a bottle of half-drunk whisky next to him.

"Thinking," he replied sadly.

"Is everything okay? I know it's not my business but…"

"You're right, it's not really your business," he snapped, taking another hefty swig.

"I was only being polite!" I snapped and slammed my glass down on the table and attempted to storm off.

"Wait," he grabbed my arm dragging me back towards him, I could feel the electricity between us. He continued to pull me closer to him, our gaze did not wither.

"I'm sorry," he released my arm and sat back down, taking a glug out of his whisky bottle.

"You won't find the answer in there," I said lowering my voice and pulling up a chair to sit opposite him, my stomach was in knots. Normally I would have walked away if someone had spoken to me in that way, but I wanted to know his story, I was desperate to be the one he confided in and understand him.

"No, but it's worth a shot," he replied miserably.

"Want to share?" I asked.

"What the whisky or my plight?" He smirked. That smile, wow, he had the cutest dimples, I was smitten for this stranger, I had never felt this way before about a boy; it was alien to me.

"Your story, it might help to tell a complete stranger." I was trying so hard to keep my cool and not be a quivering wreck, I felt vulnerable and naïve in his presence. He looked at me, narrowing his eyes,

"I don't think so, I'm just not in a great place, and I can't see a way out," he paused. "It's hard to explain," he took another drink.

"I have all night," I smiled at him reassuringly, hoping that my pushing would release his deepest thoughts. He studied me for a second, and continued sighing.

"I'm meant to be protecting king and country and I can't bring myself to even step back into a plane, it's embarrassing really!" he exhaled. We were getting somewhere now.

"Why can't you step back into a plane?" I enquired, his gaze fell down onto the table, and he rubbed his forehead, as if he was in pain.

"Ah it's hard to talk about," he took a deep breath. "I lost ma' best pal in the most disturbing way imaginable, and there was nothing I could do, I was useless." He paused briefly, "the image will stay forever in here," he tapped his head, "and I'll never get him back. I have never felt so pitiful. I've always been so strong, but I cannae seem to shake this." He did not lift his gaze from the table, but downed another drop of whisky, frustrated at himself.

"I'm sorry…" he cut me off.

"I don't need your sympathy and I don't deserve it either. I said I would protect him, have his back and I didn't, I don't deserve pity, I deserve the dcath that was meant for me, not him." We had a few moments of silence, I hesitated but could not hold back any longer, he needed to hear it, I could tell he was a good person.

"It probably means nothing coming from me, but war is not pretty, war doesn't give two shits what promises you made, war will take the weak, the strong, the helpless and the innocent, and there is absolutely nothing you can do about it. You didn't fail him that day, you didn't fail us, I bet you did everything you possibly could. Our fate is mapped out for us before we undertake any journey, and I am a strong believer that everything happens for a reason. Be grateful that YOU are alive, that YOU get to still see your wonderful family, that YOU get to live another day and that YOU can don your uniform once again and fly that Spitfire proud, for all the world to see what a hero you really are." Jack just stared at me dumfounded, not saying a word, it felt like an eternity, and I didn't want it to end. He let out a small guffaw of disbelief. He stood up and walked to the kitchen cupboard pulling out two glasses and filled them both with whisky. He smiled sweetly and handed me one.

"Cheers." He held up his glass, I clinked it with mine.

"Cheers," I repeated a little wary, and we both sipped our drinks. He didn't take his eyes from me, and began to smirk once more, he made me nervous, I could not read him.

"Quite a bold woman aren't ye'." I didn't agree and

responded with a lie.

"I try and say what I think, most of the time anyway, after all life is too short to be a mute. When I can see someone is good, and deserves happiness then why wouldn't I tell them?" I mumbled. If I truly said what I really thought I would be telling him how much I had fallen for him after knowing him for all of five minutes, I will probably leave that bit out.

"I deserve happiness? Ye' don't even know me, why would ye' think that?" His gaze suddenly intensified. I rapidly felt shy, what was I even saying. I felt like a wanted to make this man happy at all costs.

"Doesn't everyone?" I quickly inserted, looking down at the table, twiddling my hands. Our eyes met once more, my heart started beating faster, my stomach was doing somersaults. He grabbed my hand and stood me up, so I was facing him. My breath became slow and deep, and in that moment he leant forward and kissed me, slowly and tenderly. It felt right, I felt the electric between our lips. He put his hands through my hair and pushed me against the wall. Our kisses became faster, steamier; I wanted to rip his clothes off. I shouldn't be doing this, I was with someone, but I didn't care. All that was in my head now was Jack. I started unbuttoning his shirt hurriedly, all fingers and thumbs, he took my hands and he led me towards the living room. He laid me down on the floor, and just stared at me with his pool blue eyes, no kissing, just his eyes fixated on mine. He took his shirt off and lifted my nightgown over my head. I couldn't believe this was happening, I was definitely not normally this type of girl, but for him I felt like I would do anything. I lay there on the living room floor, completely naked and entirely exposed to him. I bet he did this with all the girls. I knew in the back of my head that this was just a moment of passion for him, a welcome distraction, and that tomorrow he wouldn't think twice about me, but I didn't care, I wanted to feel him. He took his trousers off and began to kiss me all the way down from my neck to my thighs. I moaned; I had never experienced such sensations. He gently caressed and kissed my breasts, watching me and smiling cheekily. He was definitely experienced in this arena; he knew exactly what to do, and he did it so well. His body was fit and muscular, and I ran my fingers down his chest back up to his cheek and into his hair. He made me feel confident and sexy, more than Harry ever had. We kissed again, more intimately, more deeply, faster and he entered me. We both moaned with pleasure. He did not take his eyes from me, I wanted him to stare at me, it made it so much more intense. I came almost immediately, as did he, in that moment it felt as if we were one person, that we should have been doing this all our lives. We made love two times more, each time better than the last. We finished, out of breath and panting for air. We lay there next to each other, naked under a faux fur throw that Mrs Watson kept on her sofa. He rolled onto his side and stared at me with a soft satisfied expression.

"How are ye' feeling?" he finally muttered. I smirked, I felt like a little girl again.

"Wonderful thanks," I replied, I could not contain my happiness.

"That ye' are," he laughed. "Thank you," he stopped smiling, his expression became serious, he stroked my cheek tenderly, "I needed ye' right now, my little guardian angel, maybe Collier sent ye' for me," he smiled once more. I knew in that moment that this was just sex for him, he needed a distraction, and I was it.

"Maybe he did. Now you need to go back out there and be the best pilot you can be, for him." He sighed and looked into the distance as if he was thinking about what the future held for him now. We were suddenly interrupted by creaks in the floorboards upstairs, *shit.* I quickly pulled on my nightgown, and Jack got dressed within seconds. I bounded towards the door that led upstairs.

"See you in the morning, soldier," I smiled, and went off towards my bedroom.

"Wait," Jack called out, "I still don't know ye' name!" I ignored him, my head spinning from what I had just done, and the thought of Harry walking in. I felt a twist of guilt in my stomach, but it was soon overcome with the joy I felt when I thought of Jack. He was the one, I just knew it, I just didn't know if the feeling was reciprocated.

Chapter 3

Jack

I cannot stop thinking about last night. I don't normally feel this way after a quick bunk up, but there was just something about her. Maybe it's the way she called me out; usually girls just say what they think I want to hear. I admit, I am not usually a relationship sort of man and I have definitely never been in love but right now, I felt like the cat that had got the cream.

After losing Collier and Elvidge, I saw no way up, no way out; it's been dark for some time, and I honestly thought I had no reason to go on anymore. It's been a couple of months and I still cannot get the image out of my head of that plane on fire, my brother suffering. I cannot go there, not today. I feel like I have a reason to smile again. What was her name?

"Good morning, son," my mother was up. I opened up to mum and dad last night; out of everyone in the world, she deserved an explanation as to why I haven't been myself lately. No one could begin to understand what I am going through, they never will however they will try, just like mum and dad have.

"Morning mum," I smiled.

"You seem happier darling; would you like a cup of tea?"

"I feel a bit better thanks, had time to gather ma' thoughts, it's nice to be home, back to some sort of familiarity…"

"And the love of your family," she placed her hand on my head and messed up my hair playfully. My mum,

Delilah Watson, was the loveliest woman I had ever had the pleasure of knowing. She was the most caring considerate, happy, giving lady. Her and my dad, George Watson, made love and relationships look like the steadiest, most effortless thing in the world. Their love is what I have dreamed of replicating. I have never found someone I wanted to do that with, until now…maybe. What am I saying? I don't even know the girl!

Mum was responsible for the fantastic childhood me and my brother Bobby had. Bobby was my little brother who spent his time travelling up and down the country as a tennis coach. He was six years younger than me, but we were close. He wasn't the most mature man you would meet, and he liked a beer and a lady more than I care to go into, but he made up for it by being a sweet, funny, mischievous, naïve soul, who I was proud to call my sibling. Mum gave us everything we needed, showered us with love and affection and was there for us through thick and thin – she was a mum in a million. It was now time for me to do the same for her, starting with not putting her through the stress and worry I had for the last month. I just needed that time to feel sorry for myself, to think about Collier, and plan what my future was going to look like. I had instead just got obliterated on whisky every night, been to the darkest depths of myself, and shagged anything that moved, all in order to try and forget.

"Thanks mum, I know that; you and dad have been great and so understanding, I love ye'."

"That's what parents do love," she handed me a cup of tea, smiling, "I'd do the same for both of you." I hadn't seen Bobby in a while, maybe that would help. The front door suddenly flew open, whom were we expecting? A man I had never met walked through the door. He looked stern, angry, a man on a mission. He seemed uptight like he had something to prove. He was dressed in a Police uniform, which meant he knew my latest love encounter, which intrigued me more. I sipped my tea slowly as I tried to fathom him out.

"Good morning, Mrs Watson," he said in a broad Cockney accent, "I apologise for coming in so late, work went on longer than expected."

"Oh no problem dear. This is my son Jack, Jack this is Harry, he's an Inspector in the Police force," she nodded towards me smiling. We shook hands; and he eyed me up and down with an insincere smile.

"Is everything okay?" Mum asked him.

"Yes of course, thanks for the tea, are Nina and Iris up?" he asked. My eyes lit up, so she is called Nina or Iris, her ears must have been burning, because they both entered the room.

"Good morning, Inspector," the older woman said. The younger girl, my girl, was stood behind the elderly lady, with her eyes fixed to the ground, all sweet and innocent.

"Good morning, Iris," he replied moodily. So, my girl's name was Nina, very pretty. I took my time to scrutinise her, she appeared quite meek in the way she stood. She would not look at me; probably embarrassed after last night's antics. She looked like butter wouldn't melt, and she was so beautiful she made the other girls I had known look like mutton. She was petite but with curves in all the right places. Her eyes were jade green, her lips ruby red, and her face like porcelain. Her uniform clung to her sexily, she looked so sophisticated and important, but with an air of naivety. I couldn't read her very well, it was

28

doing my head in.

"Nina, are you okay?" Harry asked. She finally looked at me coyly, before her eyes flicked back to mean old Harry.

"Yes, thanks sir," she muttered.

"You don't have to call me sir off duty sweetheart," he laughed looking around awkwardly. *Sweetheart? What*?

"Would you both like a drink?" mum asked. That was her go to question when it began to get a little difficult.

"Actually, I need some fresh air, I feel a little dizzy," Nina replied hurriedly, and she headed through the living room and exited out the front door. Harry put his drink down on the table and followed her.

"Oh dear, lovers tiff," Iris gossiped, "they don't like to admit it, but they are courting," she raised her eyebrows at my mum in a non-approving way. *For fuck's sake*, they are in a relationship. Of course, they were. That would explain why she looked so coy. It was about fifteen minutes before Nina and Harry entered the room again. I looked at Nina to make sure she was alright; she did not look back. Why did I even care? She was with someone, and I wasn't looking for a relationship, I should just forget it; so why was I struggling to do so?

"Right, I am going to get my head down for a few hours, keep up the good work ladies," Harry boomed as he made his way upstairs. He shot me an unsure look that I ignored; I did not like this man one bit.

"Right, Nina we best make our way out and start delivering these tickets, are you ready to go?" Iris asked.

"Yes, but first can I just have two moments please," she looked at me nodding towards the front door.

"With me? Of course," I replied setting my cup down.

Both Iris and mum looked confused, of course they did, they had no idea what we had been up to, or that we had even said more than hello to one another. I followed Nina out into the garden, and she led me down to the stream.

"I'm so sorry," she blurted out as soon as we faced each other. "I am with Harry; we have been courting for three months. Last night was…great…but it was a spur of the moment thing and… I'm sorry," she finally took a breath and shut her eyes tightly, as if she was hiding from me. "I'm not usually that sort of girl," she added in a whisper. I remained quiet, taking it all in. This morning I had woke up thinking this lady had saved me from myself, that it might have been the start of something, and that I had never felt like this about someone so suddenly. And it was gone, just like that. What could I do? She was never mine and I wasn't about to show her how much she had got to me. I'm a military man, we all kept a stiff upper lip when it came to showing people how we felt. We knew there would be another dame along not long after, as disgraceful as that sounded. It had just been sex for me initially, and I let myself fall a bit too deep too quickly, I am just overcome with emotion and grief, it was never real, I told myself. After a long minute of battling thoughts, I replied calmly.

"It's okay." She looked at me, with those beautiful pea green eyes. She really was magnificent. Her champagne blonde hair curled into a plaited bun and loose curls licked her bonny face, her cheekbones were so striking she could have been on the screen, freckles were dotted across her face like the most astonishing dot to dot. She smelled like a meadow, her wonderful scent filled my nostrils as it blew towards me in the warm wind, it was comforting and alluring in the same moment. Her gaze was so intense I didn't know where to look, what was she doing to me, I felt under her spell. I wanted her to be mine, she felt different to any other girl I had ever laid eyes on. I wanted to get to know her, I felt like she understood what I was feeling and that she could maybe help save me. Sadly, she would never get to know my true feelings about her, she had clearly made her choice, I was no one's second best. "Don't worry, I understand that emotions were high last night, please don't feel bad, it was just sex after all," I said through gritted teeth. She looked disappointed in my reply.

"Oh…right, yes I know," her gaze fell to the ground. I had upset her, but I thought that was what she wanted to hear, maybe she was as confused as I was. I gently moved a piece of her hair out of her eyes.

"It was nice to be in the moment, I enjoyed it," I continued trying to claw my way back, I had always been a fighter. She grabbed my hand holding it to her face and closed her eyes deeply inhaling, soaking in my touch. Her face felt silken and cold against my palm. I knew then in that moment that this was more than just sex, I could tell she had feelings for me; I had to push it so I could see how I felt too. Was it real or was it grief? I took a chance, leant in, and kissed her slowly but with lust. She pulled away at first, but once more, we found ourselves in that passionate embrace of the night before. I wanted her there and then, I did not care that it was broad daylight and that her lover was inside my family home, my pain of Collier faded away, the more we kissed the more like normal Jack I felt. She was my cure; I needed her.

"Nina," Iris shouted for her. *For fuck's sake.* She pulled

away and looked at me out of breath and dumfounded, she said nothing, but began to run.

"Nina…" she ignored me as she dashed towards the house. I had never felt more confused in my life.

Four hours it's been, where is she? I kept looking out of the window. I couldn't sit still, she was my new focus, it kept me from thinking about the dark thoughts that were still there, ready to rear their heads at any point.

"Are you alright, son?" my father asked concerned.

"Yep, fine and dandy thank ye'," I said so hastily my mum stopped peeling the potatoes.

"Why don't we go all go for a walk?" she suggested putting down her knife.

"I can't, I have to stay here," I instantly regretted my comment.

"Why?" mum asked inquisitively.

"I'm just not in the mood mum," I smiled, "maybe tomorrow." That would stop the inquisition I had set myself up for. The door leading from upstairs swung open with force.

"Ah good afternoon," it was the inspector, who else would be so angry at a door. I looked away, I hope he was not like this with Nina, I pondered, suddenly feeling protective.

"Good afternoon, Harry, would you like a drink? Did you sleep okay?" Mum asked, in her usual caring manner.

"Fantastic thank you, Mrs Watson and yes a tea would be lovely," he smiled and sat down on the settee opposite me. I continued to look out the window, I knew I was being childish and immature, but let's face it, I was as jealous as hell that he was the one that Nina was with. Maybe I should stop acting like an arse and be a man; it's not like I love the girl, besides I am trying not to pay too much attention to my irrational, abrupt thoughts at the moment, my mind is a muddled swamp which should be taken with a pinch of salt. After all, only twenty-four hours previous I was bedding a prostitute, which I must admit, was a new low.

"Are ye' back at work today then, Harry?" I was going to be the bigger person here. He seemed blunt in his response.

"Yes, the night shift again." He definitely did not want to talk to me either, I actually could not have cared less.

"Are you back for long from the RAF then?" Harry added. My Dad looked up at me, apprehensive but eager to know my answer. Of course, Harry did not know my story, and I could not be bothered to go into it.

"No, hopefully going back soon," I replied.

"Why are you back?" Harry interrogated.

"I lost a mate," I said bluntly looking to the ground. The disturbing images were creeping back, come on Jack, deep breaths, remember what Nina said, there was nothing I could do, be grateful for being alive.

"Ah, I am sorry to hear that, still back on the saddle hey," he quipped nonchalantly, taking the cup of tea from my mum. *Bastard.*

"Oh, I don't think it's as easy as that, Harry," my mum interjected, "they were like brothers," she sighed upset. She understood but this twit clearly had a heart of stone, no wonder Nina jumped into my bed.

"Have you ever lost anyone dear to ye' Harry?" I asked forcefully, continuing to look out the window, "because getting back on the saddle is not as easy when you've seen your best pal burning to death in his plane right in front of

33

your very eyes, because the Nazi bastards decided they wanted to play war," I snapped frankly, I despised this emotionless lump. He looked up at me with no reaction, but I could tell I had dinted his ego, behind those dead eyes a hint of anger flared. We stared at one another; the hatred was clear. He was about to snarl back when the front door opened, and there she was again, wonderful Nina.

Nina

Oh dear, both of them sat on the settee together, not what I wanted to walk into if I was honest. I had been going crazy whilst out, thinking about what to do for the best. Am I really going to consider throwing away a three-month relationship for one night of passion? One thought would not leave my mind though, was it more than just that with Jack? I have never had feelings for someone so quickly, so intensely. I wanted him to be mine but in the same breath I was not confident I could satisfy him. I was just some small town, inexperienced woman from Lincolnshire, he was an important military man, fighting in the war like a true hero, he probably had women throwing themselves at him in their hundreds. I envisaged what a future might look like with him, it involved marriage and children; I wonder what he would be like as a father. Oh, snap out of it, Nina, he just wanted one night with me, it was the soldier mentality, he even said it himself, it was just sex. I wasn't one hundred percent convinced that's all it was, but maybe it was just wishful thinking. I know Harry would marry me, and maybe one day we would have children. If I stuck with Harry, I would have stability; I don't know Jack from the next man and given his recent behaviour he was the opposite of stable.

"Nina!" Harry was talking to me, and I had not been paying one bit of attention. Jack smirked at me. I could feel myself blushing.

"Sorry Har…sir," I replied, we were on duty after all.

"Did you deliver the tickets to each reprobate?" he snapped.

"Yep, all done and dusted. I feel a bit lightheaded still, I might take a lie down if that's okay," I said dashing out the room before he could reply. I could not be bothered with that situation right now, I needed to think.

"She's been in a bit of a daze all morning," I could hear Iris talking about me; she was such a nosy cow.

I have laid on this bed for one hour and have not come any closer to a decision. Jack doesn't want me in that way I know it, I want more than just a fling, he just wants something casual whilst he's back, why would he want me in any other way, he's out of my league. I heard a creak outside the door; it slowly opened and in walked Jack.

"What are you doing in here?" I squawked, jumping up off the bed, "Harry is downstairs!"

"No, he isn't he's gone out, we are safe," he replied flashing me his cheeky smile. "Are ye' feeling better?" He sat down on the bed next to me, my heart beat faster and I felt nervous again, how does he manage to do this to me?

"Yes, I feel fine; I just wanted to leave that situation. I feel guilty for what I have done to Harry." He looked at me seriously.

"Are ye' happy with him?" The comment flustered me,

I didn't know what to say, *was I truly happy with him*?

"Yes, sort of. He makes me feel secure, he wants what I want." Jack cut me off.

"Which is?"

"The usual thing most women want, a trusting marriage and a family, one day," I sighed. "I have only just met you and I don't know you, it seems stupid of me to throw away a relationship for a few moments of passion."

"Come on, give me some credit, it was more than a few moments," he laughed. I smiled back, he was such a cheeky chap, he made me feel like life could be fun, Harry never made me feel that way. I felt like I could just lay and talk to him for hours about everything and nothing. Why didn't he want me in the same way, I felt stupid, here I was making such a big deal about this whole situation in my head, when realistically Jack just wanted a fling.

"Look Nina, in all seriousness, I don't know what is going on here, I wish I could say more. It's early days, and it would be wrong of me to lead ye' on. I don't let my true feelings be known very often, and I can honestly say that the way I feel for ye' now is not something I have felt before. I guess ye' could call me a relationship beginner, and it takes a lot for me to fall in love, I mean, I have never been in love." My heart dropped, I felt sick with excitement, *love.* I was acting like a schoolgirl, I suddenly felt giggly. "Love?" I sniggered. He smirked back, looking straight into my eyes. Oh, those eyes, I wanted him so much.

"I am still trying to fathom ye' out, decide what it is I am actually feeling, but I think it could be something, I don't know. I am gonna lay my cards on the table for ye' Nina," he suddenly became very grave and took my hand.

"I have thought about nothing but you since last night, when I first saw ye' I was taken back by how beautiful you were. Speaking to ye' has made me see what a wonderful, intelligent, funny, kind woman ye' are. You're unique, you're strong but vulnerable, and when I am around ye' I forget about everything bad in the world. I obviously want the same things as ye' one day, marriage and kids, just like my parents, if I could find someone to make me happy the way my mum and dad make each other happy, I would be a lucky man. But I am a broken man at the moment, and I don't want to make any promises that I can't keep. Ye' deserve the world, Nina, you're a special girl. I am sorry for lying to ye' earlier, last night did have an effect on me, and it was more than just sex. No one was more surprised than me at that realisation," he smiled at me coyly. I felt like I was going to burst with all the praise he was giving me, how did he make me feel like I was the only girl in the world, I suddenly felt full of confidence, and I wanted him now. I leant over and kissed him with desire, a kiss he would remember. I didn't care one bit that anyone could walk in, the door was shut, and I was having him to myself, I would take any risk for this man.

I took his shirt off and straddled him. The kisses became steamier; he unbuttoned my blouse, leaving me in just my bra and skirt. He stood up, undid his trousers and I took them down to the ground, looking up at him from the floor. I pulled down his boxer shorts, and took his hard penis in my hand, rubbing it up and down gently, he moaned. I laid down on the bed and he slowly peeled off my skirt, then my underwear. He looked at me up and down and gave me that mischievous smile; I could feel the anticipation, I was going to feel like I did last night. I was getting to feel the embrace of my Jack again, I was so eager. I pulled him on top of me and we kissed, it became hotter and sweatier, and he entered me. He moved in and out, I could feel it building, I was ready to come already, I couldn't contain it, and I let out a groan, he followed me soon after. We lay there, hot and sweaty, him still inside me, resting his head on my breasts, both panting and laying silently in pure euphoria.

"One of these days we will last longer than five minutes," I laughed playfully.

"It's impossible, have ye' seen what ye' look like? Ye' don't know what ye' do to me," he smirked. "But it does mean we can go again," he laughed kissing me all the way down to my thighs. And we did just that.

One hour later, we were finally getting dressed. The pang of guilt hit me again now I was out of Jack's trance. Did anyone hear? Did they wonder why we had both left the room? Had Harry arrived back? When I was with Jack time just stood still, he took over my mind and body, I had never felt this way about anything in my life, he was like a drug to me. We sheepishly walked downstairs, but no one was home, phew.

"I told ye' we were safe," he smiled pouring some water. The front door opened and in stormed Harry and Iris. I could feel Jack watching me, and Harry's eyes were on me immediately. I suddenly felt remorseful, like Harry would be able to read my mind.

"Where have you been?" Iris asked me moodily. I took a few seconds to answer but finally managed.

"Laying down, I feel better now." Harry seemed mad about something, what could it be? "Are you alright

Harry?" I mumbled. He looked at me.

"You tell me." *Fuck*.

"I don't know, you seem upset," I remarked back.

"I want a word…in private," he replied irritably.

"Is everything okay?" Jack intervened, he was concerned for me, I could tell.

"Fine," Harry said as he sternly walked towards the stairs. "Nina, now," He gestured for me to follow him.

"Ye' don't need to talk to her like that." Jack please don't, I thought to myself. Jack didn't realise what the real Harry was like, I didn't want Jack to be on the receiving end of that wrath.

"I don't think it's any of your fucking business," Harry bit back.

"I don't think treating a lady like that is necessary," Jack snapped walking towards Harry. Harry walked over to him speedily and put his face in Jack's.

"Mind your own business you cowardly bastard," Harry said slowly, but filled with anger, his black eyes were raging staring deep into Jack's. I couldn't believe what he had said, he was like a wild animal. Jack looked at me hurt, like I was the one who had said those awful words. I couldn't speak, I needed to say something, and make sure he was alright. Jack took a deep breath, put his glass of water down on the table, and walked out of the house, slamming the door behind him.

"Jack wait," I called out, but it was too late. *Harry what have you done*, I thought. He walked up the stairs and I followed, like a lamb sent to slaughter.

Harry was a deep, quiet, complex soul. He kept most of his past to himself, but every now and again some bits reared their heads. What I did know was that before we met, Harry had been a ladies' man. My friends had always fantasised about him, because he was so private, you could let yourself imagine what he was like without actually knowing. I know he slept with lots of women, but he never seemed settled or fulfilled, he always seemed like he was hiding something, and that deep down he was not truly happy and wanted more than just sex, but the barriers he put up would not let that be so, until me. He was a loner - boxing and running were his solace and aside from the police force, and me, he cared for nothing more. We had got together after my dad pushed for us to date, he was fond of Harry and always treat him like the son he never had and was keen for me to find a husband. His parents, who I also knew, were strict and very wealthy. His father was the sort of man to never show affection, and his mother did as she was told, which is maybe why Harry is the way he is. He did not see them anymore, and the last he heard his mum had passed away - he didn't even shed a tear. They had been friends of my father's, so I often saw them at my dad's card nights, and they invited him to their dinner parties. My dad had known his dad since school, and although they led completely different lives to one another, they never lost touch. My dad was a working-class factory worker, and Harry's dad had been a military man, rising through the ranks, earning lots of money along the way. Harry saw my father as an uncle, and although I had seen Harry as I grew up, I had never really been interested in him, or him me, until dad pushed for it. It was all very convenient. I always found there was a controlling side to Harry. He never laid a finger on me physically because I wouldn't be around there a minute longer if so, but things he sometimes said and did were not normal. I batted them away, thinking it was because of his position in his job and that he was just extra protective of me, or maybe my dad put extra pressure on him to take care of me. He was often quite possessive and overbearing, despite only being together three months. I found myself asking for his permission to see my friends; he made all our decisions, down to what we ate for meals. I received disapproving looks from him when I wore something he was not happy with, and found myself constantly justifying my thoughts and feelings, without him just accepting that's who I was. However, in front of people that we were close to, he was my rock, loved me more than anything, would die for me, and said he only did those things because of his job and how he saw other men acting around women. That I could believe, but I think he also liked the ownership of me. I could not be bothered with any more unnecessary aggravation, I hated confrontation, and decided it was an easier life to just get on and do what he said. This was not really what I wanted, but since joining the police force and becoming Harry's girlfriend, I was not as wild and opinionated as I maybe once was. Harry was very career driven, and I liked that ambitious side to him, but sometimes I wondered what more there was to him. Him being in my life just seemed to fit, it was safe. Is it convenient? Sure. Do I love him? I don't think so. More than Jack? Definitely not. But being with Jack was a pipe dream, and there was no way Jack and I would ever become anything more, men like him and women like me just did not happen.

Harry was sat on the bed, with his head in his hands, I walked in and slowly closed the door behind us, not daring to even breathe. Neither of us spoke for a good few minutes.

"Why?" He finally muttered, his head still in his hands.

"Why what?" I replied quietly.

"DON'T GIVE ME THAT SHIT NINA!" he bellowed. I was frightened, I had never seen Harry this angry with me. "You and him," he continued more calmly. I looked away, twiddling my thumbs standing with my back against the door. What could I say? He looked up at me ferociously; and stormed towards me. He backed me against the door and put both arms either side of me against the wall, so I was cornered. I was scared, this was not right. Tears began to fill my eyes; I had caused Harry to become this angry monster, he had never reacted like this before with me, I had never seen much emotion from him full stop.

"We slept together, I am so so sorry," I whispered quickly as tears ran down my face. Harry just continued to stare; he was back to the man with the dead eyes.

"I know," he walked away sitting back down on the bed.

"H-how?" I stammered.

"Iris suspected something was going on between you after you asked to go outside for a chat, and saw you come up to bed at five thirty in the morning. She watched you kiss him near the stream, as did I." I felt sick.

"She heard his little conversation with Mr and Mrs Watson too about how he couldn't hack being in the RAF because of his dead mate, weak man if you ask me," Harry gloated. I was horrified; he had seen me kiss Jack? I felt ashamed. I was also disgusted at his lack of empathy towards Jack; did this man have no heart at all?

"Why didn't you say something earlier?" I snivelled.

"You didn't give me much chance," he paused, "so do

you want him or me?" He looked at me with a blank expression. I could not tell Harry the truth of my feelings; it would kill him, and maybe Jack. I had already caused him so much pain and embarrassment, not to mention brought shame upon myself. I am not a floozy; this was genuinely my head being ruled by my heart.

"No, it was a mistake, I want you," I lied, wiping the tears from my eyes. I didn't want this drama and I was worried about what his next move towards Jack would be.

"Your dad would be disgusted with your actions these last few days Nina, positively whore-ish," he added. I felt nauseated, he was right; I hung my head shamefully.

"We are leaving to go back to Lincolnshire tomorrow," he replied, looking relieved, he stood up and walked towards me. "Are you coming back? Your dad would be deeply disappointed if you did not return." I didn't give it a moments thought.

"Yes, I will return," I whispered, I certainly couldn't turn my back on dad and my sister, Faye, and I owed Harry after the humiliation I had just brought upon him. Harry left the room, he turned back towards me and sighed.

"I forgive you," his gaze drifted to the floor, as he walked off into his room. I had to remain with him now, whether I liked it or not, I couldn't hurt him twice.

Jack did not return for dinner last night, it was a quiet, sombre affair. I did not want to talk to Iris as she had caught me out and I felt betrayed. I still could not understand Harry's calm reaction, why had he not screamed at me, ended our relationship or attacked Jack in a jealous rage. His behaviour confused me. Mr and Mrs Watson had no idea what had gone on but were concerned

Jack was not around again. Harry ate a few bites then left for work, kissing me on the cheek as he left. I had no appetite at all but did not want to seem rude so forced myself to eat. I dismissed myself from the table rather quickly after dinner and went straight to my bed. In true Nina style I did not sleep and tossed and turned until I decided it was time for a glass of water, but this time I would not expect to see Jack there waiting for me, and I was right. I looked out onto the babbling stream, praying he was safe. I could not get the look Jack or Harry had given me out of my head. Back up to bed I went and dozed off into a dream of Jack and I being forced apart and no matter how much I wanted to get close to him, I physically couldn't.

I woke up in a startle, my face wet, I had been crying in my sleep. I have never been through a break-up before, but this is what it must feel like. My head was spinning, and I felt trapped, nauseous and gloomy about my future. Jack was never really mine, and I never his, yet it felt like we got on so well, he made me happier than I had ever felt, I was letting myself believe it could work, but there were now too many reasons for it not to. It was too late and whatever I felt for Jack would have to be forgotten, I was due to go home today, never to see him again, and that was a very miserable notion. I looked at the clock, quarter past seven; I might as well get up and pack.

I was packed and ready to go and decided on a cup of tea before my travels. I walked into the living room, the radio was playing in the background and the patio door was open, letting in a slight summer breeze. It was a glorious day, the sun beamed in through the windows, and a scent of coffee and freshly cut grass blew through the air. The distant sound of a plane flying through the air drew my eyes to the blue sky through the window, everyone was living their best lives on this lovely day, and here I was unhappy and about to leave behind the potential love of my life. Where had the carefree girl that I had once known gone? I snapped out of my daydream and noticed Jack sat on the settee with a man who looked of great importance in a blue military uniform, and Mr and Mrs Watson by his side.

"Oh, excuse me, I didn't know anyone was in here," I apologised embarrassed. Jack looked at me sheepishly and his eyes fell to the ground as I looked back. The senior looking military man looked at Jack and followed his gaze to where I stood.

"Oh, don't worry dear," Mrs Watson said in her usual joyful tone, "we are just sorting out Jack going back into the air force."

"Oh," I was taken aback; there was even less hope for us now. "That's excellent news," I stifled a smile.

"This is Group Captain Staines," Mrs Watson finally introduced us. "This is Nina, she is a woman police officer you know," she said proudly to Staines, as if I were her own daughter, it made me blush. Staines stood up and shook my hand.

"Please, call me Oliver," he beamed.

"Pleased to meet you sir," I shook his hand back. I was very conscious that Jack's eyes were on me the whole time, and we still hadn't had chance to talk about yesterday's showdown.

"Well, you'll be getting your house back to yourselves Mr and Mrs Watson, as we are also heading off today," I said, hoping Jack was listening.

"You're going home to Lincolnshire?" Jack quizzed.

"Yep, we aren't needed here anymore, we are leaving at dinner." I walked to the kitchen to make a cup of tea, not daring to turn back and see his expression. It was probably a relief for him. He stood up and walked towards me in the kitchen, muttering so no one else heard.

"That's dandy for ye', ye' can plan your future with glum inspector boy now can't ye'," he said jealously, as he leant past me placing a glass on the counter and walking back to the settee. I did not expect that reaction at all.

"Right Jack, I should be heading off, but I cannot wait for you to come back, you've been missed, and I am glad you are feeling back on track," Group Captain Staines walked towards the door. He shook Jack's hand, nodded at me, and then left, Mr and Mrs Watson followed close behind.

"Jack, I need a word," I muttered. He turned back inside and shut the front door, so we were alone.

"Why are you so mad at me?" I enquired.

"I aren't mad, I'm indifferent," he replied blankly. "Me and Harry had a little chat when I returned last night, he told me about your conversation. He got immense pleasure in telling me that ye' thought we were a mistake and that ye' did not have feelings for me and have chosen him," he looked hurt. "I was a little surprised, but I am happy for ye', it's probably for the best if ye' think about it." I stared on, not uttering a word. "He also added that ye' only slept with me because ye' thought I was weak and felt sorry for me. That is fine, because now I can hand on heart say it was just sex and nothing more," he seemed wounded, as did I. I had to be nonchalant about this, what was the point in speaking frankly, when I knew what the outcome was going to be.

"I did not say that Jack, I don't think you are weak one bit, you are one of the strongest, most heroic men I know. I am angry that he said that, but I am not surprised, he wanted to make you feel humiliated, because that is how he feels. With regards to you and me, Harry is right and you have made your feelings clear. We are very different people, from very different backgrounds, you are off back into the RAF now, which is fantastic, but it is not the life I want or one that I could contend with. In another life, we would have met months ago, when I had no career of my own, and no one else who cared for me, and who knows, it may have worked out. I do care for you a great deal, I am now convinced the feeling is not mutual, but that's irrelevant because I feel it would not work anyway. I am a realist not a dreamer, most of the time anyway. What we did was fun, and it meant something to me, but if you would have seen Harry's face yesterday, he was a damaged man," I sighed.

"So, you're pleasing him over yourself?" His words hit me hard.

"He loves me, Jack," I convinced myself.

"I can't offer ye' love Nina, not yet anyway, if at all," he sighed remorsefully. "But I do care about ye', despite what I just said. I am just angry. I aren't going to ask ye' to stay, because your mind is already made up, and like ye' said I am going back into the air force, we will be miles apart. Go with him, and be happy, I won't hold ye' back," he feigned a smile, kissed my cheek, and off he walked, taking my heart with him. Will that be the last time I see Jack Watson? I suddenly felt very glum about

47

my future.

Chapter 4

January 1941

Jack

"Keep up Megson!" I laughed, jogging on ahead.

"You're too fast for me mate!" He said through coughs and splutters. I had been back in the air force for three and a half months now and it felt good, I needed the structure, the banter with the lads, and more importantly, I needed a focus. I had not yet been signed off to go back out to war, but I was getting there, it was looking likely it would be as soon as next week; I was chomping at the bit to get back behind the controls of a plane. I was apprehensive but knew I needed to get back on the horse sooner rather than later. I had spent the last few months training up new staff, and physically and mentally re-training myself. I felt in a good place – I was ready for combat.

"Time out, I'm done, you've got years on me, Watson." Megson held up the letter "T" with his hands whilst panting. Megson was, Luke Megson, a newish recruit to the RAF. Due to the urgent need of soldiers, he went out to war within a week of signing up. He was injured before he even started the tour after falling and breaking his leg clambering out of a Spitfire, so he has been my training buddy since I came back. His leg was on the mend, and he was due to go back out to fight with immediate effect. I hoped we'd be together but then again, with my track record of crewing with my mates, maybe not. We were at RAF Biggin Hill in London, the main RAF fighter camp in England, which felt electric. I loved being amongst my own again, and even happier that Group Captain Staines was based here too. I had the upmost respect for him, and throughout my career had always looked up to him. We had always been close since I had joined his squadron, and he had helped me enormously since I had lost Collier and Elvidge. I am indebted to him really, even after I left Bath, with a bit of a broken heart to add to my woes, he picked me up, plied me with whisky and helped me through it all. The looting and the riots were becoming all too frequent in London, not far from the camp. Like we weren't already fighting a big enough battle with the Nazi's, our own men were starting a war with one another too, what had our country become? I ran to the showers, washing away the beads of sweat, I always felt euphoric after a training session, my endorphins were high, nothing could bring me down today. Exercise was my medicine; it was my go-to activity whenever I felt crap, which was becoming rare now, but still apparent. I never thought, upon joining the RAF, that I would suffer so badly with my mind as much as I had done. I thought I had always been headstrong but looking back anything that ever happened that was out of my control knocked me for six - not the best attribute to have in the military. Still, I was going to beat this, and could already feel myself improving daily.

"Those bloody rioters, they are going to end up drafting us in to go help sort it out with us being stuck here," Megson whinged drying himself off. He was probably right; we needed to get back into a plane, fast! We headed back to our barracks, in the distance there appeared to be crowds gathered near the entrance. I wonder what was going on. Group Captain Staines was outside his tent.

"Good afternoon chaps," he addressed us.

"Good afternoon, sir, what's going on over there?" I asked.

"They're bringing some of the police in to stay on the barracks, you know to help with the riots," he rolled his eyes. "They won't interfere with our operations, but they need somewhere to stay as they have drafted them in from up and down the country, and due to the bombings, there is nowhere else to put them up." We walked up to the crowds to get a better look, it was just rows and rows of policemen walking single file, and then I saw an awful familiarity, my stomach churned with hate. *For fuck's sake!* It was him - Harry. How can this be, out of all the policemen, in all of the military, in all of the barracks, in all of Britain, he is called to help here, in Biggin Hill. I thought I had moved on from the hatred I felt towards him, but even catching just a glimpse of him reminded me of how disgustingly he had spoken to me that day about losing Collier, and how he had treated Nina. Calm down Jack, he isn't worth the anger; I wasn't going to let him do this to me, he was a bitter bully, and I was better than that. I wanted to avoid him for fear of how I might act, although each day I was better, some days I felt I was on the edge. Always fearing that the smallest thing would send me spiralling back into doom and anger. He was certainly not worth me losing my job over, so I quickly headed off back to the gym area to do another work out and clear my mind.

"Watson, what is going on? I was calling you!" Megson was running after me, I had been in a daze and hadn't heard him calling me.

"Sorry pal, I was in a world of ma' own," I replied apologetically.

"You look like you've seen a ghost mate," he retorted concerned. I sat down on a bench, rubbing my forehead,

"Oh, it's a long story mate."

"I've got all day buddy," Megson replied sitting down opposite me. He was a good friend, I was thankful for him, he was a good listener and I had on many occasions vented to him about Collier, but I had never mentioned Nina. I didn't see the point; she was history, never to crop up in my life again. It happened over the smallest period of just three days, it was hardly a life-changing amount of time in the grand scheme of things, so how had she got to me so much? There was no harm in telling a close friend about her, he might even be able to knock some sense into me.

"Well, there was this girl," I looked at him, he immediately smiled.

"Of course, there was!" he raised his eyebrows. I smirked continuing, "We got on really well, it was soon after Collier, and her honesty and frankness left an impression on me. She was there in my darkest moments I suppose, a bit of a distraction, a light at the end of the tunnel. It was essentially an affair, but more than just a shag, I felt like she understood me, it was strange. I haven't thought about her much since being here, but when I do, I wish I'd have done more to win her round."

"What happened?" he asked interested.

"It was messy. Ye' see those police out there? Well one of them is Nina's boyfriend, and he was at the time too, but he's a complete wanker!" I seethed. "A heartless shit, who basically guilt tripped her into staying with him, instead of taking a chance with me. He made her think she would be leaving her dad and sister behind. Ye' know we might not have worked out, but I knew she wanted to at least try, but she felt like she owed him. He's a controlling, nasty piece of work."

"Now, now Jack, I haven't got a bad word to say about you," a deadpan voice muttered from the shadows of the doorway. I turned to look, and sure enough, it was Harry. I stood up to face him with disgust in my eyes but kept my distance. He looked like the same old cock sure twat as before, except more muscular and rugged. I'm hoping it's because Nina saw sense and dumped him, so he's had nothing better to do than hit the gym.

"Can you believe that we have bumped into each other again? I thought it was you, but then I saw you walk off. I did think that is something that Jack Watson would do, run away from his problems, so I thought I'd come to you. How is life treating you?" he sarcastically added moving nearer.

"I am smashing thanks Harry, now why don't ye' fuck off," I warned.

"What's the issue mate?" he smiled condescendingly. "Surely you're not still bitter about Nina?"

"Why would I be bitter? You're the one who got cheated on mate," I retaliated, proud of my quick wit. His face turned to thunder, and he walked further into the gym, closer to me.

"Scuse me mate, I think it's time you left," Megson interjected, "we don't want no shit here, off you trot." Harry looked even angrier at the put down; he never could take criticism well.

"Well, I was leaving anyway; cowards aren't worth my

job, lucky for you. I just thought I'd stop by. Oh, and by the way, Jack, it's a shame she didn't keep the baby, but I suppose there was no point given you'll never see her again." What is he on about?

"What did ye' just say? What fucking baby?" I demanded.

"Oh mate, I thought you knew that she was pregnant. It was probably yours, but she got rid of it. No one but her sister and I knew about her dirty little secret. I suppose it does not matter now anyway. Who would want to raise a chicken's baby?" He began to walk away giving me a smug smile. I was raging.

"You're bullshitting me. Where is she?" I demanded. Harry turned to look back at me concerned.

"You mean you haven't heard?"

"Heard what?"

"After the guilt of aborting your baby, she killed herself. Anyone who gets close to you seems to just die don't they Jack?" He walked off. My head was spinning, I couldn't speak, I turned towards the window for air, but I couldn't breathe. She's dead?! Harry had his back to me, but I wanted more answers. My vision blurred and all I could feel was abhorrence and fury, I charged at him, I wanted to bang his smarmy head off the wall, but Megson got in the way and held me back.

"Mate no, it's not worth your job, let him go," Megson held me against the wall, breathless from trying to keep the monster from within me from launching its fist at Harry's face. I took deep breaths and brought myself back down to the ground.

"I'm fine, get off me... FUCK," I panted. I paced towards the toilets, I couldn't get my thoughts in order, was he lying? Did he just want a reaction? Could she have done that? Would she have done that? I vomited into the toilet basin. Why would he lie about something so terrible? He was an arrogant little fucker who probably wanted to get me back for sleeping with his girlfriend. Yeah, that will be it, it won't be true, she would have written to me about the baby. Someone would have told me, mum or dad about her demise. Was I really such a bad omen? Right now, I didn't know what to believe. All I did know was how I felt confirmed that I really did care for that girl, and now she was gone. I could feel myself spiralling again, come on Jack, hold it together, you've come so far.

My head was in knots all night; I couldn't sleep, thinking that what he said could be true. But even if it was true what did it matter now, I would never see Nina again, dead or alive. I never really knew her, and she was never truly mine, I needed to put it to rest. I fell into a light slumber and dreamt that she was the one going down in flames, not Collier; I could see her bonny face in excruciating pain, burning in the cockpit. I tried reaching for her, but it was no use... I woke, startled and sweaty, to the sound of wolf whistles coming from outside the barracks. I caught my breath and splashed the cold water onto my face from the faucet at my sink, the bitter sharpness of the icy water calmed me down, I stared at my bleak reflection, breathlessly. It's time to face another day, please tell me they're sending me far far away today, I prayed, I need a new focus. I got dressed and headed to get a cup of tea from the canteen, I was going to try and put yesterday behind me, it was Harry being a malicious twit and it was all probably fabricated. Even if it wasn't I would never see her again so what difference did it make? My head needed to be in the game now; I wanted to be back in a plane, now more than ever. Outside were crowds of soldiers just stood there gawping, again I heard the wolf whistles. Up ahead I saw rows of people walking through the main gates into the camp. It appeared to be rows of policewomen. What were they doing here? I pushed forward to get a better look. My mind flicked back to Nina in her uniform, stood innocently in my parents living room, before she met me and I ruined her life. No Jack, stop it, it is history.

"Who are all these?" I asked the airman standing next to me, trying to snap myself out of my misery.

"Goddesses mate," he replied, "policewomen from up and down the country come to assist with the riots."

"Surely it's not safe for them to be here," I replied confused.

"I dunno, think they're here for the women and children," he shrugged, "I don't give a fuck why they're here; I'm going to have a good time that's for sure," he laughed. What a twat I thought, did I used to be like him? I walked away from him towards Group Captain Staines' tent. I needed to speak to someone with half a brain cell.

"And he was just there in front of me, I have never felt such rage towards another human, if I had hit him I don't think I could have stopped, luckily Megson was there, I dunno what to believe sir," I said in despair, my head in my hands.

"Jack, if it is bothering you this much then you need to seek out the truth. If it makes no difference whether she did or did not abort your baby, or if she is or isn't alive, then you need to lay it to rest. As for the rage, you are working on it lad, and you are doing so well, do not let some maggot be the reason for all your hard work going down the plug hole," Staines advised. "What is more important, payback on some irrelevant copper or being a pilot again and doing what you have always loved, once more?"

He was such a wise man. He was a well-groomed tall chap, who looked after his appearance, being his rank, you would expect nothing less. He had dark hair, which was greying around the ears, and was quite tanned, he always smelled of soap and boot polish, and you could practically see your face in his boots. He had been more than a leader to me; he had been like a second father, despite only being nine years older than me. I felt I could speak to him like I could my own dad, which I was so grateful for. Normally the ranks of the military can be hard faced and terrifying, but Staines was warm and inviting.

As far as I knew Staines wasn't married nor did he have children, he had been career driven his whole life, and was a very young Group Captain, at only forty-years old. One night over a few too many whiskies, he told me he had dreamed of having a family, but it was never the right time. I did feel for him, he was lonely, but work was his solace, and war was his comfort, which is an odd idea to comprehend. There was a woman in his life before he joined, but she opposed to him wanting a life in the military, so it didn't work out. He told me that funnily enough she was now also in the services, but in the USA, which is where she was born. I would love for him to meet her again; he deserves to be happy. He was an incredible artist and had sold a few of his paintings when he was a teenager for hundreds of pounds, but a life in the RAF was his passion, he was more like me than I realised. I had put my relationships on hold for my career, I didn't have a family yet, and my loyalty towards this job always came first, before anything and anyone. He was a local man, but despite staying local, he did not seem to have many friends. From the little I knew of his family life, his father was strict, and his mother was a drinker. His father was also ex-military, which is what pushed him into making this his career of choice. He was an excellent Group Captain and leader, he was logical, courageous, calm, thought of every detail down to a tee, and I aspired to be like him; he was my hero, quite literally.

"What has become of me, sir? Ever since losing Collier I can't shake off the dark thoughts, I feel weak. I used to be so happy and saw positives in everything I did, and now I struggle everyday with what is going on up here," I tapped my temple. "I'm exhausted!"

"You witnessed a great tragedy, Jack, a few months of training and time out from the RAF won't fix that, stop being so hard on yourself," he patted me on the back. "Thank you, sir," I smiled sheepishly, I didn't want him to think I was feeble, but at the same time I knew I had to speak to someone, else I would go insane.

"Anytime, Jack, you need to think about what is best for you and realise what you really want in life."

"I want this," I replied looking around, "I was born to fly planes, it's the only place that I am truly happy," I added solemnly.

"Then there's your decision, leave the past in the past. Inspector boy will soon get bored trying to antagonise you, you will eventually forget about Nina, and then you can finally move on. He won't be here for long, there are riots all over Britain, they'll be shipped out before you can say, goodbye." I liked his positivity, I, on the other hand, wasn't so sure. He was right though, I needed to let it lie, what could I do now anyway? Let her death send me into a pit or pick myself up and try get on with my own life. I couldn't have prevented it because she chose Harry not me, she never really wanted me, and she could have told me about the baby.

"I best go, I have some lads I need to put through their paces," I smiled thankfully, and headed off out of his tent, thank god for Staines.

It was just after lunchtime, there was a cold winter sun in the air, I felt at ease as I headed towards the training area, my favourite place on camp, somewhere I could vent my anger through exercise and physical activity. I knew I was going to get to train with the lads and this put me in a good mood. I walked past our mess hall, which was essentially a large solid tent like structure with jute hemp doors, almost like a circus tent. The smell of burning wood came from a log burner that was located within the entrance, and smoke piped through a handmade chimney through the centre and up into the muggy air. It was our place to come and unwind in between warfare. A huge sound of laughter bellowed through the air; it was coming from the tent. I curiously opened the doors to peer in, there were around thirty soldiers in front of me also being nosy, and from up ahead I could hear a male voice booming orders throughout.

"We will not take this lying down, we have had too many of these trips where we have used the soft approach and it has not worked, we will now be going into this full pelt, using force if necessary, we are fighting a war with the world, not our own citizens." I recognised that violent voice immediately; it was Harry. *Boring*, I thought. He just loves to show off his plumage, I turned around to leave but I stopped in my tracks when I heard the sweet sound of a Northern female voice.

"Quite right, Inspector, and us women will be there to help pick up the pieces for the women and children, won't we!"

"But what happens if the men become rough with us?" An unknown female voice enquired.

"Well, we all know where a man's intimate parts are, and we all know where our feet are located, put two and two together and you've got a man crying on his knees," she replied. The audience roared with laughter.

"Indeed, Sergeant Hughes," Harry stifled a laugh back. I daren't turn around, I never knew Nina's last name, but I was confident it was her, but how could it be, she was dead? I finally plucked up the courage, I turned around slowly, and there she stood on the stage next to Harry, as beautiful as before and as alive as I was. I never thought I would see her again, confusion and nausea overcame me, what do I do now?

Chapter 5

Nina

Deep breaths Nina, public speaking isn't your thing, but you need to prove yourself in this new role, you're a female leader now, and these women are depending on you to guide them.

"So, I will be putting you into teams of four, just to make sure you've got back up, each team will have two policemen attached for your own safety. They will deal with the looters and the rioters, women you use the sensitive approach with the families, make sure the children are okay, and then retreat. This method has worked in Scotland so let's hope it works for us. If you have any concerns or questions, Inspector Ward and I are happy to listen. Are we all on-board?" There was a resounding yes sir, yes ma'am. Phew, my first address to my team, I was shaking inside but I think I held it together well.

The crowds of police officers began to disperse, Harry approached me.

"Well done, that looked like it came natural to you, all I would say is try not make a joke out of violence, but otherwise eight out of ten", he smiled condescendingly.

"Oh, okay, I thought it would calm everyone down a bit, tensions seemed to be running high."

"I get where you're coming from, just something to note that's all, remember I didn't get to inspector by laughing and joking with my peers, it was hard work. You've been given this sergeant's opportunity thanks to me pulling a few strings, you now need to earn it." He kissed me on the cheek and walked off towards the exit. I looked up at my colleague, Georgie who just stared at me wide eyed.

"What's wrong?" I asked.

"Eight out of ten? Are you going to let him speak to you that way?" she replied annoyed.

"What do you mean? He's right I need to earn my stripes now, I can't be dilly dallying," I said packing up the bag of leaflets I'd been demonstrating.

"Nina, he was so patronising towards you," she retorted disgusted.

"Georgie please, let's just drop it. I owe him." I went to put my blazer on. Georgie grabbed me by the shoulder.

"Nina, you owe him nothing, remember who you are, that strong willed, witty, woman who I joined with, not a meek, weakling who says yes to everything he says just because you're sleeping with him! He's an arsehole, why can't you see it?"

"Georgie! That's not how it is, it's complicated, I can't even begin to go into it. And we aren't just sleeping together, we are together as a couple, it's just not widely known because we aren't married, and he doesn't do things that way and neither do I. I am no longer this go with my libido sort of girl, I need to think about settling down, I need the security and so do my family." I was getting annoyed with this conversation, partly because I knew Georgie was right. What had I become? I was indebted to Harry after everything that had happened and how he had stepped up and helped me in my time of need, but did I really need to be controlled by him in my career too? "I can't even be bothered to think about this now, we have too much going on," I replied hastily. I bent down to pack away some stationary into my bag.

"Ooo, hello," I heard Georgie mutter under her breath, I followed her gaze, to where a fetching man was walking towards us; I gasped, it was Jack. I couldn't speak, I just gawped, I felt sick, sweaty and I was blushing, I needed to sit down.

"Hi, I'm Georgie," she introduced herself, grabbing his hand to shake it, "very pleased to meet you, what's your name?"

"I'm Jack," he finally responded after what felt like a lifetime. I couldn't look at him, I just looked at the ground, this wasn't supposed to happen, I was never meant to see him again.

"Hi Jack, I love your uniform, it really brings out your eyes," Georgie flirted. "Can we help you?" she fluttered her eyelashes at him.

"Actually, I'm here to see Nina," he said slowly, looking from Georgie to me.

"Oh, you two know each other? Well pardon me; I need to be getting off anyway. I'll see you later Nina," she winked, flashed me a smile and sauntered off. *Please stay, Georgie,* I thought. Jack and I just looked at one another coyly, I couldn't look him in the eyes, I felt shy and vulnerable, what was I going to say? Nothing, he knew nothing about anything, just make pleasantries and go on your merry way, simple. I took a deep breath.

"Fancy seeing you here," I stood up, finding confidence from somewhere, acting as if nothing had ever happened. "How are you?" I continued.

"I can't quite believe you're standing in front of me if I am honest," he was looking at me as if he had seen a ghost.

"Yes, it's a small world isn't it," I agreed, how have I

managed to bump into him again? Of all the people in England we have managed to find one another again, is this a sign?

"I thought ye' were dead," he blurted.

"What?" Was he drunk? Oh god, he has me mixed up with someone else, hasn't he? this is embarrassing. I looked around. "Do you think I am someone else?" I asked nervously, praying that he did remember me and that I wasn't actually just a quickie whilst he was visiting home.

"No, I know who ye' are, Nina, how could I forget," he smiled that smile, and it hit me again, I felt weak at the knees. We held each other's gazes for a short while; it felt like we had never been apart. I wanted him the same as I had then, but too much had changed, there was things he didn't know, and that he probably wouldn't forgive. There was complete silence in the tent except for the noise of my heart pounding in my ears, and the odd chatter passing the tent door. He looked at my hands.

"So, you're getting married?" he sounded surprised. I looked at my ring finger, with the large diamond sparkling in the light.

"Yep," I could have sounded happier. "No date set yet, we want to see what happens with the war first," I twiddled my fingers. I think I was the only one thankful for this bloody war.

"How have ye' been?" he asked. He sat down on a chair opposite me. I looked up at him, those eyes, dragging me into their sea blue circles like a whirlpool. He looked much fitter; he had toned up and seemed stockier. He smelled the same as before, it gave me flashbacks of our intimacy, his smell had stayed on my blouse for some time after I left Bath, I didn't want to wash it so I could remember him; now I sounded ridiculous. His voice sounded so warming and familiar; it was nice to hear. The navy-coloured uniform looked amazing on him, he suited that colour attire, it made him look so masculine, so important. I was proud in a way, proud that he had wanted me at one time.

"I've been fine, got promoted," I pointed to my epaulettes.

"Yeah! congratulations," he sounded happy for me.

"You?" This was small talk at its best.

"Aye, I've been grand, training mentally and physically to get back into a plane, shouldn't be long now," he played with his cap. He seemed more nervous than before, there was a reticence about him.

"Well done, you look like you've been training, you look great," I suddenly felt shy and blushed again, his eyes gleamed at me, he smiled modestly.

"Sarge, are you ready?" A colleague entered the tent, enquiring.

"Yes, I am!" I snapped back to reality. "Sorry Jack we are really busy, it's been great to see you though. Take care of yourself, if I don't see you again," I tapped him on the shoulder, like we were old mates. I'm not letting myself feel anything more, it was a silly dream, me and him could never be.

"Okay…yeah…bye," he responded dumbfounded. I left him stood there on his own, with his cap in his hand watching me walk away. I felt awful but to let him in I would need to tell him what I had done, and he would never forgive me, it's best to let bygones be bygones. I would rather us go on never knowing what we could have been, rather than him hating me.

I was not focusing properly today at all, luckily the women and children of the community were helping to take my mind off Jack and the whole situation. I decided I was going to do my best to avoid him on the camp. I did not want any more small talk, and being around him was too difficult, he sucked me back under his spell just by breathing. All I wanted was to just bury my head in the sand. I wasn't supposed to see him again, that's why I did what I did. I had done my best to try forget him, and here he was again, breathing the same air as me. The thought of him popping up again not only petrified me but made my heart race with excitement at the same time. He knew how to get my pulse going without even doing anything. We headed back to the camp, it was early evening, but the wintery dark nights had already come across. Taking cover under the darkness will make it easier to evade him. I got washed up and slipped into the canteen, wanting to eat quickly then go to bed. Harry was waiting at the table for me. Now I was sergeant it was even more imperative that no one knew about my relationship with Harry. It would raise eyebrows as to how I got the job, people would feel it was favouritism and I would no longer be able to assist with mutual aid due to Harry being the lead inspector. I smiled at him but knew he would figure out my anguish pretty soon, so I sat next to Georgie who was at the same table. That was a big mistake.

"So, who was that dreamy guy you were talking to today?" she asked inquisitively. Harry flicked his eyes to me immediately.

"What dreamy guy is she talking about?" he responded bluntly. Unfortunately, Georgie continued.

"Yes, he knew Nina, but he definitely had eyes for me... erm Jack wasn't it, Nina? He was beautiful." *Fuck!* I looked back at Harry.

"Yes, he's an old acquaintance, I didn't realise he was based here. It was a just a quick hello, I won't be seeing him again," I took my gaze from Harry and took a sip of water. That won't be good enough for him, but there's nothing he can say here in public. Harry murmured.

"I see." He stood up taking his half-eaten plate to the bin and walked out of the canteen without looking back. I left my plate untouched and followed him out, feeling nauseous with worry.

"Harry wait," I called.

"Are you taking the piss out of me, Nina?" he was angry, furious even.

"No not at all, we barely spoke, it was pleasantries and that was all, I swear," I justified.

"I'm going to kill that weedy bastard, why can he not just get the hint?" he seethed.

"Harry nothing has even happened, you're blowing it out of proportion, I walked away from him, I don't want him! He doesn't want me," I lied. I didn't want this. I took his face in my hands to calm him down.

"Is everything okay?" I recognised him; it was Group Captain Staines.

"Yes sir, sorry if we were too loud, just discussing work, aren't we?" I lied again. I am getting good at this. Harry removed my hands from his face with such force that I fell to the ground, he walked away chuntering under his breath.

"Leave me alone you whore." I was left alone on my knees, covered in mud, this was rock bottom.

"My poor girl, are you alright?" Group Captain Staines asked, walking closer to assist me, whilst shooting Harry a distasteful look as he walked away.

"What an awful thing to say!" I couldn't help it, I burst into tears, what had my life become? He took me by the arm and guided me with him towards a dimly lit tent. It smelled of boot polish and soap, but was warming and peaceful, I felt relaxed in here, almost shielded from the real world. He handed me a glass of whisky in a sparkling, crystal tumbler, what a kind man.

"I recognise you from somewhere," he said, narrowing his eyes.

"Yes, I was staying at Jack Watson's parents' house when you were meeting with them about trying to get Jack back into the RAF," he looked as though a light bulb had flicked on, as if he had just remembered something.

"So, you're Nina?" he asked, slowly.

"Yes," I sniffed, "Judging by that tone you know who I am?" I added. He sat back and crossed his arms

"Yes, I thought you were dead? I am confused."

"Why do people keep saying that?" I was confused too, "Jack said the same!"

"So, you've seen Jack?" he seemed surprised.

"Briefly, yes. Why do you think Harry and me were arguing?"

"Ah, I should have guessed that was Harry. You do realise it was him who has been telling people that you were dead?" I felt a wave of warmth spread across me, making my cheeks burn, was it the whisky or what Group Captain Staines had just revealed. Why would Harry do such a disgraceful thing? Then it hit me, he knew all along that Jack was here but didn't want either of us to know about one another. He was a twisted man.

"I hold no judgement against you, what you have done you have done for your own reasons," Staines continued.

"What do you mean judgement?" I felt angry, what have I done wrong? Except for the obvious abortion, but how would he know about that? Has Harry told him? Oh god.

"Ma'am it's none of my business, I am just here as a shoulder to cry on, whomever may need it," he said reassuringly. I didn't feel judged, but I knew that Jack had been having a hard time, and now I knew it was partly down to me. In a way it gave me answers, he must care about me to speak to Group Captain Staines about me. I didn't want to talk about this anymore, the day and night had been a wash out, I had a headache, and I just needed my bed.

"It's all a mess," I downed my whisky.

"It's none of my business and I don't claim to be an expert, but follow your heart not your head, go with your gut, love is war, so choose your side wisely."

"Thanks for the drink, sir." I placed my glass down on his desk and left the tent. I needed to think, I followed my heart when I climbed into bed with Jack and look where that got me.

Back to my usual Nina routine of not being able to sleep because of problems I had brought upon myself. I did eventually drift off and was awoken by the sound of birds singing, and the sun shining through the crack in the door. A new day, time to sort my life out… again. Out on the camp I headed to get a cup of tea before I had to face Harry at the morning briefing. I headed to the tent where all the police officers were sat down as they had done the day before. Harry did not show. I delivered the briefing;

my mind was anywhere but there. Where was he? The briefing finished and Georgie approached me sheepishly.

"I'm so sorry," she mumbled, "I didn't think about what I was saying until I said it, I guess you and Jack speaking bothered Harry?"

"You could say that you know what he gets like," I didn't really look at her, I was too preoccupied.

"Have you seen Harry?"

"Yes, erm, I don't know how to tell you this Nina, and I certainly don't want to cause anymore drama, but I saw him coming out of a woman's tent at the crack of dawn this morning." *Busted.*

"Really? How did he seem to you?" I felt relieved, worried, and maybe even hopeful that he had ended it with me, which would make my life easier.

"He seemed angry, tired, it was from afar, he didn't see me, I think you need to talk to him…" all of a sudden, the sound of a big disturbance came from outside of the tent. Georgie and I ran to see what was happening.

"…Bastard," I caught the end of the sentence, it was Harry, *oh god.* I hid behind Georgie, I could see Harry, he looked like he had been fighting, his clothes were all amiss and he had blood on his nose, two soldiers were holding him back, who was he fighting with? What was he doing? I continued to watch, afraid of what would happen if I got closer.

"Harry ye' need to calm the fuck down," it was Jack, my heart fluttered. What had Harry done to Jack? I couldn't see him due to the crowds of people, I needed to make sure Jack was okay, I pushed forward, slowly.

"Calm down? You're fucking everywhere, like a cockroach, I would get no greater pleasure than squashing you!" Harry shouted.

"Harry stop it," I forced myself to say. Everyone turned to look at me. "What is going on?!" I turned to look at Jack who also had blood on his face; his hair was messy; he had been fighting too… *great*.

"Oh, look who it is, my wonderful bride to be," Harry said sarcastically. I could see all the officers looking at each other, guess that cat was out of the bag now, wonder how long it will take for the bosses to take back my stripes and move me into the filing team. Jack looked at me apologetically.

"I'm sorry, Nina, he attacked me, I had to defend myself," sweet Jack, still thinking about me in all of this.

"Why are you apologising to her?" Harry shouted, he seemed drunk but surely, he wouldn't risk his job for this, nothing had really happened, he had just got the wrong end of the stick.

"This woman," he said pointing to me whilst looking at everyone, "cheated on me with him," he pointed at Jack.

"Mate ye' need to let it go," Jack said calmly, "what's done is done, she chose you," he said looking at me, regretfully. "And it's nowhere near as fucked up as ye' telling everyone she was dead!"

"I did it to keep her away from you!" he retaliated, aiming his finger at him with such anger. This was so out of Harry's character, he was normally a private man, I must have really got to him.

"To top it off everyone, she got pregnant with his baby," Harry continued. *NO,* I inhaled. Jack cannot know, please don't do this, please.

"Harry please…" I whispered but was cut off, I watched on horrified. "She then got rid of the baby using my money, now how's that for letting it go," he smiled a wicked smile, as if he was punishing me; I wanted the ground to swallow me whole. "She's a tart, and why I ever put a ring on her finger I will never know…I loved you!" He stared daggers at me, extremely inebriated. Everyone was staring at me. I daren't look at Jack; I held my head down, eyes fixed to the ground. I heard gasps from the other women, the men were silent, I felt shame. I looked at Harry, tears filled my eyes, if he wanted payback for the affair, he definitely had it. I turned back on myself, pushed past the crowds and ran away as fast as I could. I had no idea where I was going but it was going to be far away from here.

Oh god, everyone knows I chose to get rid of my baby, Jack knows what I did, I took away his child without even telling him, what an evil thing to do. I never thought I would see Jack again, how could I be a mother on my own? Harry wouldn't have stayed with me, and dad would have been ashamed. Faye would have supported me, but she's young and has her whole life ahead of her. My money wouldn't have been enough to raise a baby. Harry offered to pay for the procedure, he wanted me to go private and have it done, it was a way out.

I walked for hours, avoiding my shift at work like the plague. I found myself in a wooded area near to the camp. I was freezing but I didn't care, I deserved to freeze, it was my punishment. I should just go home, back to Lincolnshire, I thought. What is there left for me here? Harry and I are over, how he acted towards me proved there was no going back, I had destroyed him, like I had destroyed the baby. I was going back to no job because now they all know I was with Harry, and even if they let me back in the file team, imagine the looks and gossip I'd be subject to from the other women. I had single-handedly ruined my life by the choices I had made. I somehow had to sneak back into the camp and get my belongings so I could leave for Lincolnshire. I didn't know the time, it must be teatime by now, everyone will be in the canteen, so now is my best chance. I headed back to camp, and snuck through the gates, watching over my shoulder, hiding in the shadows. I got to where the incident earlier today had happened, I felt revolted. I wonder what Jack was thinking; I should have made sure he was okay. I saw my tent and headed in that direction, I heard voices in the distance, so I hid behind another tent until they had gone. I made my way nearer, more soldiers appeared at every turn, chatting, smoking and laughing amongst themselves. They must be coming out from the canteen from dinner; I have timed this horribly wrong. I snuck around the back of another tent that was in complete darkness, and waited, shivering as the icy wind crept down my neck giving me goose bumps. Through the wind I overhead a familiar voice talking nearby.

"I have looked everywhere for her, I can't find her, I hope she's alright, she won't really know the area," it was Jack. Is he talking about me?

"We will send out a team to go look for her in the woods, she will come back Jack, she's just been through an ordeal and probably needs time alone to gather her thoughts," Group Captain Staines replied.

"I absolutely despise him, where does he get off shaming her like that," he said angrily.

"How are you feeling about everything?" Staines asked.

"I don't know, surprised by it all but I don't blame her.

I never had time to process being a dad, so it makes no real odds to me, I aren't in the right mind-set to raise a baby anyway. I'm trying to get my own life back on track, she probably did us both a favour." How can he be so understanding after hearing what I'd done? If he's worried about me, I should face the music and go see him, I can't keep him waiting any longer and I would never forgive myself if I didn't see how he was before I left. I hovered near the door to the tent and slightly moved the curtain so it fell to one side; he noticed me immediately and stood up.

"Nina where have ye' been?" he hurriedly walked over to me.

"You're freezing!" he said grabbing a blanket off the bed and wrapping it around me. This was the closest I had been to him in months. I took in his wonderful scent and the warmth of his body which I had missed so much. I sat down on the bed gazing at the floor; I didn't know where to begin.

"Can I get you some food or a drink ma'am," Staines insisted - I didn't reply.

"A drink would be good thanks sir," Jack answered on my behalf and Staines wandered out of the tent. There was silence. I looked up at Jack, tears filled my eyes.

"I'm so sorry Jack," I whispered. He sighed back at me, and moved in closer to give me a hug, it felt like home. He held me tight, and I just lay in his arms crying.

"I need to explain everything because it's the least you deserve," I added, "and then I'll leave you be."

"Not now, Nina, ye' need to rest, we can talk about it tomorrow," he said calmly as I rested my head on his shoulder.

"I'm not staying here tonight, Jack, I need to leave, everyone knows what I did, how can I stay?"

"No one needs to know ye' are here, ye' can stay in my tent tonight, I'll sleep on the floor. This matter is no one's business but ours. Let them say or think what they like, all that matters is what me and you think," he said reassuringly, gently brushing the hair out of my eyes, like he did at the stream, all those months before. It felt like a lifetime ago. Staines brought in a bottle of whisky and two glasses.

"I am going to make myself scarce now but if there's anything I can do then don't hesitate to ask," he withdrew from the tent smiling a courteous smile. He was such a lovely man.

"Actually sir, if it wasn't too much trouble I could do with my belongings from my tent, I don't want people to see me leave in the morning."

"Of course, I will arrange for them to be collected and brought to you ma'am," and he walked off. Jack poured me a glass of whisky; I was still shaking from the cold. He got out one of his blazers, and put it round me.

"Here, wear this, it'll warm ye' up," he smiled. Why was he being so nice to me?

"Jack stop it," I batted his arm away, "I don't deserve this, why are you being so understanding?" He looked confused.

"Nina, whatever has happened or happens, I cannot help how I feel about ye'."

"How do you feel about me?" After everything we had been through, I didn't have the energy to be shy tonight, I wanted to know how he was really feeling, I had waited long enough.

"It took me a while to realise how I actually felt. I missed ye' when I came back here and you're the first woman who I've ever really thought twice about. I suppose, I didn't know what I was feeling because it was new to me. Then when Harry told me ye' had died, I was a mess, up here," he pointed to his head. "I wished I had done things differently the first time round, but I've been given a second chance, and I am going to take it. So, for tonight let's pretend that none of the shit happened, and let's be Nina and Jack who first met four months ago back in Bath. No Harry, no baby, just us."

"Okay," I whispered nodding my head in agreement, I felt overjoyed inside, that this man who I was irrevocably in love with, had feelings for me too. I downed my whisky; it felt warm as it trickled down my throat and into my chest. I was so grateful to be in here, just him and me. I felt drowsy, the alcohol had gone straight to my head, I laid down on his bed, listening to him breathing as he lay next to me, his arms around me. I felt safe in his cocoon, and I fell into a deep slumber.

I heard birds tweeting, *shit*, I sat upright, I should have gone first thing, before light so no one saw me. I thought I was alone at first, but then I saw him, stood in the corner, in just a towel, his cheeks were reddened, and he was panting.

"Are you alright?" I asked concerned, rubbing my eyes to see him clearer in the daylight.

"Yeah," he beamed. "I went for a run, the best way to start the day. Are ye' up for a walk away from here?" he said, as he rubbed his hair to get the excess shower water out. He looked as sexy as ever, he had the body of an Adonis. I couldn't help but watch him, the water glistening on his chest running down towards his groin, he wore his identity tag around his neck, I hadn't really paid attention to it before. I felt honoured that he wanted me, this brave man fighting in the war. He must have felt my eyes on him because he dropped his towel so I could see his bare bum. I giggled.

"Still as cheeky as ever," I felt more at ease, knowing that he felt the same way as me, I could relax and enjoy him. He turned round to face me, completely naked. My stomach flipped, I had seen it all before, but it was like the first time again, I giggled again. He strolled over to me; he had this confidence about him that I found endearing. He crawled up the bed towards me, not taking his eyes from me. I began to feel hot and excitable. He got on top of me, only the thin blanket between a naked Jack and me. He was dripping, his hair still damp, I could feel his hot breath on my face, he stroked my forehead with his fingers working his way down to my neck then to my breasts. I got goose bumps; my breathing became shallow and fast. He stared deep into my eyes, not saying a word, biting his lip.

"Right let's go," he said getting off me, and he headed towards the corner of the tent and began to get dressed. I sat up confused, he was such a tease. I threw his blazer at him, and he laughed wickedly as I stood and waited by the door, all hot and bothered. He led me out of the tent, neither of us said a word, I kept my head down as we neared the exit to the camp, I didn't want to be seen. We got to the clearing, and he took me into the woods where I had spent most of my previous day. It was a much nicer day today; the sun was shining and there was a warmth in the air. Group Captain Staines had brought me my things whilst I was sleeping so I had a jacket today, good job as I had only just thawed out. The woods were vast, the smell of ice lingered in the air, the trees were dead and wilted, and the paths were mainly overgrown, I wasn't sure if this was due to the winter season or the war. There were still birds tweeting away, and the odd squirrel running up and down the jagged bark of the tree trunks. I bet in summer this place is beautiful.

"This is where I was yesterday," I said making pointless conversation.

"This is my place of escapism, it's nice to get out of the camp just to get a clear mind," he replied.

"It's beautiful, a nice quiet place in a busy world," I answered. Although Jack appeared strong, I knew deep down he had his demons, especially since Collier had died. I worried for him, who did he talk to about his feelings? I wanted to be that person he shared his deepest, darkest thoughts with – I could try to help him. I got the impression that is what he liked in me more than anything else, I could see him for who he really was, and I understood his weaknesses but didn't judge him. He led me to a clearing in the woods, where there appeared a small, dilapidated barn.

"Follow me," he raised his eyebrows, flashed a cheeky smile, and walked off in front, he seemed happy, like a little boy reliving his childhood, exploring. There was an innocence about him that I found charming, it made me happy to see him this way. I followed behind him and he took me into the old barn, which was not an arduous task as only two of four walls remained. We descended upon some ladders and stepped out onto a floor laden with hay, the smell of grass and woodchip surrounded me. The breeze from the outside blew throughout. The roof still remained and sheltered us from the frosty chill. In the barn wall was an opening that looked out onto a babbling brook, which was teaming with fish and white, winter flowers, it was truly breath-taking. I gazed at it for a short time; getting lost in the moment; it was the first time I had truly felt at peace in a while.

"Glorious, isn't it?" Jack said, bringing me back into the room. I turned to face him.

"Yes, it's quite exquisite," I smiled.

"Jack, we need to talk," he cut me off.

"Shh," he put his finger to my lips. He leant towards me and kissed me; I was confused but didn't want him to stop. I had longed to feel his lips on mine for so long. I kissed him back, passionately, making up for the months we had lost, I was apologising for all the hurt. He eventually pulled away from me, but we both wanted more, this morning's encounter had got to me. I didn't give him an option, I needed to feel him again, I needed him to want me. I took off my jacket and unbuttoned my shirt.

"I need you Jack, if never again after this, then just for today." I leant towards him and straddled him, we kissed passionately, I could feel his hard penis against my inner thigh, and I rubbed myself against it, making me wetter. He took off my bra and began to kiss my breasts, I let out a groan, he had a way of making me lose my breath without doing much at all. He looked up at me intensely, there was no cheeky smile this time, it was serious. He pushed me back onto the hay and took off my skirt, he gently rolled down my tights, teasingly kissing every inch of my inner thigh as he did so. I pulled his shirt off over his head and unbuttoned his trousers, and we both lay there naked, embracing, him on top of me, like this morning. I couldn't feel the cold; his body heat was enough to keep me warm. He kissed me passionately and slowly pushed his erect penis inside, making me groan, in and out, faster and faster, his breathing became heavier. I called out his name and scratched my fingers down his back as I climaxed, hard, he came at the same time and we both lay there in a sweaty heap, very content. I laid on him for some time after, my head nuzzled into his chest, taking in his scent, and he stroked my arm.

"I think I love you, Jack," I said, not expecting any answer in return, it felt like the right moment to say it, he needed to know before whatever decision he made. There was a small pause, and he inhaled deeply.

"I think I love ye' too, Nina." My heart fluttered, he felt the same way, I couldn't believe it. I sat up to look at him.

"Really?" I was in disbelief.

"Aye, I don't want anyone else, I want you," and he kissed my forehead softly.

"Jack, we need to talk, we can't put it off anymore." I didn't want to start off on the wrong foot, if we really felt how we said we did then it needed to be perfect; I didn't want to ever lose him again. He sighed.

"Okay, what is it ye' want to say?" I sat up, "Aren't you bothered about what I did Jack, you seem to want to pretend it didn't happen, how can we move forward if we don't discuss it?"

"Ye' want to move forward?" He sounded surprised. I presumed that's what he wanted but why would he? He is probably disgusted with me, just because he said he thought he loved me didn't mean he forgave me.

"Of course, I do. It's always been you, Jack, I lied to

myself. I stayed with Harry for the wrong reasons. I aren't expecting your forgiveness at all, I just want to apologise for what happened. I didn't realise I was pregnant until it had been one month, the timings meant it couldn't have been Harry's," I sighed. Jack looked uncomfortable with the conversation, this was clearly hurting him, but I knew he would never admit it. I continued, "I honestly never thought our paths would cross again, I had chosen to stay with Harry, and you'd come here. When I found out about the baby, I knew it was never going to work. I had no money, Harry wouldn't raise your child, and he offered me a way out."

"I knew he was behind it… That's why I aren't furious, I don't blame ye'. Look, Nina, I already knew about the baby before Harry announced it to the world yesterday," Jack admitted.

"How?" I was shocked; he knew and said nothing to me?

"The day before I saw ye', I bumped into Harry, and he dropped it into conversation, just before he told me ye' were dead. He said you'd killed yourself because ye' aborted the baby. Now I know it was to antagonise me. I honestly didn't believe him at first, but as the night went on, I believed it more. When I saw ye' in the tent and knew ye' were alive I hoped he must have been bullshitting, but then when I spoke to ye' I just knew the baby was true. Ye' were off with me, I sensed something was up."

"Wow, he really is a piece of work, isn't he?" How could I have been so naïve and stupid?

"Did any part of ye' want the baby?" he asked curiously. I sighed.

"Yes, half of me did, I mean we had created something,

it wasn't the baby's fault in what situation it had occurred. But then Harry said the right thing to do was either give the baby up for adoption or have an abortion because he would not raise another man's child. He said I was selfish for bringing a baby into the world, especially when I could not provide for it. He offered to pay for the procedure and promised to keep it quiet until the day he died, more fool me, eh?" I looked away ashamed of my poor judgement and bad decision making.

"I agreed to an extent, in the lead up to the procedure, I often lay awake thinking how I would bring up a baby anyway. I can barely take care of myself, and the poor baby wouldn't have had a daddy," tears began to stream down my face. He wiped my tears away.

"Hey, don't do that. I forgive ye' Nina and I don't blame ye', not one bit. He is a nasty piece of work. I'm not gonna lie, it was hard to take at first, but it was thrust upon me alongside the news of your death, it was a lot to take in. I cannae imagine the stress it played on ye', I didn't expect to ever see ye' again so I know how ye' were feeling. Ye' did what was right for ye' at the time, it's done, we need to move past it, and get on with our lives." He was right, it was done, we needed to begin this chapter the right way. I had really struck gold with this one. I touched his cheek with my palm, he kissed it whilst gazing into my eyes, he loved me, I couldn't believe my luck, everything really does happen for a reason.

We lay together for an hour afterwards, chatting about our childhoods, and what we liked and didn't like, we never got to do any of this before, our relationship was a secret, forbidden, but now I was ready to shout it from the rooftops. I had learned of his brother, Bobby, and more about his wonderful parents. He told me that he played piano, enjoyed sailing, and was not usually a big drinker.

"I cannot abide wine; I had a bad experience one Christmas when I first joined the RAF. It was a bit of an initiation that Collier thought up. We had to down a bottle like it was water, and I was up first," he laughed, almost gipping thinking about it. He looked so happy reminiscing about Collier.

"That sounds quite fun, was it at here the base?"

"Yep, Staines was not impressed when I vomited across my bed sheets…and the floor… and the clean bedding he'd put on for me," he shook his head in disgust. I laughed; I bet he was so entertaining to be around.

"What about you then! What were your younger years like? I bet ye' couldn't keep the boys away!" He winked at me. I felt embarrassed.

"I was a good girl," I added defensively.

"No ye' weren't," he chuckled.

"I was often out drinking and dancing with my friends, secretly of course, my dad would have gone spare. My best friend at the time, used to have parties in her house because her parents worked night shifts. It was super; all the boys and girls in the neighbourhood would go. What else was there to do in Lincoln? And as for the boys, I've always been very particular about the lads I liked," I cheekily smiled.

"Ah so ye' played hard to get!" I laughed.

"You could say that."

"I wonder if I was at one of those parties, you'd have been interested in me!" He enquired audaciously.

"Without a doubt, despite you being old! I'd probably have had to fight off ten girls though." He looked at me lovingly.

"Hey less of the old, there's only six years between us. I'd have only been interested in you anyway," and he kissed me tenderly on the lips. I laid back dreamily, but my mind wandered. How were we going to work this out? He was still an RAF pilot due to go back to war anytime soon, and I lived in Lincolnshire, we were a logistical nightmare on paper, but what's a few cities and a World War when there's true love involved? I didn't want to ruin the moment talking about 'what next' so I left it and just enjoyed basking with the man I loved.

"It's nearly lunchtime, we better head back, I have some training I need to do at 1," Jack sat up in a rush. He continued to watch me whilst I got dressed, smiling his mischievous smile.

"What?" I asked coyly as I pulled on my blouse.

"You are the most beautiful woman I have ever seen, Miss Nina Hughes," he responded.

"Shut up you soppy thing," I laughed, throwing his shirt at him, I loved how he felt about me, he made me feel like the Queen of the world. We both headed back to the camp and as we approached the main entrance, my stomach flipped, was I really going to enter in broad daylight? Could I handle the gossip? I contemplated turning back, but Jack took my hand and flashed me a warm, reassuring smile, like he could read my mind. God, I loved him. We entered together, hand in hand, no one even batted an eyelid, what had I been worried about? I smiled at him, and we headed towards Jack's tent. I admired Jack as we walked, watching his beautiful eyes sparkle in the winter sun. The smile suddenly drained from his face and his eyes widened, I followed his gaze to the skyline. In the distance there appeared to be a V shaped swarm of birds taking over the skies, what was it? I stared with bated breath, my eyes wide watching the hundreds of black dots draw closer, Jack did the same, everything felt in slow motion. The black mess grew closer, and I realised they were planes. I saw something fall from one plane, then another deposit, and another, I heard Jack shout.

"GET DOWN!" WHOOOSH, BANG! The screeching sound deafened me and the ground shook. My vision briefly went dim, my ears were ringing, and I couldn't hear a thing. I had been thrown backwards onto the muddy ground; Jack was nowhere around me. What had just happened? Where was I? I tried to gather my thoughts and compose myself, why were my ears ringing, I held my hands to my head to try blank it out, but it made no difference. I stood up and turned around, to my horror, the camp was on fire, and grey smoke billowed like a huge, dark cloud above the airbase, we had been bombed.

Chapter 6

Nina

Where was Jack? I was panicked; I needed to get myself together. SCREECH WHOOSH BANG! The earth shook once more, another explosion somewhere in the near distance. I couldn't think straight, I was terrified, but knew I needed to find Jack. Was he hurt? I stumbled a few yards ahead, I saw bodies discarded on the side of the camp, some with limbs missing, and others face down, lifeless. The smell of burning and fuel wafted through the air. I wanted to cry, but was in too much shock, I couldn't comprehend what was going on. I knew there was a world war going on, but it hadn't felt real up to now, because where I lived, we hadn't been attacked, this was real life, and I was petrified. Where was Jack? Was Georgie okay? Had Harry survived?

Suddenly I was grabbed from behind; it was Jack. I felt relief, I hugged him tight, and I didn't want to let him go. My tears came thick and fast, he was covered in mud but was uninjured. His expression was serious, I knew he was in military mode, he acted like this was normal; unfazed by it all.

"Nina listen to me very carefully, ye' need to go into the underground shelter." I was struggling to hear him but could make out that he said 'shelter'.

"Jack, I can't hear you properly," I shouted. He tried to sign at me.

"You go down into the shelter, I need to go."

"NO! You are not leaving me Jack!" I shouted again, clinging onto his arms for balance.

"Nina this is my job," he looked at me stoically. He was right, this was his job, how can this be happening? We have just been reunited, I can't let him leave me now, what if he never comes back? I was horrified at the thought. He grabbed my hand and led me towards the centre of the camp, I kept my eyes fixed in front, I did not want to see around me. I knew it was dead men and women, but I did not want it to be true. It could be colleagues, it could be Georgie, I wanted to pretend they didn't exist. We stopped above what looked like a manhole cover, he bent down to remove the cover and inside was a deep, dark vertical tunnel that was dimly lit with ladders leading down.

"Ye' need to go in there, Nina, and stay there until I come and get ye', or someone comes and tells ye' it's safe out here," he demanded. "Do ye' understand?" I couldn't follow what he was saying, I was in shock, I just nodded in agreement, not really grasping what he was asking of me. He lent in and kissed me, I didn't want this to end, it might be the last time I ever see him.

"WATSON, COME ON WE NEED TO GO!" Megson shouted in the distance.

"I need to go, go down there now," he began pushing me into the tunnel; I got my foot steady on the rung of the ladder, and began to step down. I felt wobbly kneed and sick to the core, I clung to the handles for dear life, afraid I would fall. I looked above and saw Jack staring down at me unhappily, I think we both knew that this could be it, and then it went dark.

My eyes finally adjusted as I neared the bottom of the tunnel, it was damp down here, and very eerie. Why was it so silent? My heart was pumping out of my chest; I took a moment to compose myself. Everything had happened so quickly. Surely, I couldn't be the only one left alive. The smell was stale, like the place had never seen fresh air or daylight. The walls were covered in moss and were slippery to touch. Rusty lamps hung on the walls every three metres or so apart. I followed the cobbled path round the bends, all I could hear was my own breath, I wondered how deep underground I was, then up ahead I saw a door. I approached cautiously, I had no idea where I was, I knew Jack wouldn't lead me to danger, but I was in a unknown area and I was afraid. I was still trying to process what I had just seen above ground. I gently twisted the knob to open the door and was greeted by a room full of faces I had never seen before. They were battered and bruised, covered in mud, and wearing the uniform Jack wore. Why were they here instead of up there? I walked in and shut the door behind me, every pair of eyes were on me. I felt intimidated, but this can't be as bad as being up there.

The room was compact, but had more of a civilised feel to it, the walls weren't draped in mould and moss, they were boarded up with wood. It smelled of sawdust and soil. The seats were huge lumps of concrete pushed together to make a bench. A barrel of water was placed near the entrance, next to a bucket of what appeared to be cold beans, I guess that was our sustenance. I felt nauseous just thinking about eating and drinking the contents of those buckets. I kept my head down and walked to the other side of the room, I sighed a great breath of relief when I saw a face that I knew; it was Georgie. I ran to her and hugged her tightly.

"Oh my god, Nina, what just happened?" she cried on

my shoulder.

"It was the Germans I think, are you okay?"

"No, I'm terrified," she was shaking. The room full of men watched on, emotionless, silent, barely taking their gazes away from staring into space.

"Who were you with?" I asked.

"Genie and Maud, and some of the men. I don't even know their names really, we were just back for dinner and about to go back out and do the rounds, but I lost them, where were you?" she replied.

"I was with Jack Watson," I looked at her bashfully.

"Where is he now?" she seemed concerned.

"He had to go and defend the camp," I tried to remain brave, but she could see through me.

"I don't know what has happened between you two, and I don't want to pry, but it's going to be okay, he will be back!" I had not told Georgie anything about Jack or the baby, I trusted her, but thought the more people I told the more real it would have become. I wish I had of done, Georgie was such a good friend. She always had my best interests at heart, and she treat me more like a sister than a friend.

"It's complicated, and I am sorry I didn't tell you about it. I had no idea where to begin, and Harry said the more people who knew the more likely it was to get out. I was ashamed."

"I should have known he would have said that. I have said from the start, Nina that he was no good for you. Never trust a man who doesn't smile. I don't know Jack, but he seems like a gentleman. I hope you two are going to be okay!" Georgie reassured me rubbing my arm. I began to weep, tears dampened my face, I thought we would be okay until this. I suddenly felt mad; I turned to the room full of men who were sat minding their own business.

"Why are none of you up there fighting?" They looked at one another glumly.

"Ma'am, we're all injured," one young lad replied. I felt like an idiot.

"I'm sorry," I sniffed, feeling guilty, "please ignore me," I felt wretched.

"Did you say you're with Jack Watson?" one lad enquired. I wiped the tears from my eyes.

"Yes, well it's a long story," I laughed.

"He's a great guy Watson, he trained me through my broken collar bone, I'm hoping to be back out there again soon… wish I'd have been ready for today," he hung his head in pity. I looked around at the crowd of broken looking men, I bet they all felt that way, and there I was shouting at them, insinuating they were cowardly.

"It can't be helped, you're no good to anyone if you aren't fighting fit, are you?" I jovially responded, trying to get his spirits up. He smiled back, unconvincingly. I turned back to Georgie.

"Have you seen Harry?" I had to ask.

"No, not since the fight yesterday, he wasn't in briefing again either," she added. I felt the ground shudder again, that must have been another bomb.

"The fucking Nazi bastards!" one man stood up shouting at the wall. I looked at him, a little frightened, but understood his anger. I could not imagine being down here injured, when my colleagues, friends even, were up there fighting the fight and trying to protect their country. No one responded to him, or batted an eyelid, they clearly all thought the same.

It felt like hours went past, everyone was glum, and no one spoke a word, not even Georgie and I, we were drained. The conditions in here were grim, it was freezing and there was nowhere to use the toilet. I couldn't get the image of Jack stood at the top of the tunnel out of my head. He was already a hero to me, I just prayed that he was safe, that he wasn't under fire, or suffering. I felt myself dozing off when a large bang at the door awoke me.

"Come in," one man shouted in a monotone voice. The door creaked, and in walked Harry, with more policemen. A wave of anger overcame me, the last place I wanted to be was in here with Harry, but I was also relieved that he was alive, despite him being a first-class idiot. He noticed me immediately, staring at me with a deathly conviction. He didn't seem to have a fleck of dirt on him, he looked unbothered by the situation, like we weren't at war, and that someone had just let off a firework outside instead. How does he do that? He always ends up looking like nothing has been arduous for him, like everything has been handed to him and that nothing on this earth could cause him to have an ounce of emotion. I turned my head away; I did not want to speak to him, I no longer owed him anything. Georgie mouthed, "Are you okay?" bless her sweet soul.

"Yes," I lied. Harry took a seat opposite me, he sat with his hands fisted together in front of him and looked down at the ground. Another hour or so passed, no one uttered a word, the silence was deafening. I closed my eyes so I didn't have to see Harry, but all I could think about was Jack. My mind roamed, I could not stop myself from thinking the worst, and I needed to snap out of it. It was out of my control.

"So, where's lover boy?" Harry finally muttered, *there it is,* I thought. I knew he couldn't resist.

"Harry, please don't," I asked kindly but authoritatively.

"It's a bit too late for that?" he barked. I had really dented his pride. The other men were beginning to look.

"I don't want to fight, please can we talk about this another time, perhaps when we are not being subject to Luftwaffe bombs?" I snapped back.

"You really are just a common tart, aren't you?" he retaliated. I stood up; he was not going to speak to me this way any longer. I approached him and lowered myself so his face was directly in front of mine. I removed the engagement ring from my finger and placed it in his hand.

"Okay, so you want to know where Jack is? Well after we fucked each other again, and told each other we loved one another, he went off to fight for the country, and try to save our lives. What have you done lately other than make up disgusting lies and make a complete arse of yourself?" THWACK. I felt a sharp sting to my cheek, he had smacked me across the face. I fell to the ground with an almighty thud, dazed. My lip was bleeding, I was in shock, he had actually just hit me, all that time I said to myself he would never lay a finger on me, his true colours had really come out now. A handful of soldiers stood up and walked towards him hastily.

"Why don't you pick on someone your own fucking size you little shit," one of them snarled. Another soldier pushed him against the wall.

"Not so fucking mighty now are you, you little runt," another one shouted. Harry knew he was outnumbered. He looked at me and spat at the floor.

"I sincerely hope that coward dies out there today, your dad is going to be so disgusted with you, I hope you're happy with the choices you've made." He turned, slamming the door behind him. I realised I did owe him an explanation, but he wasn't going to be reasonable, so how could I discuss it? I had tried everything to make that man happy, he had ruled me for too long, and now the shackles were finally off and I felt free. I felt like Nina again. One of the men, and Georgie approached me and helped me to my feet.

"Th-thank you, for doing that, and for defending me, it was really kind of you," I mumbled.

"Oh, Nina," Georgie whined, dabbing a handkerchief on my lip to wipe the blood.

"I'm going to report him! Who the hell does he think he is?" she said angrily.

"No just leave it, please. That was it, he did what he wanted to do, said what he had to say, I think I'm rid of him now," I whispered. I felt out of breath, dizzy and weak. What he had said about my dad and Jack was spinning round and round in my head. I just hoped that neither would be true.

I sat with my back against the wall, in a daze. I finally fell asleep thinking about the future of Jack and I. We were going to get married, and have a family - two kids, one boy and one girl. He would be the best dad, teaching them how to play piano, playing football and flying kites with them on the green, I would be sat on the side-line with Faye whilst tea was cooking, immensely content with the little family I had. Dad would live close by, and he would come round for Sunday lunch, he would love Jack. Jack wouldn't be in the RAF anymore, there would be no risk, no sadness, no threats, just pure happiness. We would have meals out together, and Faye would babysit the children. He would tell me he loved me, and we would just laugh and chat away the night then go home and make sweet love. War would be over, Harry would be long gone, and everyone will have forgotten the bad things I had done. We could have already had our first baby on the way, but I ruined it, I will never forgive myself. I could feel myself slipping into a dark hole of thoughts, but I was dreaming, wake up, wake up - I told myself.

I awoke with a startled yelp; I look around urgently.

"I'm sorry… I was just dreaming," I apologised catching my breath; I had woken a few of the soldiers up.

"What about?" Georgie asked interested.

"Oh, the usual rubbish," I rolled my eyes and Georgie sniggered.

"How long have we been down here?" I enquired.

"Twenty-two hours," a soldier replied. Wow, surely, it was safe up there by now, how much fuel did the Germans have?

"Shouldn't we try and make our way up there now?" I probed.

"It's a war zone Miss, I would advise that we didn't," another retorted.

"Yes, but it's been a while since I've felt a bomb fall, and no one has been to get us, maybe we've been forgotten about?"

"Or maybe those who knew we were here are all dead?" another soldier bluntly added. The realisation hit me, he was right, Jack would never leave me here alone if he was alive, he would have come back to get me. I need to find out if he was alive or not. I pushed past the soldiers and headed towards the tunnel and the ladder I had entered via.

"Miss don't do this; you are going to get killed!" The same soldier responded. I ignored him, it had been ages, I needed to get out of this sewer. I began to climb the ladders; soldiers were approaching behind me, waiting with bated breath. I reached the top of the ladders and pushed with all my might on the heavy lid that enclosed us in this underground tube. And then there was daylight, my sight adjusted, and chaos met my eyes. No noise, just silence, it was as if someone had hit mute. I moved the cover to one side and began to climb out of the hole, taking my time. I looked all around me, in dismay. The camp was obliterated; the fires were no longer burning, they were smoking. Most of the tents we had resided in had burned to the ground and were now just embers. There was an eeriness in the air, the feeling when snow settles on the ground, and all the sound around it becomes muffled and subdued.

My footsteps crunched on the floor as I walked gently across the ashes and was presented with the same dead men and women I had tried so hard to avoid only twenty-four hours previous. I stood taking it all in, my eyes wide with anguish. The soldiers appeared one by one behind me, making their way across the cinders. They looked at each deceased man and woman and began to cover their bodies with pieces of unburned tent material and their uniform jackets. I choked back a tear. Where was my Jack?

"We have some here, sir," a posh English accent shouted to another man across the way from us. I didn't recognise either of these men, but they looked military, in their khaki uniforms.

"Come hither all of you," he shouted bossily. The soldiers began to make their way towards him, I waited for Georgie, and we walked linking each other's arms, clinging on for dear life. Georgie was sniffling into her hanky. We will both never forget this day.

We were all bundled into the back of a camouflaged van and sat for fifteen minutes in silence as we made the journey to our next destination, taking in the horrific sights as we drove past. The city was destroyed, there were men, women and children crying in the street, huddled together, and looking at their wreckage of a home. Rubble lay strewn across the roads, nothing looked familiar anymore, there was a smell of death, burning rubber and fuel in the air, a smog lay across the city, stopping the sunlight from shining through clearly. Aside from the cries it was silent, like a graveyard, no hope or possibility was present, just doom and destruction. The truck stopped and the posh English man appeared.

"Right come on everyone," he ushered us off the vehicle.

"Sir, excuse me, but have you seen a Jack Watson, he's an RAF Pilot?" I enquired.

"I don't know anyone by that name I am afraid, I'm Army," he bluntly replied, and ushered me to move on. I felt deflated. We were taken into a vast hall, lined with benches, there was a walkway down the middle so people could get in and out. There were already hundreds of people here, some of which appeared to be RAF, and police, but there were other civilians amongst them too. I had no idea where we were or what was going on. It smelled like an old school hall, all disinfectant and lingering sweat. The room was cold, as cold as the pit we had been in for the last twenty-four hours, and condensation clung to the small windows that were located in the roof. We were passed a blanket as we entered, I was grateful for the warmth; I hadn't been able to feel my fingers for some time.

"I presume this is a safe house," Georgie whispered. We were sat down next to each other on the benches, squeezed in like sardines. You could hear the hustle and bustle of people chatting, but there was a melancholic quality to their voices, the sort of tone you would expect to hear at a wake.

"Alright, I'm Sid…Army," he extended his arm out to the solider sat next to me.

"Now then, I'm Marty, RAF," he replied with a thick West Yorkshire twang. Sid looked at me and Georgie.

"Well, you two don't belong here," he smiled.

"You can say that again," Georgie replied hastily.

"What's ya' story?" he continued in his Geordie accent.

"We are policewomen, we came to help with the riots, the only two standing from our force by the looks of things," she said sadly looking around the hall, "except for him," and she nodded disgustingly towards Harry who was sat on the opposite side, staring into space.

"Sorry to hear that," he said solemnly, following her gaze. "Well, I'm Sid, here to help if needed," he reached across to shake our hands. We responded with our names, but I didn't want to talk, I wanted some answers. I didn't even care that Harry was there, I just wanted Jack. Twenty minutes passed and suddenly an importantly dressed man, appeared in the middle of the walkway. You could tell he was high up in the military, by his pristine appearance, the medals decorating his blazer, and the way he talked with conviction.

"Good afternoon, Ladies and Gentlemen. I am Colonel Heath. I wish we were all together under different circumstances but unfortunately, we are all here due to one great tragedy. Yesterday afternoon, as you well know, Germany opened fire with us, around 12:45pm. Biggin Hill camp was bombed, sadly taking with it many men and women. The bombs carried on into the night, destroying most of the surrounding areas, including the RAF camp. The Germans surprised us by attacking during the day, as we all well know with their current strategy; they usually strike us throughout the night. Admittedly, we were caught off guard, but our excellent Air Force came up trumps and defended us the best they could. Sadly, we lost three men in the air battle. Their families are yet to be informed so I will withhold their names for now, but our thoughts and condolences are with them and their families." A hot flush burned over me, everything became fast and loud around me, three men have died, one of them is Jack, I just know it. Before I could stop myself, I stood up and screamed.

"NO! Who was it? I need to know!" tears were streaming down my face. "Please," I whispered. The

Colonel looked confused with the interruption.

"I am sorry ma'am, but it really is not for me to say at this time," the whole room stared at me.

"Sit down sweetheart," Sid grabbed my hand and sat me down. I was in a daze, I just stared into space, and the tears fell down my cheeks, onto my neck and hit the floor. I had no energy left, I didn't want to talk or engage, I wanted to perish. I could feel everyone's eyes burning into me, I glanced at Harry, a conceited smile furnished his face, his wish had come true - I hated him.

Time ticked by slowly, everyone continued to mutter to each other. I wasn't paying attention to anything, I was in my own world, lost, trapped in my thoughts. I kept thinking of what it could have been like, whether he was hurt, whether he suffered like Collier, how would his parents be with the news? I needed fresh air. I stood to walk outside, my legs shook, and I felt so feeble, I hadn't eaten in over twenty-four hours, but I had no appetite. My mouth was dry, I realised I hadn't drunk anything recently. I headed wearily towards the door, it was as though I was in a dream, like I was floating. Everyone got louder, I started to see black, my vision kept appearing then disappearing.

"Whoa watch her; she's going to pass out!" I heard a ghostly voice shout in the distance, did they mean me? I saw people running towards me, and then as if by magic, Jack appeared in front of me. Had I died? Was I dreaming? Was it a mirage? He looked alarmed, and ran towards me in slow motion, I tried to speak but no words came out, and then it went black.

Wow it's bright in here, is this heaven? Did I even believe in that? I could barely open my eyes due to the whiteness of the walls in this strange setting. I felt fragile and tired, I eventually forced my eyes open to slits, so a little light came through. I noticed a drip coming from my arm. A nurse walked in to my view, I was in hospital. There was an antiseptic smell enveloping the room, it was warm, and my limbs felt fuzzy. All I could hear was the buzzing of the light on the ceiling.

"H-h-hello, where am I?" I managed to drone.

"You're in a military hospital dear, you passed out. We are just running some tests to see why you fainted. Can you tell me when you last ate and drank something?"

"I can't remember," I whispered. "We had been in a bunker, then a hall, and that's the last I remember... when can I go?"

"Oh, not yet dear, maybe tomorrow, we are just giving you some fluids for now, that should help, why don't you try get some rest?" I did as she asked; I was so tired I could barely keep my eyes open. I slept solidly, not even waking for the toilet; I was physically and mentally exhausted. I opened my eyes again, it was ten past two in the afternoon, I could see properly now and felt more human. The sun blazed through the window, I could now see the room was a dusky pink colour, not the whiteness I had envisaged yesterday. I was in here on my own, with only a sink, a bed and a table for company. Blinds hung down from the window, all tousled and broken. I spotted some beautiful pink roses by my bed. I picked them up and sniffed them, it took me back to a warm summer's day in Lincoln, where Faye and I used to spend our afternoons walking through the flower gardens, putting the world to rights, I missed my sister. I wonder whom these were from, probably deepest sympathy flowers from Georgie. My memory was gradually returning, and I began to feel sad, miserable at the thought of never being able to see Jack again – he was gone.

"Good afternoon, Nina," a man in a white coat and stethoscope walked in, he was clearly the doctor.

"How are you feeling?" He placed a thermometer under my tongue, felt my forehead, then lowered his stethoscope to my chest to listen to my heartbeat.

"Better thanks, how long have I been here?" I managed.

"Three days, you seem much better today, we have fed some fluids into your body as you were dehydrated, and it also appears you have an iron deficiency, so we advise you to eat iron rich foods, mainly red meats, greens and fish, and drink plenty of water, when you are discharged."

"Okay," I replied.

"Have you got any questions? If not, you are free to go. I believe your car is waiting out front for you, would you like one of the nurses to assist you to the door?"

"No, I will be fine thank you," I said getting out of bed. The doctor left the room, *what car?* I thought to myself, it must be normal procedure when someone faints in the vicinity of Army personnel, I chuckled to myself.

I looked at myself in the mirror, I looked unpleasant, my eyes were sunken, I had black rings circling underneath them, my lip was split from where Harry had hit me, and my hair was in disarray. I splashed the cold water from the faucet onto my face, it felt refreshing, giving me a little boost.

I spotted an open leather, brown bag in the corner of the room that I hadn't noticed before. A note was placed on top that read 'Self Care'. I opened the bag up curiously, inside was makeup, how strange, I wonder if Georgie has been by. I applied it generously, so I no longer resembled a snowman. I carefully painted on my ruby red lips, ran my black eyeliner across my eyelid, and feathered my mascara through my eyelashes, I always found it amazing how that black line, and those red lips can make me look and feel human again. I ran a brush through my hair and plaited it up into the bun I always wore, I felt slightly better now. I should have asked about the flowers I thought to myself, as I picked up the bunch and opened the door. I turned to look back at the room, here goes, it's time to face reality, on my own, again.

I headed down the corridor, the hospital was calm but busy, I think the worst of the bombing casualties had probably passed. I turned down a corridor that housed huge, grand windows, I could see the sun shining through the panes, bouncing off the dusky pink walls, it was quite serene. I walked slowly down it, letting the warmth catch my face, and watching the planted tulips that were in the garden, sway in the breeze. I noticed something cerise on the floor, out of the corner of my eye. I approached it, and discovered it was another rose, like the one from my bunch. How strange, maybe someone visiting a loved one dropped it; I put it amongst my bouquet. A feeling of despair crossed my mind, I would never get a bunch of flowers from Jack, I would never kiss him again or hear his voice once more, I sighed morosely. I continued to walk down the corridor, a bit more urgently now, I just wanted to get out, where was the exit? I approached a row of seats and noticed another pink rose; which clumsy soul is dropping all these flowers around the hospital? They really ought to be more careful, I thought to myself. I put it amongst my bunch and looked for the 'Way Out' sign, spotting it and heading towards it with pace. As I got nearer to the exit, I noticed through the glass windows at either side of the main door that soldiers were lined up outside, all in the RAF attire. My mind flashed back to Jack in his blues. I don't know if I can face this yet, maybe I should find another exit. I took a deep breath to compose myself, I was going to have to face it at some point, I was on a military camp, I was going to see soldiers everywhere, I needed to be brave and deal with the grief, as brave as Jack had been defending us all. I cautiously approached the thick wooden door that led outside, and slowly opened it. A nurse sat on the benches near to the door beaming at me. I smiled back to be polite, but she just continued to grin. I felt uneasy so stepped into the sun, closing the door behind me. As I stepped outside a violin began playing, I recognised the song it was Pachelbel's Canon in D, I loved this song. The sky was very blue today; there wasn't a cloud to be seen. Birds flitted between the tall trees that were planted outside the hospital gate. My mind fell into a daydream of brief calmness and tranquillity as I soaked in the sun and listened to the violin. I switched back out of it quite quickly realising I must have walked into a parade of some sort. I clumsily walked down the steps, trying not to be noticed. As I approached the soldiers that I had spotted through the glass, they began to salute, one by one; I was confused, I looked behind me expecting someone of rank to appear, but it was just me. Was I in some form of coma? I looked around in dismay; every one of them was staring at me. I walked past them, eyeing them all up dubiously, and as the last one in the row stepped aside, I saw him - It was Jack. I didn't know what to do with myself, was I dreaming again? He looked so dashing in his blue uniform. His dirty blonde hair was perfectly styled, and his sapphire blue eyes gleamed at me, he looked flawless. He didn't take his eyes from me. There was a row of red and pink roses leading towards where he stood. Georgie was on one side of him, beaming with happiness, Group Captain Staines was on the other, grinning. Tears began to stream down my face, it had sunk in, it was really him, "JACK!" I cried.

"Here I am," he flashed his playful smile. I began walking towards him, my pace getting quicker, and as I approached, he got down on one knee, brandishing a small, purple, velvet box. I stopped in my tracks, I felt like my heart ceased beating for a moment, my mouth went dry.

"Nina, ye' don't know what it feels like to see your beautiful face again. Since I met ye', you're all I have thought about. I never believed in soulmates, but I do now I have *you* in my life. In that plane all I thought about was getting back to see ye' again – ye' were my motivation, my reason for fighting to stay alive, and I am not letting ye' out of my sight again. I have never loved anyone the way I love you." His eyes filled with tears. "Nina, will ye' do me the honour of becoming my wife and making me the happiest man in the world? Will ye' marry me?"

"Yes, yes, yes, yes, yes, yes!" I shouted, overjoyed. Everyone cheered and clapped, I ran to him, and he placed the most beautiful diamond ring on my finger, which sparkled in the glorious sunshine. He kissed my hand, like I was his lady this time, not Clara, not anybody else, just me. I jumped on him and wrapped my legs around him, happy tears creeping down my face. I kissed him so hard; I never wanted to let him go. My Jack was back, and we were getting married, I couldn't have been happier if I tried.

Chapter 7

Nina

Three weeks had passed and today was the day; Jack and I were getting married. I could not contain my excitement; it had not been long since he had proposed to me, but we weren't taking any chances after everything we had been through. We wanted to be man and wife, Mr and Mrs Watson, and there was no stopping us. Jack was due to go back to war in the coming week and had even been promoted to Wing Commander making the day even more special. We'd had three weeks of bliss, getting to know each other, and falling in love that little bit more each day. The wait and pain we had both faced over the last few months had been worth it, it had dissolved away. We just fit together, like pieces of a jigsaw. I still couldn't believe our paths had led to one another again. I was a strong believer in fate and destiny, and he was finally mine.

"Oh, Nina you look beautiful," my sister Faye finished applying my lipstick. My dad and sister were both down for the wedding. I had gone up to Lincolnshire to see dad, to explain everything that had happened with Harry, immediately after Jack proposed. He was not best pleased at first, but after I told him what Harry was really like, he saw how happy I was, and with some gentle persuasion from Faye, he finally came around. He met Jack, and immediately loved him, like I knew he would. They both liked rugby, fishing and playing cards. Jack promised to take dad to see a Spitfire when it was safe to do so, but their main common ground was they both wanted the best for me. I didn't see Harry again, which was still too soon, but that part of my life was gone, out of my mind. I had new, exciting things to think about now. Gratefully, he never told my dad about the abortion. Let's see if he reacts to Jack and I getting married – I winced at the thought. Oh well, not today, happy thoughts only from now on. I did a twirl and Faye and Georgie wolf whistled, I giggled playfully. I looked at myself in the full-length mirror and barely recognised myself. Faye had done a wonderful job at making me look and feel like a princess; my lashes were long, my eyes gold and sparkly, my lips ruby red and my hair was curled like a corkscrew, with the side pinned down using a hair grip decorated with real pink roses. There was a smell of perfume, coffee and flowers in the air. My wedding dress was something a queen would wear. It was snow-white lace and silk, the neckline swept across my collarbone and the skirt dangled like a waterfall down to my feet. There were small diamantes encrusted within the chest that sparkled as I walked, and the hem was lace. My shoes were like Cinderella's glass slippers when she met her Prince Charming, and I certainly had met mine. My earrings matched the diamantes of my dress, and my nails were painted a rose pink to match my bouquet. I was glowing, I felt elegant and classy, I was getting the wedding day I had always fantasised about and marrying the man of my dreams – I felt like the luckiest woman alive.

"Oh, girls I cannot tell you how happy I am! I can't believe today is finally here, I am finally going to marry him!" I shrieked gleefully. There was a knock at the door, it was Mrs Watson, Jack's mum.

"Oh my gosh, Nina, you look like a starlet!" I blushed.

"Thank you, Mrs Watson," I smiled and kissed her on

the cheek.

"Please, call me Delilah!" she continued, "Jack is going to melt when he sees you - simply stunning. I still can't believe my little boy has finally settled down! I am such a proud mother; it won't be long before the pitter patter of tiny feet!" Let's not go there I thought, changing the subject.

"Mrs... Delilah, this is my sister Faye, and my best friend Georgie," I introduced them.

"Lovely to meet you girls, you also look gorgeous," she smiled at each one of them.

"Aww Neen, I can't tell you how proud I am of you, everything you've been through, it makes my heart swell, I'm so delighted for you, you deserve to be happy after everything you've had to endure," Faye grabbed my hands. I smiled bashfully, I loved my little sister, she was like my best friend and sibling rolled into one. She was three years younger than I was, and I had been like a mother figure to her, since our actual mum walked out and left dad on his own to raise us. We had a special connection that no one could break. We told each other our deepest, darkest secrets, and always had each other's backs. It became apparent after me and Harry had split, that Faye had warned Harry to stay away from me in the very beginning of our relationship, as she knew he was bad news. He retaliated by threatening to tell dad that she had had been smoking and drinking underage, and she had no choice but to remain quiet. What an awful man he really was. Us Hughes girls might not do things by the book, we may like to have a bit of fun, and not all our decisions might be deemed socially acceptable, but we were happy, and that's all that matters.

"Thanks Faye, I hope you and dad move down here one day. I don't know what I will do without you!"

"I'm not going to be far away, I will always be here whenever you need me," she teared up, as did I. Nope, don't ruin the makeup, Nina.

"The car is here," my dad shouted up from the bottom of the stairs. I couldn't wait for my dad to walk me down the aisle; it's what most little girls dream of. I approached the staircase, with Mrs Watson, Georgie and Faye in tow, and slowly walked down the stairs towards dad.

"Oh my, Nina, you really look like the most beautiful bride I have ever seen," his eyes began to fill with tears. He leant in for a hug and squeezed me tight; I couldn't help but weep a little, today is going to be an emotional day.

"My little baby all grown up getting married to a military man, I am so proud of you!"

"Thanks daddy, how I am is all down to you, thank you for everything," I squeezed his arm. My dad was a rotund, short, balding man but had the biggest heart of anyone I knew. He was strong in his morals and principals, and sometimes came across as over opinionated, but deep down he wanted what was best for Faye and me especially after mum left and broke our hearts. He worked in a cotton mill back home, and provided for Faye, as he always had done for both of us. We both loved our dad with our whole hearts, and admired how humble and hard-working he was, he shaped who we were, and made us courteous, polite, well-mannered people, who did not take nonsense from anyone; most of the time anyway.

"Dad, this is Delilah, this is Jack's mother," I introduced them.

"Pleased to meet you Delilah, I'm Glen," he went to shake her hand, but Delilah went in for a hug.

"Lovely to meet you Glen, I have heard lots about you; Jack is very fond of you!" My heart melted, and dad smiled, he was happy with that assessment.

"That's very kind, I am looking forward to meeting your husband too, George, is it?" He asked.

"Yes, I am sure you two will get on like a house on fire!" she smiled. I neared the door and looked outside, the most beautiful pure white Rolls Royce Phantom was parked on the road, wow I really am being spoiled. Jack had picked the car for me to arrive in; I knew he would pick something luxurious and classy. The inside of the car was lined with red leather, and the bonnet was decorated with pink roses. My dad was very impressed with the car.

"Wow this is excellent," he said running his fingers down the bonnet. We never had much growing up so this was as exciting for my dad as it was for me. I wanted this day to be about all of us, because these were the most important people in my life. The chauffeur stepped out and opened the back door for us to climb into. My dad sat in the front and me, Delilah, Georgie and Faye stepped into the back. I took a deep, nervous breath.

"Here we go ladies," I smiled an excited smile. I was about to become Mrs Nina Watson.

Jack

"Give me another swig of that," I said grabbing the hip flask from Bobby. I was beginning to feel the nerves and needed that whisky, like I needed the air that I breathe. I had finally committed to someone, I wasn't regretting it, not one bit but this was a big deal. I would no longer be a lone ranger; I was going to be someone's husband. Not just anyone's, I was going to be Nina's husband, that alone made me feel better.

"Don't be getting drunk before she arrives you idiot," Bobby laughed. I had asked my brother, Bobby to be best man today, everyone who I love had made the wedding, except Collier, but I had his picture in a frame pride of place next to the alter, he was here in spirit.

"I won't be getting drunk, I'm just taking the edge off," I took one last sip and passed it back to my brother. My dad looked at me smirking.

"I don't think I've ever seen you so nervous son." I laughed back.

"I don't think I've ever felt this nervous, being in a plane is a piece of cake compared to this!" I couldn't keep still. Dad was one of my groomsmen, along with Megson and of course Group Captain Staines. Numerous soldiers were guests in the audience, along with close family and friends of both of us, from back home. We didn't want a big elaborate affair, we wanted the wedding to be intimate, and special, so we could celebrate us being together, with those that mattered the most. The venue was a church next to a country house, in the outskirts of Bath; it was a picturesque, quiet village, with one pub, a guesthouse and a few residential homes. It was so relaxing to hear the birds tweeting in a morning, instead of car engines and horns beeping. Not to mention the stench of war and smog that oozed out of London. My mind was at ease and had been since I had proposed, Nina was my medicine - I needed her. We had wanted to get away from the city life and had picked this place, so we had somewhere peaceful

111

to relax for a few days after the wedding, before I went back out to war. I was delighted to have been promoted to Wing Commander and Staines really saw the potential in me and I couldn't wait to teach him that he was right to have that faith in me. My life was so different to just a month ago, and I couldn't believe how lucky I was. It was going so well for me, I dared let myself believe that all the shit was over, and that now it would just be plain sailing, as it once was. I looked at my watch, fashionably late so they say, but I couldn't wait a minute longer to marry her, hurry up!

The winter sun shone through the church window, and the chattering stopped. My heart started palpitating, was she here? The organ started up, and the wedding march began to play.

"Fuck this is it," I muttered under my breath to Bobby who shot me a cheesy smile and nudged my shoulder with his, wishing me luck. *Derr der da der, derr der da der*, and the doors to the church opened. I turned to face the door and in walked the bridesmaids, Faye and Georgie; they looked beautiful, my mum walked behind them dressed up to the nines, grinning at me like a Cheshire cat when she saw me. I smiled back; then there she was - breath taking. I mouthed *wow*, she saw me, smiling her wonderful smile at me, she looked like a goddess. I couldn't take my eyes from her; I was so in love with her. How had I managed to get this innocent beauty to be my wife, she made my eyes ache with her magnificence, I couldn't stop staring. Her dad walked beside her as proud as punch, linking onto her tight. I could tell he was filled with emotion; he nodded at me as he left Nina at the altar, giving her a kiss on the cheek and a squeeze of the hand.

She stood beside me, her golden hair loosely curled, dangling down to her shoulders. Her elegant, snowy white dress flowed to the floor, her ruby red lips shined, and her green eyes pulled me in. She smelled of roses, I was sure every man in the room was extremely jealous that she was mine, she truly looked like an angel.

"Ye' look incredible," I whispered to her. She timidly put her head on my shoulder.

"So do you, Mr Watson." My nerves washed away, I knew I was doing the right thing, I wanted to make that woman mine, I couldn't imagine a day without her now, I was a changed man.

"Dearly beloved, we are gathered here today, to witness the marriage of Mr Jack Thomas Watson and Miss Nina Gloria Hughes...now for the vows," the vicar looked at me and smiled. Nina looked at me raising her eyebrows, confused, she had no idea I had written my own vows, I smiled cheekily. Here goes.

"So ye' know I am a man of many talents," I raised my eyebrows, the guests and Nina chuckled. "Well, I have written a poem for ye'," she seemed impressed. "When I first met ye' I was so lost, I didn't know what to do, ye' saved me from the winter frost, and for that, Nina, I love you. We had our obstacles and beat them all, we were meant to be together, for the rest of our lives, the long haul, and in any kind of weather. Today ye' do me the honour of becoming my wife, and spending your life with me, I promise never to cause ye' strife, and will love ye' for the rest of eternity." Tears appeared in her eyes.

"You soppy thing," she smiled wiping them away.

"And now you Nina," the vicar encouraged. She looked around nervously.

"Well, I am not as talented as my soon to be husband," she laughed awkwardly. I loved how shy and sweet she was, her purity made me see life in a completely new way. "Jack, you had my heart from the moment you set eyes on me, and I you, you made me weak at the knees with those beautiful blue eyes staring deep into my soul. I was yours from that very first day, and there is nowhere else I'd rather be than by your side. You and me, were meant to be, and our fate was mapped out for us, from that night we sat in your mum and dad's kitchen putting the world to rights. I love you with my whole heart, my body, my mind and my soul. I am forever yours, for now and always. I'm your guardian angel, sent from above remember." I smiled proudly; she always speaks from the heart. I remembered the conversation we had after that first night together; I looked at Collier's photograph and glanced up towards the skies.

"Now it's time for the rings. Do you Nina, take Jack to be your lawfully wedded husband…?" Faye passed her the wedding ring, in a blue silk bag; the colour of the bag matched my uniform. I had worn my uniform today as my wedding attire, I wouldn't want to get married in any other piece of clothing, I wore it with pride. It was who I was, and it was why I had met Nina, I owed everything to the air force.

"I do," and she placed the ring on my wedding finger, beaming with happiness.

"And do you Jack, take Nina to be your lawfully wedded wife?" Bobby passed me the box containing the ring, this was it, the official mark that she was to be my wife forever, I felt elated, "I one hundred percent do!" she giggled, and I placed the ring on her slender ring finger, squeezing it as I drew my hand back.

"I now pronounce you husband and wife, you may kiss the bride," I would get no greater pleasure. I took her in my arms and kissed her passionately for all the room to see, my wonderful wife, Mrs Nina Watson. The room erupted with applause; this was easily one of the best days of my life.

Music blasted in the hall, our wedding reception was underway, and everyone was full of joy. There was laughter, dancing, chatting and love in the air. Waiters were handing out champagne and canapés; some of the soldiers had latched on to Nina's friends and were dancing together on the dancefloor. I eyed up Bobby who had located Georgie, I knew he would, I raised a glass to him and winked smugly, he raised his glass back. That's my bro, I thought. I was stood at the doorway, alone, nursing a glass of champagne, taking it all in. I had been watching Nina meeting and greeting the guests. I had held out for a woman who I wanted to call my wife for so long I began to think it would never happen and that she didn't exist, yet here we were.

"Penny for your thoughts," Faye sneaked up on me. I jumped.

"Ye' scared me then! I'm just taking it all in, admiring the view." Faye followed my gaze to Nina.

"You two are so cute, she's honestly so smitten for you. I'm sure my dad already has or will but I'm giving you the father talk now," she became serious, and I laughed.

"Don't fuck her about like Harry did, or I will chop off your balls and post them back to you!"

"Wow, I thought Nina was the bold one!" I sniggered.

"How I am is down to that girl, she deserves the world,"

she continued.

"Faye, I love your sister, I aren't gonna hurt her, I promise," I saluted her.

"Good!" and she clinked my champagne flute and walked off. That told me, I took a sip of my champagne. I continued to look around the room. Nina had chosen the décor, it was rose pink and white, there were flowers on each table, and garlands of real roses hung around the room, it looked elegant and classy, just like she was. I would have expected nothing less from *my wife*, wow my wife; that sounds crazy! The wedding cake was on the main table, where piles of gifts and cards had started to appear, it was three tiers and pure white, except for rose pink frosting, and edible roses on top. We got seated at the top table and was served our wedding dinners, everyone tucked in, except Nina, she didn't touch much at all.

"Are ye' feeling okay?" I squeezed her hand.

"Yes," she smiled back, "It's just the nerves of today getting the better of me."

"Here," I poured her a glass of champagne and toasted our love with a clink, I downed the whole glass, it was taking the edge off, Nina took a very small sip and placed it back down. I hope it was just the nerves. Clink clink – it was time for the speeches, I couldn't wait to hear what Bobby had to say, I didn't expect it to be clean.

"Hello ladies and gents, so here we are gathered today for my big bro's wedding day. I cannot believe he managed to bag a girl as beautiful as Nina, especially with that ridiculous Scottish accent, I don't think she quite understood what she was getting herself into," the room laughed, I nodded smiling and Nina squeezed my thigh.

He continued on, "...I have never known Jack to fall for a woman the way he has Nina, normally it's wham bam, thank you mam, but not with this girl. He doesn't wear his heart on his sleeve and has never been one for speaking about how he really feels, but with Nina, I couldn't shut him up, that's how I know she is the one for him. I cannot wait to see their love blossom further and for them to eventually make me an uncle," I looked at Nina and muttered whilst laughing.

"Maybe not just yet eh," she gave an insincere smile back. I shot her a look of concern, she just smiled back and grabbed my hand, I wasn't convinced. Maybe what he had said about me sleeping with other girls had irritated her? Now it was time for my speech.

"Where do I start? First of all, Nina, thank ye' for making me the happiest man in the world and becoming my wife. No one will ever say this, but if it hadn't have been for the war our paths would have never crossed, and for that part of me wants to say thank ye' to Hitler," the room laughed, ironically. I continued melancholically. "My best pal Collier should have been here today, but in a very strange way, he was the reason we got together and for that I thank him. I would love for us all to raise a glass to the most brave, courageous man I have had the pleasure of knowing," everyone raised their glasses, and it felt good to respect the hero. I looked at Nina and she grinned back at me reassuringly. "Today has been the most special day of my life, I always thought my life was the RAF, and although I enjoy it and I am so proud to be part of it, meeting *you* Nina has made me realise what else there is, and how happy I can truly be outside of work. You're the other half to me, ye' are what I have been searching for and I am so proud to call you Mrs Watson." I leaned over to kiss her, and she grabbed my face and stroked it, I took in her smell, sweet and floral, and kissed her.

"Get a room!" one of the soldiers shouted laughing, I looked up.

"Shield your eyes ladies and gents," and I kissed her again harder. Mr Hughes went on to give his speech, it made Nina and Faye tear up. I am so glad me and Mr Hughes get on so well, I was worried when meeting him how he would react to me, and what Harry would have said to him, but he took me at face value and made his own opinion of me up, and that just showed what a strong, gentleman he really was. I had a lot of time for him and respected him greatly. After the meals everyone mingled until it was time to cut the cake, we posed for the photographer and then it was time for the first dance. We had chosen 'Our Love Affair' by ol' blue eyes because ironically it reflected how our relationship had been, up until today. We swayed to the music, embracing one another, forgetting there was anyone else in the room. I was disappointed when it ended but knew this was just the beginning of many wonderful moments alone with her. Unexpectedly Staines began to clink his glass for attention, I was curious to know what he had to say.

"I know it's not my place to say something at the wedding so forgive me but hear me out. I have known Jack since 1932 when he was a young fresh-faced lad starting out in the RAF. He's always been like a son to me; he is going to go far I have no doubt of that. He has always been a happy go lucky chap, but I have never seen him happier than when he is with Nina. I welcome my surrogate daughter Nina; I am here for both of you. I may have had a few whiskies, so I am being a bit sentimental, but after everything Jack has been through this last year, I just want everyone to raise a glass to him on his and Nina's wedding day…here here," everyone raised their glasses. I was taken aback; I knew Staines and me got on well but for him to say those things about me meant the world. I raised my glass to him; he smiled. Everyone was in such good spirits. I glanced at Nina, and noticed her sip her champagne, then spit it straight back into the glass. What was going on? She put her glass down without spotting that I had seen her, and walked off towards the toilets, I followed her.

"Nina," I grabbed her arm and pulled her towards me, "what's going on? I feel like you've been a little iffy today, I aren't sure if it's nerves or you're overwhelmed or what, but please talk to me," I smiled, moving a strand of her hair out of her eyes. She looked at me seriously.

"Jack, I have something I need to tell you, but let's talk tomorrow, I am fine so don't worry, but it can wait," and she began to walk outside.

"Ye' can't say that to me and not expect me to ask why, tell me what's going on, are ye' regretting marrying me? Was it what Bobby said about me sleeping with other women?" I had to ask. She turned to face me.

"God no! To both! Everyone has a past Jack, and the best thing I have ever done is marry you, I couldn't be happier, I love you... It's just something you said about children and it not being the right time." Oh, is that all? I relaxed a little.

"I just thought it's pretty soon after everything that's happened, and I don't want pressure putting on ye'. We both have to be ready for that sort of commitment." I

119

grabbed her hands and interlinked our fingers. A few moments passed.

"Jack, I'm pregnant," she blurted out and looked away. What? I didn't know what to say. Did she just say she was pregnant? Fuck! I wasn't expecting that.

"Wh-…okay," I couldn't get my words out.

"I knew you'd be unhappy, I'm so sorry," she hung her head.

"Erm, it's sudden, we've only been married three hours," I laughed, trying to make light of the situation. I took a moment to process this. How did I feel? Was I unhappy? No! My wife was having our baby; she was going to have a mini version of her and me! I was scared and nervous but which first time parent isn't?

"Nina, I am fucking over the moon!" I grabbed her, not too tightly, and hugged her.

"Really?" she gasped.

"Yes, it's scary as hell, don't get me wrong but we are going to be parents, that's amazing!" I stroked her cheek.

"I am so glad, Jack, I thought I was going to scare you away, I have known for a week," why didn't she tell me straight away, carrying this around with her all week leading up to the wedding must have been tough.

"Ye' need to start talking to me about things, I don't want ye' carrying all this heavy information around with ye' anymore. Let's start our marriage off the right way. Today has been perfect. I really have some fast swimmers don't I," I sniggered. She laughed back, I kissed her on the forehead, and we swayed together in the setting sun, the breeze licking our faces. I was going to be a dad, I didn't think it possible, but this day just got even better.

Nina

The wedding was incredible, everything about it was perfect from start to finish, and the news at the end just made it even more special. The baby was going to be mine and Jack's secret for a few more weeks, we wanted to get a bit further along then we could begin to share. Jack and I had been married one whole week, and it was bliss. We honeymooned in the place we were married, as we didn't want to go too far away, and each day was spent relaxing, laughing and having lots of sex, I was so happy. A dark cloud, however, loomed over me like a blanket over a cage; Jack was due to go back out to war tomorrow and I couldn't believe our time together was nearly over. We had quickly found a home, and for the last two days, we had been living in the outskirts of central London in a place called Ruislip. We wanted the peace it brought for me, and now the baby while Jack was away. Areas around Biggin Hill were just too dangerous, it was a huge target after the last bombing, and the fact it was the Britain's main fighter jet RAF base made it high profile. When Jack was at war he would be staying back on the base, and the thought of that haunted me deep within, but what choice did I have? We had discussed living near to the sea before the wedding, because Jack had grown up in Bath and loved living so close to it. The plan was when he finally retired from the RAF, he wanted a place like Bath to live and raise a family, so we settled for Ruislip, for now. It felt strange for me being so far away from home permanently, but Faye and dad could come visit at any time, and one day I envisaged them moving down here. Mr and Mrs Watson had already began looking for houses nearby, which I did not mind, they wanted to be close to us so they could be nearby for when we had children, little did they know it was about to be sooner than they anticipated.

Our house was wonderful, it had three bedrooms with a huge back garden, lots of cherry blossom trees and plenty of bright, colourful flowers, including those pink roses. The front looked out onto a cobbled street that led down to the sea. Our master bedroom had its own little 'beauty room', where I could get ready without disturbing Jack. Our lounge was open plan and led out onto the veranda, and the kitchen was so modern and spacious. The décor was already to my taste, it was spruce green and white in most of the downstairs rooms, with high ceilings and decorative coving. The prettiest glass chandelier hung from the dining room and landed just above the table. Upstairs was rose pink and white, with harbour grey wooden flooring, it was classic. We had room in the dining area for a piano, so Jack could play, and the third bedroom we were going to make into a playroom and keep the second bedroom a guestroom until the baby came along. The bathroom was tiled with pure white brick squares and had a stand-alone bathtub in the middle of the room, which was glorious and big enough for two, as we had tried out a few times already. It was the perfect family home, and I was so excited to create our future here.

Jack sipped his tea whilst reading the newspaper as I looked out onto the warm botanical style garden from our veranda, it was a warm day for early March, and I had already begun to feel nauseous due to the baby, so I gently sipped water taking in the slight breeze. Jack looked up at me and shot me a cute smile with his fine-looking dimples, I still could not believe he was my husband; I looked down at his wedding finger, where he brandished his gold ring, the mark that he was mine.

"Are ye' feeling okay honey?" he asked continuing to smile. We had lately joked about how all married couples somehow seemed to adopt these ridiculous pet names for each other, his mum and dad called each other baby bear and rose bud, which sounds sweet, but it made us both cringe a little, and laugh a lot.

"I am fine my sweetness," I laughed, "baby is just playing havoc with me today, I feel a bit ill," I sipped some more water.

"Why don't ye' go lie down angel and see if some sleep helps," he answered.

"Good idea cutie pie, this name calling is making me feel worse," I laughed, standing up.

"I'll come wake ye' when it's time go for lunch darling," that one was genuine, I winked and walked off to our room.

I woke to someone gently stroking my forehead, I felt better but felt like I had been asleep for ages. Of course, that someone was my Jack.

"Hello sleepy," he whispered sweetly leaning over and kissing my forehead. I smiled at him; I didn't feel as sick anymore, thankfully.

"How's baby Watson doing?" he asked gently rubbing my stomach.

"Much better now, thank you, how are you?"

"I'm okay," he looked troubled. "I can't stop thinking about how I really don't want to leave ye' tomorrow, it makes me feel sick just thinking about it, especially now you're pregnant. What sort of irresponsible husband am

123

I?" He was giving himself a hard time.

"Jack, you're a pilot, you have to do this, and we understand," I said putting his hand back on my stomach.

"I've been thinking, maybe we should tell someone about the baby so ye' have someone when I'm not here?" Jack added. He had a point, he was going away, and I was not sure, when he would be back, I was already feeling nervous about everything, I had never done this before, it couldn't hurt to tell one person.

"Like who?" I asked.

"Anyone of your choice, I would suggest my mum and dad because they're moving here so will be close by. I know Faye or Georgie would be your first port of call, but they're in Lincolnshire and if, God forbid, something was to happen, it would take them such a long time to get down. It's completely up to you though darling."

"You're right, we will tell them at lunch today," I had butterflies, telling people made it even more real.

"We best get going then, we are due to meet them in fifteen minutes," he said kissing me on the forehead as he stood up. Here goes.

"Oh, look at you beaming with joy!" Mrs Watson kissed me on the cheek, "you really do have the new bride glow," she continued, little did she know it was from being sick three times a day.

"How are you son?" she gave Jack a hug.

"Good thanks mum, just soaking up our last week together before I have to go back," Jack swigged his beer regretfully.

"Oh Jack, I feel for you both, but you are doing the right thing, as hard as it seems, it's what you love doing, and with a lovely, supportive wife like Nina, you know you can do it but still have a wonderful, loving home to come back to. To make you feel better, you will have us soon, Nina so you won't be on your own, and you'll make friends in no time. What are you doing for work? Is there a police force down here you can work for?" she finally took a breather. Jack looked at me coyly.

"Well mum, Nina isn't going to be working for the police anymore, it's too dangerous… in her condition," he smiled. My stomach did summersaults, how are they going to react?

"Condition? dear, are you okay?" she asked concerned.

"Well Mr and Mrs Watson, actually we're going to have an addition to the Watson clan," I smiled looking at Jack.

"I don't follow," she replied.

"We're having a baby!" Jack shouted happily. There was a moment of silence, Mr and Mrs Watson looked at each other briefly. Oh dear, this didn't seem like a good reaction. Mrs Watson turned to face me, her hands were covering her mouth, and tears welled in her eyes.

"Oh my, I am SO happy for you both, congratulations," she finally answered. She hugged me and Mr Watson kissed me on the cheek.

"Fantastic news sweetheart." Jack and his dad hugged, and Mrs Watson held his hands.

"Oh son, this has made my year, I couldn't be happier for you, I am so proud right now. Oh, I am going to be a grandma, George, we are going to be grandma and granddad!" The realisation hit her.

"One small request, we ask ye' to keep it between us for now if that's okay? Nina is four weeks pregnant so it's early days. We told ye' because with me going away, I want to know Nina has support, and can talk to someone about the baby, or come to ye' if she needs to," Jack spoke earnestly.

"Of course, we completely understand, son," Mr Watson replied. I suddenly felt a bit more relaxed about Jack leaving. I didn't want to admit it to him, but I was terrified of being alone and pregnant, I just had to get through the next few months until Jack would be home, and hopefully this damn war would be over.

The meal ended and we said our goodbyes to Mr and Mrs Watson. It had been decided that they would stay in our house for a week until the house they'd made an offer on was cleared. They had already sold their house in Bath, so this meant I was going to be on my own in the house for at least two nights, until they came across. Why was I so nervous? I had been alone before, but the thought of Jack going off to fight, not knowing when I would see him next, and now the extra protection I felt for the baby, meant I was scared of being alone at any point. I didn't speak much on the walk home; I went straight upstairs to run a bath as soon as we arrived; all I wanted to do was cry. Our little magical bubble was close to ending, and the reality was about to start, and I wasn't ready for it. I shut myself in the bathroom as I ran the bath, I didn't want Jack to see me upset, it would make it harder for him. There was a small knock on the bathroom door.

"Hello, can I come in?" Jack asked. I was a mess, tears wouldn't stop appearing, I know my hormones won't have been helping but I felt like my eyes were leaking, and there was no tap to turn them off. I tried to hold in the sniffles.

"Won't be long honey." He definitely knew I was holding something back now; I never call him honey,

126

honey I thought, what an idiot. He didn't ask again, he just walked in; I should have locked the door, damn. He looked at me and sighed.

"Don't pretend you're okay, Nina, I know ye' aren't," he walked towards me. I was sat on the toilet with the lid down; he perched on the edge of the bathtub.

"I'm sorry." I completely lost control of my emotions. I was sniffling, crying, you name it, it was happening. He looked at me, not knowing what to say, what could he say? "Jack, I didn't want you to see me like this, because it's not your fault, I am just a little hormonal and tender, and I am going to miss you more than words can express." I put my head in my hands. He crouched down next to me, rubbing my knee and my hair with each hand.

"I'm going to miss ye' too, Nina, I can't even describe what pit I have in my stomach right now. I want to go AWOL, I'm that sad about going back and leaving ye' both, but I have a duty. I'm going to be fighting for the future of that little one in there," he said looking at my belly. "I want to do him or her proud, and I want ye' to be honoured to have me as a husband too," his eyes filled up.

"Always, Jack, there's nothing you could do that would make me think any different. I…we love you more than life. You go and do us proud soldier, we'll be just fine," I smiled through tears and kissed him. We embraced tightly for a few minutes, neither of us speaking, just holding one another taking each other in. The bath was nearly finished.

"We can save on water if we both get in at the same time," I said cheekily trying to raise spirits. He raised an eyebrow.

"Ye' don't need to ask me twice Mrs Watson," and he began stripping my clothes off. He gently unzipped my

127

dress and it fell to the floor, leaving me in my shoes and underwear. I kicked my shoes off and slid down my stockings, promiscuously. He sat on the bath watching me, as if I was putting on a show for him. I kicked them at him one by one, he laughed whilst wolf whistling. I approached him, swaying sexily as I walked, his head was in line with my breasts, as I neared him, I put my hands through his hair and he began to kiss my breasts, slowly but sensually. His breathing got deeper so I moved back playfully so I was out of his reach. I wanted to make him wait a few more seconds so he could really appreciate me. I teasingly approached him again, this time he stood up and unhooked my bra and kissed me. I was so ready, but I wanted to make him wait. I stopped kissing him, and began to unbutton his shirt, slowly undoing each button one by one; I did not take my gaze from him. His shirt fell to the floor revealing his masculine torso. I kissed his chest and bent down, kissing his stomach as I crouched lower and lower. I could see how hard his penis was through his trousers, I kissed it above his trousers, and he inhaled deeply. I stood back up, and unbuttoned his trousers, making sure I rubbed his hard penis with my hands as I did so. His breathing got faster.

"You're teasing me," he smiled naughtily.

"Maybe… you see two can play at that game," I laughed back insatiably thinking back to that day in his tent. I stood back from him and gently teased down my knickers, so they fell to my ankles, and I was naked in front of him, but not close enough for him to touch me.

"Why don't we have some fun?" I smirked and reached across to the basin where I had left my hair ribbon from yesterday. He stood with his trousers unbuttoned, bare chested and I walked around the back of him, so I was stood behind him. He didn't move, I loved this power. I put the ribbon over his eyes, and he smiled.

"You are a wicked girl, Nina Watson." I said nothing; he had no idea where I was. I moved beside him and with pressure rubbed my palm down his chest towards his hard genitals, he moaned. I moved and knelt in front of him, and began to finish unbuttoning his trousers, gently pulling them down to his ankles. His penis was so stiff, I felt if I touched it one more time he would explode. I pulled his boxer shorts down to reveal it. He kicked off his trousers and underwear and he stood completely naked in front of me, I took a moment to appreciate the sight. I stood up towards him once more, and kissed his lips, he kissed me back like there was a magnetism between us. Faster and harder, we interlocked lips and tongues. I kissed his neck, his chest, his stomach and moved onto his penis. I put it in my mouth, sucking and licking it, each time making him moan harder and harder. I wanted to please him; this would be the last chance I get for a long while. I kept going until eventually he let out a great moan and orgasmed into my mouth, his penis throbbing with every release, holding my hair tightly for balance. He was out of breath, and he sat on the bathtub, smiling at me tiredly, with the hair ribbon in his hand.

"Wow," he exhaled. I smiled nonchalantly as if it had been nothing at all, and I hopped into the warm bath. Jack leaped in after me and we sat at opposite ends, smiling at each other hazily.

"I love you," I told him for no other reason than I just wanted to say it and I wanted him to hear it.

"I love ye' too," he squeezed my leg and closed his eyes.

We sat there in silence, relaxing for ten minutes, soaking in the closeness and both thinking deep down how this was going to be it for a few months, at least. I moved across to his side and sat in between his legs and lay back on his chest, he stroked my arm, like he did in the barn, and we cuddled. I wanted to feel as close to him as possible, I wanted to stay in this moment forever. He gently began to nuzzle my neck, now it's my turn I thought, excitedly. I turned my head sideways to face him more and he began to kiss me harder, he moved his arm down from mine towards my vagina underwater, gently scraping my thigh. He gently rubbed me, slowly at first then faster; I was so ready it wasn't going to take long. I could feel the build coming, I began to moan, he kissed me faster, as his hands moved up and down over my clitoris, and I orgasmed, pulsing in his fingers. He began to slow; his kisses became tenderer, my body felt weak and relaxed. We lay there for a few moments more and got out, drowsy but satisfied. I didn't want to bring it back to normality, but I had to ask.

"What time are you leaving tomorrow?"

"I need to be away by 5 am," he looked at me apologetically; I smiled back, dying a little inside.

The rest of the evening was spent eating dinner, Jack packing his belongings together and me sitting on the veranda alone, a taste of what was to come I expect. We finally lay in bed together, eyes wide open looking at the ceiling. I snuggled into his chest.

"What names do you like for the baby, Jack?"

"Ermmmm, for a boy I quite liked the idea of calling him Louis, as that was Collier's name," he said thoughtfully.

"Oh, I love it!" I exclaimed, what a lovely way to remember him too. "And what about a girl?"

"I haven't really thought about girl names, what about you?" he looked down at me smiling.

"I like so many girls' names, Florence, Lily, Grace, Daisy," I stopped for air. Jack laughed.

"How about ye' pick the girls name, and I will agree with anything ye' choose?"

"Deal!" I looked up and kissed him. "Have we got time for one more round?" I asked cheekily.

"Ye' might even get a third if you're lucky," he chuckled sliding on top of me. And I did.

Four thirty am, I could hear movement in the bedroom, I rubbed my eyes and yawned.

"Sorry I didn't mean to wake ye'," Jack apologised.

"Its fine, I want to see you off!" I exclaimed. He was stood at the foot of the bed dressed in his ones; he looked so handsome; my heart wanted to burst with pride.

"I have to go shortly, Nina," he said solemnly. I felt sick, how was this day here already? I put on my dressing gown and followed him out of the bedroom down the stairs towards the front door. His bags were stacked ready to go, he was walking to the train station to get the train to the camp, so had packed lightly, you don't require that many belongings fighting in the war, I suppose. He stood at the door and observed me, I stared back, I didn't know what to say - good luck, I'll miss you, kill the Nazi bastards and get home quickly - nothing seemed right.

"Nina, whatever happens I love ye', always remember that. I will be back home soon and will write to ye' at every opportunity I get. Please take care of yourself and little one," he stroked my stomach.

131

"My mum and dad will be here very soon to help take care of ye'," he fondled my hair, looking at me lovingly, but with an urgency in his voice.

"Please be careful out there Jack, we need you to come home. I love you with all my heart, thank you for finding me and making me your wife," the tears arrived, great, I thought. I had tried to be strong, but ever since baby Watson had begun to grow inside me, I found myself crying at thin air, let alone the love of my life about to walk out and maybe never return.

"Don't talk like this is the end, I will be back, stay positive, I've made it to ye' twice before, nothing is going to stop me a third time!" He was right, positivity was key here. I nodded in agreement, he kissed me on the lips tenderly, and put his forehead to mine.

"Love ye' Mrs Watson."

"I love you more," I whispered weakly. He turned to collect his bags, opened the front door and without looking back he walked away, closing the door behind him, and taking my whole world with him. I watched him walk away through the window, he didn't look back once, I knew he was in war mode now – go get 'em Soldier, I thought.

Chapter 8

Nina

Jack had been away for two months now; my body was aching from how much I missed him. He was in the same country as me and yet I couldn't see him. It felt like an eternity since I had held him or kissed his lips. We were nearing the summer months; the nights were lighter, and the sweet smell of summer lingered in the air. The trees were green and full of pink blossoms, I only wish Jack was here to see the view, his view will have been black smoke, death and devastation. The Blitz, as they were calling it, had grown much worse, and the Germans bombed Britain in the middle of the night on a daily basis. I knew my Jack will have been worked to the bone, protecting our country, I was so proud, yet everyday more and more terrified of what might happen to him, and not knowing when it might end made it worse. We had been sending each other letters once a week, and every Friday morning I looked forward to the postman arriving to see what Jack had been up that week. Today was Friday, my favourite day of the week, especially at eleven am, I was like a child waiting for Santa Claus to arrive. My pregnant belly was visible for all to see now, I was three and a half months pregnant and everyone knew. I was so happy to share the news with everyone, but it was bittersweet that Jack was missing out on the baby growing and that he wasn't by my side when I announced the amazing news. Faye and Georgie were absolutely over the moon, and my dad could not wait to be a devoted granddad. Faye and dad had visited me twice in the last couple of months, which was brilliant; I often got lonely clattering around in the house alone. They had stayed a full week on their last visit, and I nearly asked them to move in until Jack was back, but stopped myself because it was a big ask, and I didn't want to worry them about how hard I was finding it. Mr and Mrs Watson now lived only a five-minute walk from our house, and they checked in with me daily, but they had their own lives to lead, and although they visited for a cup of tea most days, I still felt alone. I had taken a part time job in the local bakery just for company and made friends with a lovely woman named Sophie. She was a little older than I was, but had a four-year-old girl, so I knew I could speak to her about anything mum and baby related; it helped take the pressure off me a little. Any little twinge or question and I would visit or telephone her for a check-up; she was most probably sick of me and thinking about quitting the bakery for some peace. I had become such a hypochondriac since becoming pregnant, but I knew it was because I had nothing else to think about, other than Jack, and no one else to share my woes with. If Jack had been here, I know he would have told me to relax and not worry, he always had an air of calm in whatever he did. I missed him so much. I spoke to Georgie most days on the telephone too, she hated the police force, and Harry had become even more of a prat than usual. He had been promoted to Chief Inspector, dear god, and was exerting his power left, right and centre. He never asked about me, which I was glad of. Deep down I knew it was because he didn't want to know how happy I was without him. Bobby, Jack's brother, was also looking to move to the area. He had taken a break from tennis coaching and was looking for somewhere to live nearby, for when Jack returned. I had considered offering him our guest room until Jack returned; I still might do yet, might be nice to have some company. Ten fifty-five am, not long until the postman gets here, I felt excitement – what had Jack been up to this week? His previous letters had told tales of Germans being shot down by him and his comrades and that we definitely had the upper hand in the battle. Megson was doing well back out fighting and Group Captain Staines was checking in on me all the time. Jack was missing us greatly. I told him of all of the goings on here, and my little job. I pretended he was reading the letters out to me when they arrived, so I could imagine his voice, it made him feel closer. *TAP,* the letterbox went, and so did my stomach, yes, it is finally here! I ran to the door, but was disappointed, it was just a bill, where were Jack's letter? For two months without fail, they had arrived on a Friday morning. I opened the door swiftly and chased after the postman.

"Excuse me, sir," I shouted slightly out of breath. He turned round to face me.

"There must be a mistake, I normally receive a letter from my husband on a Friday morning, have you misplaced it?" I quizzed. He checked his bag.

"No ma'am, I have no other letters for you I am afraid," he smiled and began to walk away.

"Can you check again please? It always comes on a Friday because the military always send their post on the same day! My husband is in the RAF you see," I exclaimed. He looked back confused but checked again.

"Ma'am, I am sorry, I have nothing for you." Why had he not sent me a letter?

"It may come tomorrow ma'am, sometimes the post is

late, or it could be at the sorting office still?" he explained, clearly lying, I could see the pity in his face, or was I just being paranoid?

"Yes, yes that is probably it, I will wait until tomorrow then, thank you," I began to walk slowly back to the house; he just stayed where he was watching me saunter away. I knew what he was thinking, the same thing as me - was Jack okay?

Knock knock –

"Only us, Nina," Mrs Watson shouted through the front door as she opened it. She entered with Mr Watson and Bobby in tow.

"Good afternoon," Mr Watson took his hat off and tipped it towards me, Bobby smiled

"Well look at you!" he looked down at my growing belly, I smiled and rubbed it lightly. I hadn't seen Bobby much since the wedding, but he looked well, there was an air of maturity about him, Jack would have been proud.

"Can I make you all a cup of tea?" I asked.

"Let me do that," Bobby approached the teapot and filled it with water ready to put on the stove.

"So, are you officially back home then, Bobby?" I enquired.

"Yep, staying with mum and dad until I can find a place here. Ruislip is very sought after, there's nothing anywhere!" I hesitated before speaking.

"Look I may be way off the mark here, so feel free to say no, but I don't know when Jack is back, and I am rattling around in here on my own. Why don't you take the guest room for a month or so, until you get somewhere?" Bobby looked at Mrs Watson.

"Are you sure, Nina? I wouldn't want to encroach on

your space, and Jack will probably want it to just be you two when he gets back."

"Yes, I am sure, and when Jack gets back, you can maybe just move back to your parents until you find somewhere, if you haven't already."

"Well, it's a nice offer and it does make sense Bobby," Mr Watson replied.

"Nina is in here on her own, and a man around the house will be a help, I am sure," he laughed.

"I can easily do a man's job, Mr Watson," I retaliated wittily, "but probably not as I get bigger," I looked at my ever-growing bump. Bobby smirked.

"Nina could probably do more with a screwdriver and some nails than me anyway. Well then it's a deal, thank you!" he shook my hand to make it official.

"Fabulous, why don't I cook us all some dinner this evening to celebrate?" Mrs Watson asked.

"That would be lovely," I replied pleased that I had finally got myself some company.

"Is tomorrow too early for me to move in?" Bobby enquired.

"Not at all, it makes no difference to me whatsoever."

"Have you had your weekly letter from Jack then Nina?" Mrs Watson asked excitedly, changing the subject. I looked away, I felt sick thinking about it.

"No," I managed. They all turned to look at me.

"Nothing?" Mrs Watson continued.

"Nothing," I looked up to meet her gaze.

"Well, I am sure it's just been delayed," Mr Watson tried sounding optimistic.

"Yeah, probably," I muttered. "The postman said it will probably come tomorrow," I feigned a smile.

"Well, there you go then!" That was enough for Mrs Watson, and she began cutting the cake she had brought round to have with our tea - myself, Mr Watson and Bobby looked at one another, we weren't convinced.

I tossed and turned all night last night; the nausea had finally passed but now my lack of sleep was down to worrying about Jack. I strolled downstairs and poured myself a cup of tea; that always makes things better. There was a knock at the door. I bounded towards it, hoping it was the postman, it was Bobby and a load of his belongings.

"Hi roomie!" he joked. I smiled back hiding my disappointment.

"Good morning, need a hand with anything?"

"In your condition? I don't think so! Now I am around you will barely have to lift a finger," he smiled at me.

"Bobby, I don't need you to do everything, I am quite independent you know, just because I am with child doesn't mean I am incapable," I snapped.

"Sorry, no, I didn't mean it like that, I just meant to say thank you, and for you to make sure you get rest, I didn't mean to offend you," he looked at me as if he was in trouble.

"Sorry, I just didn't sleep well, ignore me, I appreciate it, thank you," I smiled back apologetically.

"Not heard from the postman yet?" He started to unpack some pots, whilst looking at me wonderingly. I looked back at him, then away immediately.

"No, there's still time," I tried to appear positive. The door squeaked open.

"Only us," Mrs Watson walked through with a bunch of flowers in her hand and Mr Watson followed behind. "A housewarming gift for you both, mainly Nina really, just to say thank you for thinking of Bobby, it's helped him out a lot, and he was adamant he didn't want to live with his old mum and dad," she laughed.

"Don't be silly mum, it's just once you live alone, you don't want to abide by your folks' rules again!"

"Don't you be treating this like a party house, Bobby, this is Nina's house and if you step out of line just once, I ask that she comes sees me and you'll be ejected immediately," Mr Watson said sternly. Bobby was known as a bit of a party animal, and was always socialising with someone, especially where alcohol and pretty ladies were concerned – I suppose he was young, free and single; why not?

"I respect Nina and Jack too much to even contemplate doing that, dad, I am just grateful to her for letting me stay for a bit, I'll be out of her hair as soon as I can!" he responded earnestly. We had a cup of tea and a chat whilst Bobby began unpacking his things upstairs and around the house. He had some fairly nice pieces of art and furnishings; I was quite impressed with his taste. *Knock knock knock;* the postman? I jumped up and marched towards the door as fast I could. I opened it hastily; it was not what I wanted to see. Group Captain Staines stood in the doorway, accompanied by another RAF chap.

"Mrs Watson, lovely to see you again, may I come in?" he asked politely. My heart sank.

"Hi, please call me Nina, and yes do come in," I sounded monotone, but I wasn't in the mood for niceties.

"Hello Group Captain Staines," Mr Watson greeted him, I stepped out the way and closed the door behind him, I dare not turn to face him. I felt sick and breathless –

maybe I am jumping the gun, he hasn't actually said why he is here yet, I should hear him out before jumping to conclusions.

"Can I get you a drink Oliver?" Mrs Watson asked.

"I don't mean to be rude sir but why are you here?" I interrupted. The room turned to look at me, shocked at my retort, I was always the polite, pleasant one, but this time I wanted answers. He looked deflated.

"I am not quite sure how to tell you this," he looked in my direction. I felt unsteady on my feet, I held onto the kitchen table for support. "On May 3rd 1941, Jack was on duty flying his Spitfire across the English Channel as part of an attack on the Germans, defending British soil… unfortunately he never returned back to base," Group Captain Staines hung his head. My mouth was dry, what was he saying? Is he telling me my husband is dead?

"What do you mean? Have you found his plane?" I murmured.

"Not yet ma'am, we are searching for it as a matter of urgency. None of his crew mates saw where his plane went down," he continued.

"Well, why the hell not? He managed to see Collier land during crossfire, where the hell were they looking?" I was uncontrollable in what I was saying.

"Ma'am, they were in the middle of an exchange with the Luftwaffe, I am afraid their concentration may have been on defending themselves from that," the other officer replied protectively.

"Well have you asked them? What did they say?" I demanded.

"Both returning officers have been questioned about the matter ma'am, we've had an area to search for his plane wreckage," he tried to stop himself but had already spoken the words.

"Wreckage? That's all it is to you isn't it, another man down, another plane destroyed, now onto the next one to fill his shoes." I couldn't contain myself; I knew I was being hard on them, but I needed to vent.

"Nina, you know how fondly I think of Jack, I assure you we are doing everything we can to find him, I am putting everything I have on this, I promise you," Group Captain Staines looked at me sincerely, with a stoic expression upon his face.

"So, at this point you don't know if he is dead or alive?" Mr Watson probed.

"Not yet, Mr Watson, there is always a possibility that his plane went down and he parachuted to safety and was picked up by the Navy or another vessel. Enquiries are ongoing, but we had to let you know," Group Captain Staines smiled empathetically at us all. I had no words; I sat down biting my nails and staring at the kitchen table. Mrs Watson began to sob, and Mr Watson comforted her, Bobby stood opposite me staring into space.

"We will leave you alone, I am sorry we couldn't meet in better circumstances, and I wish we had better news. We will be in touch with every update we have. I am so sorry, thank you for your time," he nodded as he left the house, closing the door behind him. None of us spoke, we sat there silently, all wishing that what we had just heard was a lie.

"I'm going to get a bath," I said with no emotion.

"Nina..." Bobby called after me.

"Just leave me, please," I said walking up the stairs, I didn't want to talk to anyone. I lay in the bath, crying, rubbing my stomach, how can this be happening again? Were we never destined to have a happy ending? Did he suffer? I kept playing the same scenario repeatedly in my head – Jack going down in flames, as he had described Collier's demise. I put my head under water, trying to blank out the images. A thought suddenly crossed my mind; what if he got out? This stress isn't good for the baby, I should be thinking positively. There's no plane yet, they are checking with the Navy, no one saw him crash land, maybe he is alive, just maybe. He survived a plane crash once before, what is to stop him surviving again? I wanted to share my theory with the rest of them. I jumped out the bath and quickly got dry; I put on my dressing gown and made my way downstairs. Mr and Mrs Watson were just leaving.

"Wait!" I called. They turned to face me; mascara ran down Mrs Watson's face. "We need to be thinking positively!" I sounded weirdly energised. "He has survived a plane crash before, what is to stop him doing it again? He didn't tell you he was home until a whole month after the last one, and he had survived. We are thinking too negatively here, he's going to come back, as if he would miss this one being born!" I pointed to my stomach. They looked at each other as if they were holding back some secret I wasn't meant to know about. Bobby looked at me and weakly smiled.

"Yes, maybe Nina." They didn't believe me; did I even believe what I was saying? I was in denial, no, I am thinking positively. Mrs Watson approached me and held me in a tight embrace.

"You take care of yourself dear, get some rest tonight please," and she stroked my face and her and Mr Watson left. Did they think I was having some kind of breakdown? Maybe I was. Bobby sat down on the sofa, it was dark outside, rain clouds had emerged, and the wind howled. A small lamp lit up the living room, Bobby just stared at me, he was trying to read me.

"I am not having a breakdown," I felt I had to reply to my own analysis out loud.

"I never said you were," he replied frankly.

"We need to think positive Bobby, for this one's sake, it could be true – I need to believe it's true, please," I begged as I approached him.

"Of course, you're right, hopefully the Scottish twat will get home soon then!" he smiled, and he squeezed my arm. I smiled back.

"Thank you." Rain started to pour outside, the weather was glum, I was not taking this as a sign.

"Shall we play cards?" Bobby asked jovially. I was so grateful he was here.

"Yes, that would be nice," I replied, I needed a distraction.

"And then I am going to cook dinner, a surprise, as a thank you, not taking over!" he added holding his hands up to admit defeat. I smiled back weakly.

"I can deal with that!" He dealt the cards to me as we sat in the dim living room, both praying that Jack was still alive.

Two weeks had passed, and still we heard nothing. I was nearing five months pregnant now, and my bump had grown to the size of a planet, or so it felt. All hope was beginning to die out for Jack's return. The Blitz was over, the Germans had retreated, knowing they couldn't take control of Britain; my Jack will have been part of that defeat. Group Captain Staines rang me almost daily with any piece of news he had. He had checked with the Navy, they had searched the perimeter they believed he had crash-landed in, and they had sent submarines out looking for wreckages that could have sunk, but there was nothing. I still didn't let myself believe the worst though, he was going to come home, he was just stuck somewhere or laid up in a hospital and couldn't reach us; but it wouldn't be long. I hadn't slept properly since the news, and probably got the best part of two hours a night, it was insomnia at its best.

"Would you like a tea, Nina?" Bobby shouted up to my bedroom.

"Yes please." Bobby had been my rock; we talked about Jack every night and being with Bobby made me feel closer to him. Mr and Mrs Watson popped by every day still and we had them over for dinner once a week, and we went to theirs once a week for dinner in return. I was so grateful for having them all close by, I don't know how I would cope if I didn't have them. Faye was visiting me this week, and I couldn't wait. She had been so worried about me since the news dropped two weeks ago but was unable to visit immediately. Dad didn't yet know, and I didn't want to worry him unnecessarily - Jack will be back soon anyway. I went downstairs and was greeted with breakfast.

"Are you fattening me up?" I joked.

"Maybe," Bobby laughed. "In all seriousness I have been a bit worried about you, the baby needs feeding, and I noticed you haven't eaten very well these last couple of days," he added disapprovingly.

"Jack...I mean Bobby, I'm sorry, I can't believe I just

did that," I felt stupid.

"Hey, it's okay, easy mistake to make," he smiled reassuringly.

"Yeah, it's just something he would have said, always looking out for me," I gazed at the table; I missed him so much.

"That's why I am here, to watch over you whilst he's out there," and he placed the plate in front of me and squeezed my hand. I looked up at him and smiled back, I felt saddened but comforted, it was a strange feeling.

"What is this?" I asked picking up a round patty like food. Bobby laughed.

"It's a codfish cake, don't they have them up North?"

"Erm yes but not for breakfast," I was disgusted. Bobby laughed at me.

"Why not?"

"Who has fish for breakfast?" I continued.

"People have kippers. Plus, fish is good for the baby; Jack loved these as a kid!" he replied.

"Jack, Jack, Jack," I muttered disapprovingly, shaking my head and reviewing the cake on the fork. Bobby continued to laugh at me.

"Just eat up, fussy!" I cut into one and took a bite.

"They're nice, just odd for breakfast, but I will eat them just this once," and before I knew it, I had devoured two, maybe I was hungrier than I thought.

"Do you fancy going for a walk somewhere today?" he asked.

"Yes, that would be nice, but not too far, you know I am carrying a lot of extra timber these days!" and I smiled down lovingly at my belly.

"I'll walk slowly," he smiled, taking my plate from me.

I needed a nap after that, I felt lethargic.

"I'm just going to get my head down for half an hour then we can go." I rested my head on the bed and was out for the count quicker than I could say, 'goodnight'.

There was a light knock at my door, I sat bolt upright, what time was it?

"Hello," I enquired rubbing my eyes.

"Hi, Nina its Bobby, sorry to wake you but I just wanted to check you were okay, you've been asleep for four hours!" Oh my god, I must have been exhausted. I jumped out of bed and swung the bedroom door open.

"Oh, Bobby I am so sorry, I didn't realise I was that tired, thanks for waking me!"

"It's no problem, its 1pm do you still fancy going?" he asked.

"Yes, definitely, I have lots of energy now, let's go!"

We headed out across the backfield; it was a lovely summer's day, the golden sun beamed down, and the blossom-fuelled breeze rattled through the trees. The smell of flowers wafted through the air and the colourful tulips and lavender danced across the field. I felt at ease, for the first time in a while. Bobby had packed a small picnic and some water to take with us. We bumbled on through the wooded area behind our house, it felt like we were in the eye of a storm, everything was serene, dreamlike and calm. We had been walking for around thirty minutes and I decided I needed to sit down. Bobby unpacked the blanket and we clambered on.

"Thanks for suggesting this, Bobby, I wouldn't have done it on my own, or even suggested it, it's nice to get out of the house." I took a large swig of the water.

"No problem, it's been nice to get out and about too, I

know the waiting game is taking its toll on us both," he closed his eyes, leaned back on his elbows and put his head towards the sun, taking in the heat. In all my selfishness, I had not even thought about what this might be doing to him. Yes, I loved Jack more than anyone on this earth, but had only known him nine months. Bobby was his brother. They grew up together, were related by blood and had many memories. If I thought anything could have happened to Faye, I would be beside myself.

"I am so sorry; I have been so wrapped up in my own despair I didn't think about how any of this has affected you."

"Oh, don't be daft, it wasn't a sympathy call," he smiled back, painfully.

"Talk to me, Bobby, how are you feeling? A problem shared is a problem halved," I smiled, wanting him to open up. He sighed.

"I guess I'm just hurting, not knowing where he is, whether he's okay, or even alive. He's always looked out for me, and now I want to do it for him. The best I can offer now is to make sure his lovely wife and unborn child are taken care of. He's the reason I came here, I just hate the not knowing more than anything. It leaves you open to dark thoughts and interpretation and, eurgh, I can't put it into anymore words, Nina." I could see he was getting tense and upset about it, his fists were clenched, and tears were in his eyes, I had never seen Bobby this way.

"It's okay, I am sorry for asking," I approached him and hugged him. We embraced – both feeling like we had the world on our shoulders. Part of me didn't want to let him go, he was the closest thing to Jack that I had right now. We parted and gazed at each other, our faces close, I suddenly felt awkward and retreated, what had just happened? I felt there was something between us for a split second, surely not, it's Jack's brother, I am just grief stricken, that's all it is. He clearly felt awkward too because he cleared his throat and packed up the picnic and the blanket without saying a word.

"Let's head back," I said hastily, and we walked back towards the house, not a word passed our lips. As we approached the house, I noticed a car parked outside, it was a military vehicle; was Jack home? I ran as fast as my bump would allow me, Bobby followed behind me. No one was in the vehicle, where were they? I flung open the door to my kitchen and Mr and Mrs Watson sat at the table with Group Captain Staines and the same RAF officer from before. I looked around, hoping to see Jack, but he wasn't here.

"Is there news?" I asked hopefully, catching my breath.

"Please sit down, Nina," Staines commanded. Whatever he was about to tell me Mr and Mrs Watson already knew, they wouldn't make eye contact with me. He didn't waste time.

"We found Jack's plane, well part of it, it had floated down to some marsh land near Calais. Calais is currently occupied by the Nazi Germans," he gathered his thoughts. "Nina, there was blood found in the plane, a considerable amount of blood. I am sorry, but at this moment in time, we presume Jack to be dead. If not dead, then captured and taken to a prisoner of war camp." I cut him off.

"What happens there?" Staines looked at Mr Watson. "Well, erm, they are held captive…"

"Nina, it's all over the fucking wireless, if you get captured and taken there, you fucking die!" Bobby

148

interjected furiously.

"So, you're telling me he's either already dead or soon will be?" My voice broke as I held back the tears. He looked around awkwardly.

"I'm afraid so, Nina, I'm so sorry. We have no other hopes at this moment in time. We have to look at what we have been presented with." I felt faint, and immensely sick.

"Get out," I stood up to walk towards him, "get out of my house and go look for him, can't you send someone to go find him? I will go look for him!" Tears were streaming down my face now. I was lost in emotion – I went to put on my coat, as if I was going to head to Calais and rescue a prisoner of war from Hitler and his army of despicable humans. Suddenly I felt a twinge in my stomach.

"OW," I doubled over in pain.

"Nina!" Bobby ran over to me, "what's wrong?"

"OWWW," the pain in my stomach was sharp, and it ran straight down to my bladder, I looked to the floor and blood was streaming down my leg.

"Call an ambulance!" Bobby shouted, "she's bleeding." After that I don't remember a thing.

Those damn bright lights, I presume I am in hospital…again. I opened them gradually trying to adjust. There would be no flowers waiting for me this time, no Jack waiting outside to see me, he was dead. My heart was broken in two, I felt like I wanted to stay asleep and for this whole nightmare to be over.

"Nina, how are you feeling?" My vision focused and I realised it was Bobby. I stared at him blankly. Mr and Mrs Watson were sat at the bottom of my bed.

"How are you love?" I ignored her. I didn't want to talk, but I knew they were grieving too, both had lost a son and a brother, I forced myself to speak.

"Better," I whispered. Realisation suddenly hit me that before I blacked out, I had been bleeding, I panicked and tried sitting up.

"How is the baby?!"

"She's fine Nina, just relax please," Bobby calmly pushed me back down to the bed.

"Did you say she?" I realised as tears pricked my eyes. Bobby looked at his mum and dad.

"Sorry, I didn't mean to say that it's just the midwife said you are carrying the baby quite low and she said from her experience that means you are having a girl," he smiled, "and she's doing brilliantly."

"Nina, the doctor will be in shortly to explain everything," Mrs Watson said as she rubbed my leg. I couldn't hold back my tears, I sobbed, I closed my eyes and laid my head back on the pillow, I couldn't have stopped if I tried.

"Jack should have been here for this!" Why was this happening? I am carrying our baby and we cannot be together again, and this time there is no hope of his return at all. I will never see his beautiful blue eyes again, never hear his warm voice, never feel his tender touch, or smell his familiar scent. The feeling of grief was stronger than any feeling I had ever felt, I felt lacklustre, I had no energy and I felt like I didn't want to carry on, but I knew I had to. I eventually snapped out of my bubble, and realised Mrs Watson had left the room, I had probably upset her, Bobby had gone after her, and it left Mr Watson and me alone.

"I just want you to know, Nina that me and Delilah are going to be here for you every step of the way. Even though Jack has…" he couldn't say it, "is no longer with us, you are part of the Watson family, and you and that baby are going to be so loved and taken care of, do you understand?" I smiled at him, thankfully. The doctor entered the room.

"Mrs Watson, good morning," he said chirpily, not the tone I wanted to hear right now, "how are you?"

"I've been better," I wasn't lying.

"Everything is absolutely fine with the baby. I understand you have been under immense pressure and stress lately, which has likely caused yesterday's bleeding and black out, we haven't been able to determine any other issues. You are also extremely low on iron, so I advise you to take these pills, once a day, and eat a well-balanced, healthy diet, as much as you can in these hard times," he finally finished.

"Okay," I had nothing else to say. I was delighted that baby, *she*, was okay, but I just wanted to go home and crawl into bed with some of Jack's belongings and cry myself into a watery stupor. I took the pills and ushered them out of the room so I could get dressed. Mr and Mrs Watson dropped me home; no one said a word in the car. Every so often I could feel Bobby's eyes on me, he was clearly worried but he needn't be, I wouldn't put her in harm's way, she was the only thing I had left of Jack; the most precious thing in the world to me.

I did exactly what I said I would do and cried in my bed wearing and holding Jack's possessions, for around two weeks after I left hospital. I barely came out of my room, and when I did, it was for a walk on my own so the baby could get some vitamin D. I was taking my pills but couldn't stomach much food; most mealtimes were spent force-feeding myself. Bobby had slipped back into his old ways somewhat, he was getting drunk more, and coming home at dawn, after clearly spending the night with a woman. We were both struggling, and neither of us could get it together. Mr and Mrs Watson were the only sane ones, they brought Bobby and I home cooked food at least three times a week, and instead of popping for a quick cup of tea daily, Mrs Watson would sit downstairs for hours, mostly on her own in silence. Part of me thinks it was just to be close to Jack, and I was okay with that, we were all grieving. Mr Watson didn't let emotion get the better of him and held it together for us all. He encouraged Bobby to play tennis matches and have regular walks. He managed to keep him off the alcohol for two nights in two weeks, which in itself was a small victory. *Knock knock knock* – every time someone knocked at that door, they brought bad news, so I just ignored it. *Knock knock knock* – they repeated four times, it was annoying me, so I mustered the energy and walked downstairs to answer it, still in my dressing gown. I opened the door and a man dressed smartly from head to toe, all in black stood in front of me, with a briefcase and a cardboard box at his feet.

"Can I help you?" I enquired.

"I'm Edgar, are you Mrs Nina Watson?"

"Yes, why?" I answered lacking the energy to continue the conversation.

"I have a Mr Jack Watson's belongings here," and he looked down to the tatty looking box near his feet.

"From where?" I was suddenly interested.

"These are from RAF base Biggin Hill ma'am, I work with the families of those who have lost loved ones in war."

"And offer what exactly? I don't need anyone working with me, now if you don't mind, I'll take my dead husband's last possessions and you can be on your way." I leaned down to pick up the box. It was quite heavy, but I was not having some stranger of death in my house, I slammed the door in his face and placed it on the table. A few moments later I heard the man get in his car and drive off. I stared at the box, daring not to open it. I was startled when the door went and in sauntered Bobby.

"Hi," he was surprised to see me out of bed, "how are you?"

"This box just arrived from the camp, it contains Jack's things," I replied ignoring his question.

"Oh, well are you going to open it?" he enquired, taking off his jacket and placing it on the coat stand.

"I daren't, it'll be the things I saw him pack the night he left, it's just more memories to add to the ever-growing pain inside me," I sighed.

"We'll do it together if you want?" and he pulled up a chair and sat down beside me. I smiled at him reassuringly.

"Thank you," and I slowly peeled the lid of the box open. Bobby waited with bated breath. Inside, perched on top of Jack's belongings were four letters, entitled 'Mum and Dad', 'Bobby', 'My wonderful wife Nina', and 'Baby Watson'. Tears sprung from my eyes. "I can't do this Bobby," I stood up and backed away from the table.

"It's okay, Nina, in your own time. But at some point, we have to try, it's part of the process, we need to start trying to get past this, for that little girl's sake," and he looked at my bump.

"I want to read mine in private," I insisted.

"Of course, Nina, I'll go to my room," and he took his letter and walked away. I couldn't read it straight away and instead rifled through the other things in the box. I studied his comb looking for traces of his hair like a mad woman. His spare uniforms lay neatly pressed on top of the blanket that he had wrapped around me the night I creeped back into camp. Enfolded inside the blanket was a photograph of us together at our wedding. I studied it, we were so blissful, the happiest day of our lives, just him and me. My mind flashed back to our wedding dance where we held onto each other, never wanting to let go. That day we had no worries, we were carefree, and in love. I studied his face, I never wanted to forget it. I will forever remember the first time I saw him stood in his mum and dad's house, slightly inebriated, but handsome as ever, those excitable feelings I got when he looked at me for the first time. I loved him from that very day; why didn't I marry him sooner? I had so many regrets. He could have watched our last baby grow if I'd have done the right thing and took the chance on him instead of Harry, instead I chose to get rid and now he will never have the opportunity. I sniffed the blanket, it smelled of his pink pepper scent, I took the letter and the blanket with me up to my bedroom and climbed into bed holding onto them for dear life. I lay there for what felt like hours, I heard voices and movement downstairs, but I had no urgency to get up. I finally convinced myself to read the letter, so clicked on my bedside lamp. The day had begun to close, and the night was beginning to creep in. I peeled the envelope and opened the letter up, it read: *'To my wonderful wife, Nina Watson. If you are reading this, then I am regrettably no longer with you. This letter was the hardest letter I have ever had to write. Up until the day I left this earth I loved you with my whole being, and I will continue to love you thereafter. I am sorry that I have left you and our baby behind, it was the last thing I ever wanted to do. I hope that what I did has made the future better for you both. I have written a letter for our wonderful child; would it be possible to give them this on their 18th birthday please? I want them to know how much I loved them, despite never meeting them. Please talk about me; I want them to know what type of man their father was, and how happy we made each other. Every night I lay here, thinking of our wedding day, the happiest day of my life. The way you looked at me as you walked down the aisle, and how much of an angel you looked in that beautiful, white dress. Thank you for coming into my life, Nina, I never knew love until I met you, you were the other half of me, and we were one when we were together. I will die a blissful man knowing you walked beside me and that we made each other happy at one time. Please don't be sad, I know this is not how we planned our future, but our baby needs you to be strong. Can you do that for me? I will live on in their eyes, and you will always see me when you hug them, see their smile and put them to bed on a night. I want you to try move on as best you can, if it means finding someone new then you have my blessing. I don't want you to be alone, you deserve to be happy and loved; both of you do. I hope my family are standing by you, I know they will, you are a Watson after all. Please remember me; I will be your guardian angel from now on, until we meet again my darling. I will be waiting for you at the old barn near the babbling brook.*

All my love, Jack x'

My tears dripped onto the letter, I screamed out, why had he been taken from us? Footsteps boomed up the staircase and Bobby flung open my bedroom door; I sat in a heap on the floor, wailing. He approached me and seeing the letter on the floor next to me, he said nothing, he just hugged me tightly, and he didn't let me go.

We all gathered in the living room. I laid down on the sofa staring into space, my legs resting across Bobby's lap, my head resting on my hands. Mrs Watson sat opposite, clutching her letter from Jack, and Mr Watson stood with a glass of whisky in his hand. None of us spoke, we were just amongst each other, thinking, dreaming, and wondering. I had no energy left, being pregnant and widowed was not a healthy combination, my body felt like lead, I was exhausted, mentally and physically, I kept thinking back to the line from Jack's letter, 'our baby needs you to be strong,' how Jack, how?

"Right, I just wanted us to have a chat, see how we are all keeping. These last few weeks have been tough, and I know we are all grieving. Some days it feels like there is no tomorrow, but we need to think about the future. Jack was a strong man, and he wouldn't want us to wallow in misery. We need to try pulling ourselves together, especially for that little one in there," Mr Watson pointed to me. He spoke with courage; he was finding this as hard as we all were. He continued.

"So, Bobby, I think it's best that you have no more alcohol, it is not the answer, and I said before I would not have you treating this house as a place to come and go from your drunken nights out."

"I'm not doing that dad," Bobby spoke indignantly, "I have just been letting off some steam, I am happy to give up alcohol, and try put my efforts into something else," he continued. He didn't want to be another problem in our miserable lives.

"I understand it's not easy son, but together we can work through this," he smiled a brave smile.

"Have you considered teaching at the school, Bobby?" Mrs Watson finally spoke.

"No, but it sounds like something worth looking into mum, thank you," he smiled back warmly.

"You could be a sports teacher? The kids would love it!" Mrs Watson sounded happier, "I will speak to the school Governor, I am well connected there, or I was when I hosted my bridge nights before all of this," she sounded proud of her connections. Bobby sniggered.

"Thanks mum, you little socialite," she laughed back, and I smiled within.

"That brings me to you, Delilah," Mr Watson continued.

"You could start hosting those bridge nights again, and your dinner parties. It is something you love doing, and if anything, it might help alleviate the pain that you are going through, a gentle distraction. Just because you decide to socialise again, does not mean you are forgetting Jack. Bringing back some normality into your life will make you begin to feel like yourself again, and Jack would want that."

"True mum, and Jack loved how sociable you were. He said you and dad must have been a Lord and Lady in a previous life, hosting banquets and dinner dances," Bobby laughed. She pondered the proposal for a short while.

"You are both right, I will get one organised, maybe it could be in memory of Jack. It could be a ticket entry and we could send the money raised to a charity we know Jack would approve of, or something RAF related?" You could see the ideas spinning around her mind as she spoke; she seemed to have her glint back briefly.

"Fantastic idea sweetheart," Mr Watson concurred. He then turned to look at me; I hadn't moved an inch throughout this conversation or taken part in any of the discussions.

"Nina," he said softly. I didn't move, there was nothing he could say that would get the fire back in my belly, as it had done for them.

"Maybe we should leave it for tonight now, eh dad," Bobby looked at Mr Watson hinting him to leave.

"Yes, of course, well good night to you all," he smiled and headed for the door. Mrs Watson approached me, she rubbed my belly

"It will get easier, Nina, just hang in there, sweetheart," and she left without giving me chance to respond. Bobby rubbed my legs, I could tell he did not want to ask me how I was feeling, again, but that was his way of letting me know he was there for me. I sighed.

"I'm sorry."

"What are you sorry for?" he asked surprised.

"I'm really struggling, you all seem to be taking it better than me, I feel like I'm in a pit, and I'm too deep in to climb out," tears approached my eyes again.

"Hey," Bobby got onto his knees on the floor and faced me.

"Don't be silly, everyone is dealing with this in their

own way. You've not just lost him, you've got your baby to think about too, no one is expecting anything more from you, Nina," he spoke calmly.

"I know, what sort of a mother am I? I can't even feed her what she needs whilst she's inside me, what am I going to be like when she's here?"

"You're doing the best you can for that baby girl, now stop being hard on yourself. I am going to run you a bath, and you are going to have an early night, no arguments. We will take care of her together whether she's in there or out here. I am here for you both, remember that." He moved the hair out of my eyes the way Jack used to. We stared at each other, not speaking for at least a minute; I had so many thoughts in my head at once. I thought he might kiss me, I am misreading this surely, he wouldn't. I awaited hesitantly, not daring to say another thing in case I had completely got the wrong end of the stick and looked stupid for even thinking it. He finally pulled away.

"I'll, erm, I'll go run you that bath now," and he walked away hurriedly. Why did we keep having these awkward moments?

I laid in the bath, the wedding picture was perched on the bathroom sink counter so I could see it, I just stared. My mind wandered back to the day before he went, the quality time we had together, which I took for granted. Why did I go nap for so long? Why did I sit on the veranda whilst he packed instead of helping him? Why did I let him leave at all? I suddenly felt a thud from within my belly, oh my god, what was that? *Kick*, there it was again! It felt like flutters in my tummy, *kick,* oh my gosh my baby is kicking me, I had to tell someone. I jumped out of the bath and made my way downstairs in my bathrobe.

"Bobby, feel this!" I exclaimed. He looked at me startled.

"What?"

"She kicked; she just kicked for the first time!" I was so happy. Bobby put his hand on my belly; she had stopped doing it now.

"Rub my belly gently," I urged. He rubbed and *kick,* she kicked again for him.

"Oh my god!" he was just as excited as me, "that is amazing; I can't believe she is kicking you, god it makes it all feel so much more real!" I smiled at him, this girl was going to give me my purpose, starting from now, and I needed to make some drastic changes.

Chapter 9

Nina

"Dinner is ready," I shouted to Bobby, I waddled to the table and lay it down, he had just finished his day at the local school after taking his mother's advice and becoming a PE teacher, and he was loving it. I was eight and a half months pregnant now, and the size of a car, I felt like I might give birth at any minute, and I wish I would, I was so uncomfortable. My reason for not sleeping now wasn't thoughts of Jack, it was just the inability to get comfortable and I spent many a night trying to sleep sat up. We had held a memorial for Jack in July, and no further news had come back about him. My mind still wandered most days to what he must have had to go through, but I couldn't go back into that pit. I had tried my hardest for three months to clamber my way out of it for my unborn daughter, and I needed to be stronger, for when she arrived.

"Thank you," he smiled at me. The last few months had been strange having to adapt to having another man in the house, knowing my man wasn't coming home. I debated asking him to move out, as a mark of respect, but I really needed the company. If I had learned anything about myself since Jack had left, it was that I was weaker than I imagined. The thought of doing this alone terrified me to the core. Bobby and I had more awkward encounters, but we just let them pass, we knew it was grief, and nothing more. I loved having him around; he had not attempted to find another house, he wanted to be here too, and truth be told I needed him. Georgie was due to come down this evening for a few nights and I couldn't wait to see her. Mr and Mrs Watson seemed back to their usual chirpy selves and were back hosting parties and getting excited for their granddaughter's arrival. It felt like life had moved on, sadly. I had accepted it wouldn't be the same again and to just go with it, because the other way made me too unhappy.

"How was your day?" I asked whilst loading my fork. My appetite had come back, and I suddenly couldn't get enough, the baby, as I liked to blame, loved apples and mashed potato, so that is what I was having for dinner. Bobby smiled looking down at my plate.

"You've tried a new variation for dinner today then? Mashed apples and mashed potato, yum," he laughed sarcastically. I laughed back.

"Well although I love a whole apple, I get bored of gnawing them, so thought stew it, mash it, eat it."

"Have you ever thought of working in advertising, that tag line could work wonders," he raised his eyebrow smiling a cheeky smile. Some days I could see Jack in him, which was another reason I liked having him around, he was familiar to me, and it brought me comfort.

"So how was your day?" I smiled, ignoring his comment.

"Great, getting paid to teach kids sports, I think myself very lucky," he had changed a lot since moving in with me. Jack had always described him as being quite immature, but I had rarely seen the childishness. I know the situation probably meant he had to step up, but he was doing a mighty fine job.

"And what did you do with yourself today ma'am?"

"Well," I paused. "I ran a marathon, dug up the back garden and redecorated the bathroom," I jested.

"I always said to dad you'd be better at DIY than me," he laughed finishing his meal.

"Georgie is coming tonight you know," I winked at him. He looked behind him.

"Are you winking at me?" he joked.

"You know she likes you, why don't you ask her on a date or for a drink or a walk?" I insisted.

"I don't think so, Nina," he picked up our plates and took them to the sink.

"Why not? She's very pretty, she would make a wonderful wife, and she has a good job, plus she is a laugh," I persuaded him. He turned to look at me, deadly serious.

"Thank you, but I will pass, she is a lovely girl, but she's not my type."

"She's beautiful Bobby, and I saw you together at the wedding, has something happened between you?"

"No, I just aren't into dating," he shrugged his shoulders. That was a lie, and then it hit me.

"I get it, you feel like you can't date because you have to look after us? Bobby, that's silly, you don't owe us anything. I want you to be happy, and we aren't going to hold you back. Whether you date or not, you'll still always be a part of our lives." He didn't seem convinced.

"If it will stop you whining at me, then I will go for a drink with her, okay?" he held his hands up.

"Perfect, tonight it is then!" I quipped.

163

"What? She is only arriving here tonight, surely you want to see her first?"

"I do, she will be here in a few minutes, but I am really tired today, and to be honest you will be doing me a favour, I can try and sleep and then tomorrow I have her to myself for a girly day," I smiled.

"I best get washed up then hadn't I," he rolled his eyes.

Right on queue there was a *knock knock knock.*

"Yoo-hoo, it's only meeeee," here she was!

"Hi Georgie," I ran over to her and gave her a big hug; I have missed her so much.

"Hello beautiful mummy to be," she looked at my stomach and mouthed, "wow, you look glowing Nina, it suits you so much."

"Thank you, I feel like a beach ball but otherwise it's amazing, can't quite believe she could be here any day," I rubbed my stomach lovingly.

"I have a surprise for you!" I couldn't wait to tell her.

"You do? I am intrigued," she placed her luggage down on the floor.

"You have a date," I smiled a big cheesy smile. She didn't seem as happy as I had expected.

"Oh, with who?"

"Bobby, you know you said you fancied him at the wedding, well he's asked to take you out for a drink, tonight," I clapped my hands together, I loved playing matchmaker. Georgie still didn't seem as happy as I had wanted.

"Tonight? okay, well what about you?" she seemed astounded.

"Well, I am tired today so bed beckons, but you and him tonight, and then me and you from tomorrow, you aren't happy, are you?" I asked disappointed.

"Of course, I am, I am just taken aback that's all, it's sudden, erm, let me get some makeup on and into a new dress and I will see you down here. Am I in the same room as before?" she asked walking towards the stairs.

"Yep, I would follow you up, but it takes a good three days," I joked feeling a little irritated. Bobby came down smelling fresh and dressed smartly.

"Look at you who said he wasn't ready to date, you look dashing," I smiled. I hadn't seen him dressed up much before; we spent a lot of our time indoors or going for walks. He smiled coyly and sat opposite me.

"Are you alright?"

"Yes fine, your date will be with you shortly," I smirked. Bobby rolled his eyes and laid back in the chair.

"You owe me!" he moaned.

"I am doing you a favour, Georgie didn't seem best pleased either, what is wrong with you two…oh my gosh, have you been with each other before?" The realisation suddenly entered my mind, had they got together at the wedding?

"No, we never did. We chatted to each other but that was all, in all honesty I just can't be bothered but I will do it for you," he replied. Oh, I thought I had cracked why they were both acting strange, maybe I was just reading the signals wrong, I am tired after all.

Georgie's heels clinked on the last stair as she entered the living room, I wolf whistled, and she laughed. Bobby got to his feet; you could tell he was pleasantly surprised. What was not to love, she was a blonde goddess, with chocolate brown eyes, legs up to heaven and a body to die for, and she was the funniest, kindest, most loyal woman I had ever met. If I were a man, I would choose her.

"Georgie, this is Bobby, Bobby this is Georgie," I introduced them.

"Pleased to meet you again," Bobby replied holding his hand out, Georgie extended hers and he kissed her hand, what a good start. I feigned a yawn.

"Oh my gosh I am so tired now, bath and bed for me, wow is that the time? Best be off, have fun," and I winked at them both as I headed up the stairs. Within a few minutes, I heard the door shut behind them, and they were gone.

I lay in the bath thinking about the romance I could have just created, I envisaged myself as Georgie's bridesmaid, walking in front of her down the aisle, and Bobby stood at the altar, dressed like a true gentleman. By this point, my little girl would be here, and she could be a bridesmaid alongside me, with flowers in her hair, holding onto mummy's hand. The thought made me smile, but quickly my mind fell back to Jack. All the things he was missing, I had to be both mummy and daddy for that little girl, his memory would live on forever in me, and I would never stop talking about him. We had received a framed picture of Jack in his RAF uniform from Staines, that he had painted, and it took pride of place in our living room. Every morning I looked at it and blew a kiss towards it, I knew he was watching down on us. I was truly exhausted today, and for once felt like I could sleep in any position. I climbed into bed and fell into a deep slumber.

It's a new day, the birds were tweeting, and I was

feeling rested after sleeping nine whole hours, I could not believe it. I was excited for my day with Georgie, and even more excited to learn how their date had gone. I got dressed and briskly walked downstairs, Bobby was sat at the table with a newspaper, he smiled a warm smile when he saw me.

"Good morning, Bobby," I headed over to pour myself a tea from the teapot.

"You're full of energy this morning," he noticed.

"I got nine hours sleep last night, I told you I was tired. I think I slept soundly knowing I had set my best mate and brother-in-law up on a date that could change their lives forever," I jested. Bobby didn't appear remotely interested.

"Tell me how it went then," I urged.

"It was okay, but there were no sparks, I'm sorry," he bluntly replied.

"Wow, how?" I was confused. "You seemed happy when she came down the stairs."

"She is a very attractive girl, Nina, but I aren't in that mind-set, she's not the one for me," he replied buttering his toast.

"Well, who is?" I wondered. He spoke like he already had someone in mind. He looked at me, about to reply, when Georgie walked in.

"Morning mama, morning Bobby," she acknowledged him and beamed at me.

"Morning, how did you sleep?"

"Very well, I am so excited about our girly day today!" she buzzed. Bobby looked awkward.

"I'm going to work, have a good day," and he briskly left.

"Eurgh, that was awkward, did it not go well?" Georgie paused briefly.

"It was alright, nothing to write home about, come on eat up I want to go out!" She poured herself a tea and changed the subject.

"What are we doing then?" I was confused but got the hint that neither wanted to talk about it so decided I would interrogate her later.

"Into town for coffee and cake, and a bit of baby shopping," I excitedly announced.

"Oh yes! I am so excited, she is going to be the most loved, spoiled little darling," she beamed.

"Can I have a piece of the Victoria sandwich and a cup of tea, and my friend will have a scone with jam and cream and a water please," I handed the waitress the money and returned to my chair. We had purchased bags of clothes for baby Watson, and I couldn't wait to see her in some of the cute little outfits, it was all becoming so real.

"Neen, she's going to look adorable; I want one now," she laughed.

"Well, you need a man for that!" I replied speedily. We were alone now, and I wanted the low down.

"What happened with Bobby? It started so well, and you seemed really off with each other this morning. Tell me. I was planning your wedding last night," I quipped. She looked at me seriously.

"I haven't been honest with you, Nina, it's early days, and every man I get with ends up cheating on me, or being scum, so I wanted to keep this under wraps for a short while. I am engaged to someone!" she announced.

"Oh my God, Georgie that is a shock but it's

incredible, who?"

"Do you remember when we were in that big hall after the bombing at the base, and a man named Sid introduced himself? Well, it's him!" I was stunned, I remembered it well, Jack was alive then.

"Congratulations! How did this happen?"

"Well, he wrote to me a short time after, and when I came to your wedding, I ended up meeting him. I stayed with him for a week, and it was magical. I didn't think anything would come of it, but we fell in love, and now he's asked me to be his wife," she was elated.

"Georgie, I am so happy for you, you deserve complete bliss, I wish you had told me though!" I was a little sad.

"Nina, you have had such a lot going on, the last thing I wanted to do was rub your face in how happy I was. I wanted you to vent to me, and tell me what was on your mind, not the other way round. Do you forgive me for keeping it a secret?"

"Of course, I do, I can still plan a wedding then?" I laughed.

"I wouldn't want any other woman to be my chief bridesmaid than you, Nina Watson," she squeezed my hand.

"We are not planning on getting married for a while yet, we want the war to be over before we commit, I can't go through what you…" she stopped herself from finishing the sentence. "Nina I am sorry that was so heartless and dumb of me," she looked embarrassed.

"Don't be silly, I wouldn't wish this on my worst enemy, Georgie, you are doing the right thing. Don't get pregnant yet either, it plays mayhem with your emotions," I laughed off her comment, I was hurt but didn't blame her, why would she want to be in my position? Widowed and pregnant at twenty-six, it's no life for anyone is it? I finished my tea, feeling foolish deep within.

"So, what did happen with you two last night?" I changed the subject.

"Nothing, we had a couple of drinks, mainly talked about you to be honest…" she paused, "Nina, I have to tell you something," she became stern.

"Who else are you engaged to?" I laughed.

"He…" she was interrupted as Mrs Watson entered the café and approached our table.

"Well, hello you two, I was just passing by, Georgie, how lovely to see you!" She said kissing us both on the cheek. "Oh, that looks lovely," she said eyeing up the cake.

"Would you like to join us Mrs Watson?" I asked.

"My my, it's Delilah dear, you're practically my daughter now," she laughed, "would you mind? I am just on my way back home, apparently Bobby is helping George with some roofing, a few tiles fell off the roof in the night," I look at her quizzically.

"I thought Bobby was working today?"

"No dear, it's half term now, they broke up yesterday," she replied gesturing over the waitress. Oh, maybe he went into work forgetting, silly Bobby, I bet he was just gutted that Georgie was with someone, and wanted to save face, that would explain the awkwardness this morning. We spent the rest of the afternoon with Mrs Watson, talking about Georgie's engagement, it was a lovely afternoon, I missed having my best friend round the corner.

We all totted back to the house together, Georgie was cutting her stay short, as there was to be a rail strike and she needed to get home, I was gutted, it was nice having a bit of normality in my life again. Mrs Watson had volunteered Mr Watson to take her to the train station.

"Nina, can you give me a hand with packing please?" she ushered me upstairs.

"Of course," I waddled behind her, Bobby and Mr Watson were chatting on the settee as Mrs Watson poured herself a cup of tea. She closed the door behind me.

"Nina, I need to tell you something before I go, urgently," she seemed panicked, I was suddenly worried, Harry popped into my head, could he have told dad the truth of the first baby?

"Me and Bobby were speaking last night, and as I said it was mostly about you. Well, I don't know how to tell you this but, he told me he was in love with someone." *Phew,* not Harry related.

"Really? That's great news; I thought you were going to tell me something awful then. I always thought he was holding back because of me and little baby so I am happy to hear it."

"No Nina," she cut me off, "he told me he has fallen in love with you!" My heart skipped a beat.

"No, you're mistaken, he's Jack's brother, I am Jack's wife, he's family, you must have got the wrong end of the stick. What exactly did he say?"

"He said, he knows it's wrong but he's in love with you and has been for a few months, he said grief has pushed you together, but it's love. He was a bit drunk when he told me this, but I have no doubt he is telling

171

the truth Neen, you saw how awkward he was this morning," Georgie gawped at me waiting for a response. I sat down on the bed astounded, I didn't know what to think, Bobby can't be in love with me, this was just bizarre. Then I started to piece things together - the looks he gave me, the awkward silences we had in such close proximity of one another. Have my affections towards him, like the hugs and putting my feet on him led him on, and given him the wrong signals? I felt foolish and confused.

"What are you going to do?" Georgie asked.

"I don't know, what can I do. Does he know you were going to tell me?"

"No, I said I wouldn't say a thing, but how can I not? You're living with him for heaven's sake; you deserve to know the truth!" She packed up the last of her belongings and zipped up the bag.

"Are you ready dear?" Mr Watson shouted up from downstairs, "your train will be here in fifteen minutes."

"Just promise me you will think long and hard about this," she grabbed my shoulders.

"What's to think about?" I asked confused.

"I aren't saying you are going to replace Jack, Nina, but could you learn to love Bobby? You need someone who can help take care of you and your baby girl, and he is a nice man with your best interests at heart, would it be so terrible?" What was she saying? I am not going to shack up with Jack's brother just so I'm not alone.

"Georgie, no! It's wrong on so many levels."

"Is it? You need to think of number one now Nina, I hate to say this but as your friend, you need to hear it. Jack is not coming back, Bobby is here, and he loves you, just please think about it." I couldn't process what she was saying to me. She kissed me on the cheek and hugged me. "I will ring you through the week, I love you," and she waltzed out the room. My head was spinning.

I left it ten minutes before I dare go back downstairs, what do I say to him? Should I say anything? If I don't mention it, it might never be spoken of again, but can I live with myself knowing something so huge about him and not addressing it? Eurgh, why can't life be straightforward. I gradually made my way downstairs, where Bobby and Mrs Watson sat on the sofa discussing the roofing, I felt muddled.

"Hello dear, would you like a tea?" Mrs Watson asked, jumping up and heading to the teapot.

"Erm, yes, thanks," I dare not look at Bobby.

"How was your day with Georgie," he asked. Damn I have to speak to him now.

"Oh, you know, it was good, wasn't it Mrs Watson," I quickly tried bringing her into the conversation as a diversion.

"Yes, she is such a bonny girl isn't she, it's a shame you didn't get in there quicker Bobby," she laughed. Bobby sighed.

"Just because a pretty girl is single doesn't mean I am always interested mother," he replied, flicking through the pages of the newspaper disinterestedly.

"Oh, what's wrong with you today!" she asked jokingly, "think he got out on the wrong side of the bed," she whispered towards me. I wanted to push the Georgie thing a bit more, I wondered if he would ever be honest with me.

"So, you won't be seeing her again then?" I continued.

"She's engaged," he looked up at me confused. Damn, course she was.

"Of course, yes, I knew that, well there's a few eligible women in the town I could set you up with," I added.

"Thanks, but I am all set," he didn't take his eyes from the newspaper. Georgie must have got the wrong end of the stick, if this was him in love with me; I would hate to see what he was like when he had no feelings for me whatsoever.

"Right, I am going to bid you adieu, thanks for the help with the roofing dear, take care Nina and little one," Mrs Watson blew us a kiss and left. Just me and Bobby now, let's see what happens.

"Thought you were at work today?" I quizzed sitting opposite him.

"I got my days mixed up, ended up helping dad with their roof," he replied nonchalantly.

"I see, what time did you get in last night then?" I continued.

"Late," he replied, these one-liners were odd.

"I see, were you drunk?" I asked.

"Nina, why don't you just cut to the chase, I know Georgie told you," he looked directly at me. I didn't know what to do with myself; I was shocked that he had been so brazen.

"Told me what?" I played dumb.

"You know what," he replied knowing full well what I was doing, "I didn't expect she would keep it a secret," he added.

"So, you wanted me to know?" I asked.

"So, you do know!" he replied.

"Bobby, just talk to me, I want to hear what is going on from you, not Georgie," I sighed. He took a deep breath, put the newspaper down and leant forward in his chair.

"This is not ideal for either of us, but since I have lived here, and got to know you more, and spent time with you, I have found myself feeling things."

"Like what?" I was curious. He looked embarrassed.

"When I see you, I feel excitement, I want to be around you, I think you are a beautiful woman inside and out. I have changed since moving here, I have grown up, and it's thanks to you, you've made me a better person."

"Maybe you are just confusing gratitude with something else," I pushed.

"No, it's not that, I have to be honest with myself, and you, I am falling in love with you," he stared into my eyes. How could this be happening?

"Bobby, I am married to your brother," I whispered.

"I know that, but he's not here now, and I know it's strange, but he would want me to…"

"NO, he would not, Bobby, listen to yourself. Do you think he would want you telling his wife you loved her?"

"Nina, if he were alive of course not, but he's not, is he," he looked down at the ground and rubbed the back of his neck awkwardly. "As I said, it's not ideal, and in a way, I am glad it's out in the open because I am struggling. I can't help but want you Nina," he walked towards me. "It's not just about sex, I want to love and look after you, both. I'm sorry," he stopped in front of me. Georgie's words went through my mind, would it be so bad, he wouldn't do me wrong; he would love the baby as his own because they shared the same blood. Eurgh, what am I saying, I aren't thinking straight.

175

"It's just grief, Bobby, you feel like you are closer to Jack, if you get closer to me," I empathised. "I feel the same in that respect, some days I look at you and I see glimpses of him."

"It's more than that, Nina," he walked towards me closer, so we were only inches apart. I couldn't lie and say I hadn't felt a little excitement when he looked at me a certain way, or when he touched me sometimes, but everyone wants to be wanted, and he felt familiar, he felt like Jack. That is all it was for me, I wanted Jack and couldn't have him, and he was there. He didn't give me much time to process things, as he leaned forward to kiss me. I pulled back immediately.

"No Bobby." I suddenly felt a trickle down my leg. I looked down at my feet - I was stood in a puddle of water. Oh my god, my waters have broken.

"Owwww," the pain was coming thick and fast now; Mrs Watson was holding my hand as they rushed me into hospital.

"Deep breaths dear, all those months of waiting and she's on her way!" she said excitedly. I was so excited to meet my daughter, to look at her and see Jack again. Mrs Watson was going to be in the room whilst I gave birth. Dad, Faye and Georgie were going to come see us as soon as the rail strike was over, great timing, I thought. Mr Watson and Bobby had stayed at home; there was no need for them to be here. I had been in labour for around four hours at home; I didn't want to go into hospital too early to see whether I could last, and I couldn't, this was the worst pain in the world. My stomach tightened every two minutes, Mrs Watson said that means the baby is very close to being born. Bobby had no hands left after taking the brunt of my pain, we didn't mention the failed kiss after my waters broke, it was not the right time, but having left it the way we did, I know it was a topic for discussion when I returned.

"Owwwwwww," I screamed.

"You're doing so well dear," she stroked my sweaty head with a wet flannel as we pulled up into my delivery room. The doctor measured my dilation.

"Wow, you're at ten centimetres already, you are keen to get this baby out," she laughed. You could say that again, I thought. I had longed for this day since Jack had died.

"We are ready to push Mrs Watson, let's go," I felt a wave of nausea go across my body, this was it, I was going to meet her, half of me and half of Jack, bring it on. *Pushhhhhhhhhhhhhhhhhhhh,*

"Aarghhhhhhh," I screamed.

"Keep going, keep going," the Doctor ordered.

"I can't, give me a minute…right," I gathered myself and pushed again, *pushhhhhhhhhhhhhhhhhhhhhh.*

"The head is out Mrs Watson!" the Doctor shrieked.

"Oh Nina!" Mrs Watson began to cry.

"And push again," the Doctor ordered once more. *Pushhhhhhhhhhhhhhhhhhhhhhhhhhhhhhhhhhhhhh.*

"Wahhh wahhhh," the sound of my new-born daughter – she was here at long last. The Doctor passed the most beautiful bundle of joy to me; she lay on my chest with her eyes closed, gently whimpering, tears filled my eyes. She was mine, look what Jack and I had created.

"I already have a name for her in mind," I sniffled, "I want to call her Jacqueline after her daddy," I looked at Mrs Watson. She put her forehead against mine, and we both sobbed, happy and sad tears. It was a bittersweet moment.

I walked through the living room door carrying my wonderful little girl and was greeted by bunches of flowers and a round of applause from Bobby and Mr Watson. They both approached me cautiously.

"Oh, my, the most beautiful little girl I've ever seen," Mr Watson cooed over her.

"She's adorable, Nina, well done and congratulations," Bobby smiled at me proudly.

"And guess what Nina has called her?" Mrs Watson added delightedly.

"Meet, Jacqueline Rose Watson," I beamed.

"That's a nice touch," Bobby welled up and looked up at Jack's painting, I followed his gaze and stared at Jack too, I wish you were here my love.

We spent the rest of the day, into the early evening, just staring at her; she was the most beautiful baby I had ever seen. She had not cried once and was content just laid in my arms and being passed around the family. I suddenly felt as if I had purpose once again; she was going to be the most loved little miss.

"Right sweetheart, I don't want to, but we best be heading off, you both need your rest, thank you for blessing us with our granddaughter, Nina," Mrs Watson kissed my cheek and stopped to look at Jack's painting on her way out. Mr Watson followed, gently stroking Jacqueline's head as she lay in her Moses basket. Then there were three, I was so tired from the ordeal of giving birth, I needed sleep.

"I am going to go to bed, I am exhausted," I stood up a little unbalanced, Bobby assisted me. We hugged each other, I rested my head upon his chest, and he stroked my hair.

"Well done, Nina, you are the strongest woman I know, Jack would be so proud of you," he whispered. I closed my eyes and thought of how Jack would have been with Jacqueline, he would have rocked her, and sung to her, kissed her forehead and we would have laid together on our bed cuddling, we would be the happiest people alive.

"Thank you," I managed back, feeling a pang of sadness and despair. The antics from the other day had been put to one side, I just wanted to be held. I took Jacqueline from the Moses basket and headed upstairs.

"Night Bobby," I called back.

I woke up three times to feed Jacqueline last night, I was tired, but she was so worth it. I dressed her in a beautiful frilly dress ready for grandma and grandad to come see her again. Bobby had offered to pick my dad, Georgie and Faye up from Lincolnshire and had set off first thing to do so. I was so excited for them to meet her. She was such an angel baby, she barely cried, I couldn't believe it, she was like a little doll. I walked downstairs and introduced her to her daddy's painting.

"Jacqueline that is your daddy, his name is Jack, who you are named after. He was the bravest soldier ever, and he loved you very much. He is in heaven with the angels, and he is watching over us daily," I began to well up. Enough of that for now, I thought. Mr and Mrs Watson popped their heads through the front door.

"Hello, my two favourite girls," Mrs Watson whispered, she brandished a large chocolate cake, which she had baked for us.

"Oh, that is beautiful," I thanked her passing Jacqueline to her and began to make a drink for us all. They cooed over her on the settee, laughing at the funny faces she was pulling, and sniffing her beautiful baby scent. I felt like I was on cloud nine, it was not how I expected to feel at all.

"Would you like to feed her?" I passed Mrs Watson the bottle, and she took it from me delighted with my request.

"Hello, only us," I recognised the voice, it was Faye. I ran towards her and gave her a huge hug.

"How are you?" she asked.

"Amazing, oh, Faye she is astounding," and I led her to the settee where Mrs Watson was feeding Jacqueline. Faye began to weep.

"Oh, my word Nina, what an adorable, beautiful little lady." My dad came through the door carrying his suitcases.

"Hi daddy!" I ran towards him and hugged him tightly.

"Hello, my girl," he replied sweetly. Dad had been quite upset with me for not telling him about the Jack ordeal when he had first gone missing. I understood why, but he knew I did it because I needed to believe he was still out there. Dad has been a great comfort these last few months, the way he spoke so fondly of Jack made me miss him ten times more, but it was so nice to think that dad loved him and respected him as much as I did. Georgie followed behind and smiled at me.

"Hello beautiful mama, I didn't expect to see you again so soon!" she laughed. She had only left the house two days ago, leaving me with the bombshell of Bobby's feelings. Each and every one of them couldn't take their eyes from Jacqueline and were delighted with my name choice. They all took turns in cuddling her, and we spent the day into the evening discussing the birth and our plans for the future. I was in my element, there was just one person missing. I remembered that I needed to notify Group Captain Staines about the birth; I will write him a letter as soon as I get chance. It wasn't long before I was feeling tired and bid everyone goodnight, taking Jacqueline with me. Georgie followed behind me.

"Did you speak with Bobby?" she whispered.

"Yes, we didn't get to finish the conversation though, as I went into labour," I added.

"Did he tell you how he really felt?" She quizzed.

"Yes, he did…he kissed me," I replied coyly.

"What?! How do you feel about it?" she exclaimed.

"I don't know, I am not over the moon if I am honest, but I don't want to think about it now, I just want to enjoy Jacqueline, and Jack is too much at the forefront of my mind right now, it will have to wait," I sighed.

"Take your time, he won't be going anywhere, you know where I am if you want to talk it out," she kissed me on the cheek, and I went up to bed. The two weeks with my family flew by, I didn't want it to end, priceless memories had been made. We took Jacqueline to the beach, and for a walk into town, and my dad babysat her for the afternoon whilst me, Faye and Georgie went for a pamper day. I told Faye about everything that had been going on with Bobby, she wasn't impressed with his actions at all, and said he was being inappropriate, and catching me at a vulnerable moment. I saw her point, but we were both vulnerable, he couldn't be blamed for it all. She advised me to follow my heart; the trouble was my heart was still with Jack, and where is that going to get me? I wanted the girls to stay for longer; it was nice having someone to vent to, and not have to make all the decisions on my own, especially seeing as all I ever seem to do is make bad ones. I was really missing Jack being here this week, even more than usual. Holding his daughter in my arms made my heart ache that he couldn't be here to enjoy her. Every morning I took her to see his painting, and talked about how brave, cheeky, funny and courageous he was.

A friend of Mrs Watson's had made a blanket out of one of Jack's jumpers, and Jacqueline adored it, she slept the most peaceful when she was wrapped up in that, she knew her daddy was close. I said my goodbyes to my family and suddenly felt a wrench of sadness, I felt like I was coming down off my cloud, keep strong Nina, I thought. The next week went by slowly, Bobby was working a lot as he had started tutoring children who were hoping to compete in a local tennis tournament, it was nice that he was doing something for himself. It meant a lot of time was spent just me and Jacqueline, which I adored, but the sleepless nights were starting to get to me. She woke up a lot through the night and I was exhausted. Bobby had offered to do some night feeds, but I wasn't ready to let her out of my sight yet, but by the time the week had closed to a halt, I was ready to start sharing the load. My eyes were like lead, my back ached from rocking her back and forth to sleep, and although I wouldn't change her for the world, I admitted to myself that I needed a break.

"Why don't you let mum and dad take her for a night?" Bobby suggested as we watched her sleeping in her

Moses basket, finally, "you can catch up on some sleep then!" It wasn't a bad idea, and I trusted them with her completely, the way Mrs Watson fussed over her, it wouldn't surprise me if she just sat up in the corner of the room watching her sleep all night, like a hawk.

"Yeah okay," I replied hesitantly, she had been with me protected for nine months; this was going to feel strange.

"It'll be okay," he smiled at me reassuringly, "they are practically next door if they need anything or have any concerns, I will ask them for you, how about tonight?"

"Tonight, that is a bit soon!"

"Nina, if you're tired there is no better night than tonight, and you've got plenty of time to prepare for it because it's only 11am," he looked up at the clock. He was right.

"Okay," I muttered. I knew I needed this, but it felt so hard. Bobby arranged it all, which was sweet of him, they were picking Jacqueline up at 3pm, so I had time to enjoy my evening a little before sleeping, I felt nervous about letting her out of my sight. Mrs Watson arrived, I could see how excited she was, it put me at ease.

"Oh, Nina, thank you so much for letting us have her for the night, she will be under my watchful eye from now until we bring her back tomorrow, you just relax and have a glass of wine, now that you can!" I kissed Jacqueline goodbye, sniffed in her beautiful baby scent and handed the bags over to Mr Watson and they took Jacqueline with them. I took a deep breath, I missed her already.

It felt strange round the house. Bobby had gone to teach tennis and I was sat in the bath, with no bump, and no baby, it didn't feel right. I got out of the bath and pampered myself, rubbing creams here, and lotions there. I got changed into my nightwear and strolled downstairs, feeling so relaxed I could have fallen asleep walking. I might treat myself to a glass of wine after all, before I hit the hay. I poured a glass and sat on the settee, the sun was setting now, and the birds were tweeting, I felt like I was on a minibreak, I looked up to see Jack's painting, and raised a glass to him, God, I missed him. My mind started to wander when the door burst opened and in walked a sweaty, panting Bobby.

"Wow, are you on the verge of a coronary?" I laughed. He laughed back through sparse breaths.

"I just ran...home...because I lost a bet...with one of the lads..." he puffed and sat on the floor near the door catching his breath. I laughed; this was highly amusing.

"What was the bet?"

"Best of three games... and I bet that I could lose graciously, it appears I am a terrible loser, and used many expletives," he walked to the sink and poured himself some water; I laughed some more.

"Well, I could have told you that, we have played cards many times and you are like a child when it comes to losing." He looked at me jokingly hurt.

"Did mum and dad get Jackie?" he asked. No one had called her Jackie before, it was sweet, it sounded more like her daddy's name.

"Yes, about two hours ago," I replied sipping my wine.

"I am just going to get washed up and I will be down, I am going to cook you your favourite dinner, to celebrate three weeks of being a mum," Bobby smiled a coy smile and headed upstairs. I stayed where I was, admiring the view and drinking the icy, dry white liquid, I hadn't realised how much I had missed wine. I had come such a long way from the dark pit of despair that I once was in, I felt like I had accomplished something. Familiar footsteps walked towards me, and Bobby sat across from me, smelling fresh, it was an appealing scent.

"Are you hungry?" I was ravenous.

"Yes! I haven't eaten properly today at all, what are you cooking for me then chef?" I jested.

"Well, I managed to get us some steaks!" he was proud of himself.

"Were you really running from the police when you got back here, did they find out you'd been buying from the black market?" He laughed.

"No, but I have a friend who is a butcher and he managed to secure me two, it's not what you know, Nina," he tapped his nose and walked off to start the prep.

The sounds of sizzling and chopping came from the kitchen and Bobby whistled to himself as he prepared the meal.

"Dinner's up," he called. I walked to the table; a meaty aroma filled my nostrils and my hunger suddenly intensified. I sat down feeling a little tipsy from the wine, that's what nine months of no drinking does to you, after only one glass. I took a bite.

"Oh, this is divine," I exclaimed.

"I do surprise myself sometimes too," he laughed. We finished our meals, laughing and joking about various things, and he cleared my plate away, poured me another glass of wine, and one for himself.

"Nina, I am glad I have got you to myself, I think we

need to talk," he sounded serious. There it is, I thought. I knew it was coming at some point, it was weeks ago since he tried to kiss me.

"Why do we?" I responded, "let's not spoil it, Bobby, tonight isn't the night, let's just forget it happened," I added calmly.

"I don't want to, Nina, I can't go on like this." I felt sick.

"What do you mean?"

"I see you every day, and it breaks my heart that I can't touch you or kiss you or be with you. I want you to be with me, and if I can't have you then I don't think I can stay," he put his head in his hands. He can't leave me too.

"Bobby, please don't do this, I need you, Jacqueline needs you, but you are asking a lot from me. I can't pretend I don't love Jack."

"I aren't asking you to stop loving him, I know he will always be number one, but for me, I am happy being number two. I love you, Nina," his voice cracked. He stared at me from across the room. Emotions ran high, I felt confused, tipsy, but I also felt a small twinge of lust for him; it was the wine, it had to be. He walked towards me, taking my face in his hands and pulled me towards his lips. We kissed passionately, he pushed me up against the wall, I still felt confused, it was happening too fast. My mind was swimming with thoughts. Did I even want this? Was I doing it so he stayed? He pushed me down, so I lay on down on the floor, and he began to unbutton my nightdress. I didn't have a moment to think, he kissed my neck down to my breasts and I moaned, I had not felt a touch like this since… Jack, no I couldn't do this.

"Bobby, stop, please," and I pushed him off me and buttoned up my nightgown, "I can't do this, it feels wrong," I whispered suddenly sobering up. He looked at me, panting, and closed his eyes for a short while, when he opened them again, it was as if he was someone else. His eyes were black, he pushed me back down to the floor, and holding me down he continued to try lift up my nightdress. "No Bobby, get off me, what are you doing? I said no." He ignored me; his upper body strength was no match for mine. He continued to try and pull down my underwear, kissing my chest, and restraining me. "GET OFF ME!" I screamed. I didn't know what else to do other than bite him, it's all I had to use to my advantage, so I clenched down on his shoulder with all my might, he winced and retreated, falling backwards.

I stood up, shaking, nauseated, what had just happened? I felt scared; I needed to get out, away from this monster. My mind was racing at one hundred miles per hour, I ran upstairs and locked myself in my bedroom. I wish Jack was here, I sobbed uncontrollably into the blanket that Jackie used – Jack, come back to me, please!

Some hours passed, it was pitch black outside, and the chirping of the crickets circled the air. I was curled up in the corner of my room, I had no idea where Bobby was, I hadn't heard a sound since the ordeal. What was he thinking? I had never seen this side to him before, how could he do this to me? *Tap tap tap,* there was a knock at my door - my stomach churned and I dare not answer.

"Nina, it's me," Bobby mumbled through the door. What if he has come back for round two? I looked about my bedroom for something I could use to hit him with and settled on a lamp.

"Go away," I muttered back.

"I am sorry, Nina, I don't know what I was thinking, please let me in, or at least come downstairs so we can talk about this, I don't want you to be frightened of me." How could I not be frightened? The man I have been living with for months, who I trusted, who is around my baby daughter, who is the brother of my late husband, had just attacked me; and I thought I knew him.

"I don't want to speak to you, Bobby, I have nothing to say," I snapped. He sighed.

"I think the whole Jack thing is getting the better of me. I have such strong feelings for you that I let them rule me, I am truly sorry," he sounded sorrowful. I should at least hear him out.

"Go downstairs and I'll be down shortly," I responded, and I heard his footsteps walk away. I unlocked my door, lamp still in hand, and headed slowly down the stairs. I entered the living room cautiously and saw Bobby sat on the settee, his packed bags stacked high at the door. He looked at me through teary eyes, I felt sorry for him.

"Nina, I am so sorry, I cannot believe I did that," he looked anywhere but at me. "I guess I just wanted you that bad, I thought maybe if we had sex, you would want me too, and would forget about Jack. Now I know that's never going to happen, is it?" I studied him for a moment, he looked genuinely disgraced with himself.

"No," is all I said back.

"I am going to stay at mum and dad's, I can understand you don't want me anywhere near you now, and I don't blame you. I just want you to know I am not a violent person, and I have never raised my hand to a woman, we weren't brought up that way. I cannot explain what just happened," he cried, his head in his hand, he was truly ashamed of himself, "I'm sorry," he whispered. I set the lamp down and wearily approached him, he had convinced me that he meant no harm, and most of me believed it, this was partly my fault, I had led him on unbeknownst to me.

"I am sorry too. Bobby, if we had met in another life and Jack hadn't been involved who knows. I care for you deeply, as a friend, and I honestly do love you, as Jackie's uncle, but we could never be together. I've just had Jack's baby, he's only been gone since May, and I will never stop loving him, and to get with anyone else is going to take a while, let alone his own brother. To sleep with you tonight would have been for the wrong reasons. Do you understand?" He looked at me sadly for a moment.

"Of course, I do, I am sorry for pushing my feelings onto you, you don't need this in your life, I won't mention it again," he stood up and walked towards the door. Why did I feel so bad that he was leaving? I was going to be alone with a baby; I was not ready for that. I am not strong enough for that. Part of me still needed him.

"Where are you going?" I hastily walked after him.

"To mum and Dad's," he started to open the door.

"No, you don't need to," I pleaded. He looked at me surprised.

"Nina how can I be around you after what I have just done?"

"I aren't saying you are forgiven, but I understand, let's just put it behind us...keep calm and carry on," I feigned a smiled. He turned to look at me sorrowfully.

"Okay, I'll stay, if you really want me to," and he walked back in, closing the door. He approached me slowly, holding out his hand to shake mine. "I'm sorry," I shook it hesitantly and turned to go up to my bedroom. He had almost raped me, and I had just let him back in to my house and life, due to being terrified of being on my own, what a fucking mess, I thought. Where had that strong twenty-one-year-old Nina gone? I cried uncontrollably as I walked up the stairs, mostly in despair of what an absolute mess my life had become.

Chapter 10

Nina

Obviously, I did not sleep much last night at all, which defeated the object completely of Mr and Mrs Watson having Jacqueline. Thoughts of what Bobby had done, how easy I had forgiven him and what a situation we were in swarmed through my mind. There was a small knock at my door.

"Good morning, Nina, I have made you a coffee," he was grovelling. As much as I needed him around, I was hopeful that he was going to try keep his distance from me. I felt wary of him, and I didn't want Jackie noticing that. I knew no harm would come to her, he doted on her as if she were his own, and I believed him when he said he had never lifted a finger to anyone before, this was all my fault. I had decided in the midst of overnight thinking, that I was going to ask for more help from Mr and Mrs Watson with Jacqueline, because they doted on her anyway and I was struggling. I needed to be the best I could be for her; and without Jack around to help, his family were the next best thing.

"Thanks," I managed, "I will be down shortly." His footsteps marched away, and I heard the sound of the front door opening and closing. I exhaled relaxing and fell into a deep sleep.

I awoke to a silence, which was strange, because I thought Jacqueline would be back by now. I got dressed, looking at the clock it was midday, I felt extremely lazy.

I brushed my teeth, tore a brush through my hair, put on my makeup and headed down the stairs. I was more than surprised to find Group Captain Staines stood in my living room, and Bobby sat on the sofa with Mr Watson, both looking as if they had seen a ghost. Had he told Mr Watson already?

"Good afternoon, sir," I spoke to Group Captain Staines but looked at Bobby concerned, he just stared back at me gravely.

"What brings you here?" I continued.

"I hear congratulations are in order, Mrs Watson," he smiled proudly and tipped his cap.

"Oh, thank you, I was going to write to you, I promise, it's just been chaotic adjusting to life with a new-born." I continued to peer at Mr Watson and Bobby sat on the sofa, both were not listening to a word I had said, what was going on?

"Speaking of which, when is Mrs Watson bringing her back?" I shouted to Mr Watson, to try snap him out of the spell he appeared under.

"Sorry dear, erm, yes about that, well…"

"What has happened?" I became serious, "is she okay?" I began to reach for my coat in a panic.

"Nina please can you just stop for a moment, we have something to tell you," Group Captain Staines replied sternly.

"Is Jackie okay?" I demanded.

"Yes, she is absolutely fine," Mr Watson replied, please listen to the Captain, Nina," he pointed towards Staines. I turned to face him.

"I aren't sure how to say this, I am still coming to terms with it myself to be quite frank. British soldiers managed to break through into Calais; we managed to take back the prisoner of war camp, where we believe Jack was held." I felt sick, they had found his body hadn't they? I interrupted him.

"Sir, please…I don't want to hear what state he was in; you've found his body haven't you? With the greatest respects, I imagine him being that man over there," and I pointed to the painting, "it will give me nothing but nightmares to think of him any other way, or to hear that he struggled," I put my hand to my face. There was a firm knock at the door.

"Actually, no that's not what I was going to say," he continued as a military man entered the house, followed by a shabby looking man wrapped in a green blanket, I did a double take… it was Jack! It couldn't be real, was I dreaming? I looked at Bobby and Mr Watson who stood facing the door, both in disbelief. I stared at him and rubbed my eyes - he looked painfully thin, his chin was covered by a huge beard and his hair was longer yet straggly. He wore mud-stained trousers and a brilliant white t-shirt which was illuminous against his deeply tanned skin. There were cuts upon his face, and he looked exhausted. He didn't gaze at me once; he just stared towards the ground like a child that had been told off by its parents. Was it really him?

"Son," Mr Watson walked towards him, Jack finally looked up at him, it was definitely my Jack, I could spot those shocking blue eyes a mile away. My heart palpitated - I thought he was dead, I grieved for him, I was still grieving for him, his daughter was only a mile or so away and he had never met her. How had he survived?

"Hi, Dad," he managed. My heart broke; he seemed meek, what had they done to him over there?

"Why don't you come in, Jack?" Group Captain Staines ushered him in, he walked further towards the living room, I stood back observing, as though I was watching the animals at the zoo.

"Would you like a drink of something?" Bobby enquired, not knowing what else to say.

"No thanks," Jack replied. I still daren't speak, and Jack had still not looked at me, had he even noticed I was here?

"Take a seat son."

"I'm good as I am thank ye'" Jack replied quickly to his dad, he didn't want to make conversation. My breathing was heavy yet shallow, I needed to say something, I just couldn't think of what to say. I tried to speak, but the words wouldn't come out. Staines looked at me understandingly and put his head down.

"Jack was found in the prisoner of war camp that we took over, along with ten other soldiers," Staines continued. Jack bowed his head once more; what was going through his mind? My poor man.

"Jack," I whispered, it didn't mean to come out like a whisper but my throat was so dry. He looked at me, finally, my eyes pricked with tears, he was back, but it was as though he didn't recognise me. There was no joy in his eyes, he looked lost, and troubled.

"Hi, Nina," he whispered back.

"I thought you were dead," I muttered holding back sobs, "can I…" I looked around, "come to you?" I asked. I didn't want to overstep the mark, I had no idea what he was thinking, maybe he didn't even love me anymore.

Jack didn't seem to know how to answer; he just stared at me, unsure, like a rabbit in headlights. I started to approach him gingerly; our eyes did not fall from one another. I got a few inches away from him, so we were standing face to face. I could see the pain in his eyes, he faintly smiled at me, and I didn't think for another second, I leapt forward and hugged him tightly. At first, he didn't respond but eventually he raised his hands around me and embraced me back. I sobbed on his shoulder.

"Jack, I have missed you so much!"

"I've missed ye' too," his familiar voice replied as though it didn't mean the words that it spoke, it was Jack's body, but it didn't feel like the same soul. The whole room just watched on as we hugged, I didn't want it to end. I eventually pulled away, holding onto his hands.

"Would you like me to run you a bath? Or cook you some food? Or you could sleep? Jacqueline will be back soon, but she won't keep you awake, I promise." He looked at me wide-eyed.

"Ye' had a girl?" He didn't even know he was a dad.

"Yes," I beamed, "she is three weeks old, and I named her Jacqueline, after you," I smiled. His eyes filled with tears, he looked at Group Captain Staines.

"I cannae do this," and he stormed out of the house, leaving the green blanket in a pile, discarded on the floor, like my heart. I was left stood alone again, even more confused than before, did he not want us?

"Nina, it is going to take time to adjust back to normal life, he has been through a terrible ordeal, and missed out on his daughter being born, it's going to be hard for him. God only knows what he went through in there," Group Captain Staines patted my shoulder empathetically and followed Jack outside.

"I understand," I forced a smile and turned to face Bobby, he put his head down, I was losing everyone I cared about.

"Why don't Delilah and I have Jacqueline again for tonight, just so he can get adjusted? It is probably not the right time for him to meet her," he was right, I wanted the transition for Jack to be as easy as possible.

"Yes, that is fine, I will come to yours for a short while, and let him get sorted here on his own, and I can see Jacqueline then too."

"I'll leave you to it tonight too, I'll stay at mum and dad's," Bobby added.

"Thank you," I smiled, grateful for Jack's family once again.

I spent the afternoon with Jacqueline, which left Jack and Group Captain Staines in the house on their own. I was half expecting to get a visit from Staines to say, Jack doesn't want you to return tonight, but that never came and now it was time to go back and see him. I was feeling apprehensive about what was in store for us, but also frightened that he no longer wanted Jackie, or me and that I would lose him all over again. I walked back to the house slowly, taking my time and practicing what I might say, it didn't come naturally to me like it used to, he was clearly not the same man. I slowly entered the house; only the lamp was on in the living room, it was deathly quiet. I thought I was alone and that he must have gone back with Staines.

"Hello", I shouted, checking for signs of life. There

was a small bang upstairs followed by footsteps. My heart was pounding, I felt dizzy and sick, what was he going to say to me, was he just getting his belongings together about to leave? He entered the living room timidly, looking so familiar to me. He had shaved, and his hair was styled in the same way as before he went to war. His clothes were his own from our wardrobe, which I hadn't wanted to throw away when I heard about his sudden death. They hung off him slightly as he was much thinner, but he was still my handsome Jack, stood with his hands in his pockets, mirroring the Jack I first met in Mr and Mrs Watson's living room.

"Hey, just so you know, if you want to be alone, I am happy to go stay at your parents, you take as much time as you need," I smiled warmly. He surprised me and smiled back.

"No…it's fine, please, it's your house," he replied.

"It's our house, Jack," I added reassuringly.

"Yeah," and his gaze fell to the floor.

"It's so weird to see you here, in the flesh, I can't tell you how many times I dreamt about this happening, I can't quite believe it is you," I choked.

"I'm sorry," he whispered.

"Sorry for what?" I asked.

"For leaving ye', letting ye' down, missing the birth of our daughter," he seemed broken.

"Jack, please don't, you have nothing to be sorry about, none of this was your fault," I began to approach him. "I can't imagine what hell you've had to endure, but I am here if and when you want to talk about anything," I got nearer to him, he looked away and clenched his jaw, he was really messed up, he held back tears, and backed away from me, heading towards the sofa. After a few moments of silence, and getting himself together, he looked up at his painting.

"Handsome chap, isn't he?" I joked. He smiled at my attempt at humour.

"I'm afraid I won't be much company for a while, Nina," he apologised. I didn't care, I just loved having him near me.

"I don't mind, I am just so glad you are back where you belong," I sat next to him, but left enough distance so I wasn't crowding him. He looked at me gratefully.

"Let's play cards," I quipped. He looked up at me dismayed, I knew he just wanted a small ounce of normality, something to take away the months of pain and suffering for us both, he wasn't ready to talk. He smiled.

"You've not changed."

"Nope, still as annoying as ever," I laughed. Little did he know everything that had gone on here, I had changed, but I wasn't about to let him know.

"No, you're wonderful," and he looked at me intensely, "thoughts of ye' got me through that hell hole," he winced. I looked at him, waiting with bated breath at whatever it was he wanted to say next.

"Our wedding day became too painful a memory, but the one that got me through the hardest times was sitting out there on the veranda, watching the world go by, listening to the birds tweeting, and looking across the table at ye', sat there with your little bump," he fondly smiled looking out of the patio doors. "That gave me courage, and the energy to face another day," he tapered off. I reached for his hand, and he didn't move it.

"So, you still love me?" I asked meekly, scared of what he might say. He grabbed my hand tightly with his other hand, so our hands lay rested on one another.

"So much," he began to sob, I hugged him tightly, crying back, and we sat in a weeping embrace. We hugged for an hour; I didn't dare let him go again. He was so fragile; I thought he might break if I turned my back on him.

"I'm quite tired now, I might try sleep if that's okay?" he asked.

"You don't need to ask me, Jack, you do whatever you want, I just want you to feel at ease," I smiled back at him lovingly. He collected his jacket and started to walk upstairs, I considered kissing him, but I was not sure he was ready for that sort of intimacy just yet. I was in a predicament; I didn't know whether I could get into our bed if he was there, would he want me there with him?

"Let me just get my things out of our bedroom and then you can have it to yourself," I shouted after him, hoping this would give me my answer; I prayed he wanted me near him.

"Actually, I was going to sleep in the guest room," he added. I felt disappointed, it answered my question, but I knew he just needed time.

"Okay, no problem, just to let you know, erm, Bobby moved in, he's been staying in that room," he glared at me with a serious expression.

"But the other room is free, the one that is going to be Jackie's playroom, I can make the bed up for you," I smiled, he seemed mad.

"Why did he move in?" he replied confused.

"It was a spur of the moment thing really, I was getting

bigger, and lonelier, and he wanted to move to Ruislip, and he couldn't find anywhere, so I just suggested it," I answered coolly, I didn't see the issue, but Jack seemed really put out.

"When did he move in then?" he probed.

"Erm, May time, you were still…" I put my head down awkwardly, daring not to finish the sentence.

"I was still what?" he enquired.

"Alive," I looked at him sadly. He didn't know what to say, I could tell he had not thought about the fact we had all grieved for him; he sat down on the stairs and ran his hands through his hair. He shook his head.

"I am in my own bubble at the minute, Nina, I honestly didn't think about how ye' would all have moved on," he huffed.

"I don't expect you to think about that now. We didn't move on, I definitely didn't, but naturally we grieved, we held a memorial for you," he looked upset.

"Well thank god for Bobby," he said, almost jealously, it was as if he could read my mind, I felt like he knew about what had happened.

"Please don't be like that, I was lonely and very pregnant, and you were…at the time I had no idea where you were. I waited for your letter, but it never came. The plan was he would live here, then move out when you got home, but you never came home!" I was raising my voice. I don't know why, it wasn't Jack's fault, but I had never said my feelings out loud, I felt robbed of my pregnancy and the time I could have had with Jack. Did he expect me to just stay at home alone forevermore? Jack stared at me, with no emotion.

"I understand," he stood up and walked upstairs with

nothing further to add. How had we just had such a heated discussion so close to his return. He had come back from the dead, I was overjoyed to see him, yet we had bickered. I felt guilty and wretched; he just needed more time that was all. He slept in the spare room, and I slept in our room, I didn't sleep a wink, I was distraught for letting myself become so overridden with emotion that we had more or less argued. It was my fault; I was trying to push him too hard to be like the old Jack, when he might never be him again. I bet he didn't sleep either, the first time back home after whatever he went through must be peculiar. I had so many questions for him. I contemplated going into his room in the middle of the night to show him I was sorry and that I was close by, but I thought that may overstep the mark. It was hard to believe he was my husband at this moment in time. I eventually got up and made my way downstairs, Mrs Watson was sat with Jack on the sofa, he had the same expressionless look on his face, he observed me as I entered the room.

"Morning, dear," Mrs Watson said quietly.

"Morning, I am going to go see Jacqueline, I'll leave you to it." I wanted to give him the space he needed. I put on my coat and walked out of the house. I didn't know how to act around him, and I missed my daughter incredibly, I needed a cuddle, and some familiarity. I took the long way round to Mrs Watson's house, I had acted like an idiot, the truth is I didn't know how to be, and I wasn't good at dealing with my emotions. You would think I'd be a professional at it by now.

"Hi beautiful baby," I walked in and took Jackie in my arms, "oh, I have missed you," and I kissed her on her forehead. The only piece of normality in my life right now.

"How did it go?" Bobby enquired pouring us both a cup of tea.

"Awful," I was honest; he was probably delighted at that.

"Why?" he quizzed.

"He didn't take well to you living with us," I explained. Bobby seemed confused and hurt.

"Why not?" I whispered, "I don't know but I felt like he could tell something had happened."

"Did you tell him?" He seemed panicked.

"Of course not!" I replied with conviction, still wary of Bobby, "there is nothing to tell anyway," I lied, taking my gaze away from him. Bobby stared at me hurt.

"Right," and he poured the milk. I changed the subject away from me and him.

"I don't know how to be around him, he puts up a barrier, which I expected, but then to show the emotion he did when I said you moved in for company was strange."

"Actually, is it strange, Nina? He has been gone since February, and the man closest to him has moved into his family home to take care of his pregnant wife?" I hadn't thought of it like that.

"But he shouldn't want me to be alone!"

"He doesn't, but you've been pushed into living with another man, and he must sense something about how I feel, it was written all over my face yesterday."

"Bobby let's not go there," I insisted. "I think you should all come for dinner tonight, he needs to meet Jacqueline, and when he sees us together, he will realise that there's nothing between us."

"I don't think I can pretend, Nina," he answered seriously.

"Bobby, please, he doesn't need to know, don't you think he's been through enough?" I snapped. He slammed my cup down on the table and stormed off, I seemed to be making enemies left, right and centre here, I cuddled my baby girl and closed my eyes. I was coming off as the bad person in all of this.

Mrs Watson came home, and I knew she wasn't going to be overjoyed with how I had just left the house, she was going to be overprotective towards Jack, and she had every right to be, but I did it to give him space, surely they can see that. I felt like I was having to justify every decision I was making at the minute, it was exhausting.

"Are you alright, dear?" she quizzed taking her coat off.

"Yes fine," I lied. I quickly changed the subject before she asked any further questions. "How do you fancy dinner at mine tonight? All of us together, for Jack."

"Splendid idea, I will make my famous dessert, he loves my bread-and-butter pudding!" and she totted off into the living room. I followed behind snuggling Jacqueline; she was the only person I felt secure with now. I stayed there most of the day, not daring to go back home, I wasn't sure how I would introduce Jacqueline, or what it would even do to him, but it might also make him feel more at ease. It neared two pm, I left Jacqueline with Mrs Watson again and headed back home, they were due to arrive in two hours, so I needed to brace the subject with Jack. As I neared home, I saw

Jack sat on the veranda; I stopped to enjoy the view. I knew he was in his happy space there, the place that brought him solitude and hope when his life was bleak and close to death. He didn't know I was watching him; it was so nice to see him home where he belonged, he looked the most at ease that I had seen him yet. I walked slowly towards the veranda, and he spotted me walking across the garden, he took in a deep breath of preparation - that's how I felt too. I smiled.

"Hello," I tried to be breezy.

"Hi," he looked at me, there seemed to be more of a glimmer in his eyes.

"So, your parents and Bobby were going to come for dinner tonight, if that is okay?"

"Yep" he nodded. I cleared my throat, "and Jacqueline, I mean, if you are ready." He nodded his head but he looked doubtful. "Jack don't feel pressured, there is no rush," I tried to ease his mind.

"She's my daughter, I will have to meet her at some point," he seemed worried.

"Don't be nervous, Jack, she already loves you and hasn't even met you yet, you're her daddy remember! She has slept in your blanket since she was born."

"I know, I know," he replied quietly. I smiled a reassuring smile and walked away, I wasn't going to get much more from him, and I didn't need it, we were making small steps. I began to prep dinner feeling a little more cheerful than this morning. I was going to make Jack's favourite, a hearty beef roast, something to make him feel at home. As usual I hadn't given myself enough time, so I was spinning plates as Jack walked in. He had stayed outside most of the afternoon.

"Can I do anything to help?" he could see I was flustered, and displayed a slight smile on his face, maybe he did miss my chaotic nature. I really wanted him to be involved; this was the most engagement he had shown me.

"Yes, that would be great; could you maybe peel the potatoes?" I smiled. He walked over to the kitchen counter and picked up the knife, he examined it for a while, I looked at him out of the corner of my eyes, what was he doing? He held it in his hands, studying it intently; it was as if he couldn't bring himself to use it, as though he was frightened of the blade.

"Are you alright?" I asked.

"Yes, please stop asking me if I am okay," he snapped throwing the knife onto the kitchen counter. He stormed off upstairs, once again I was failing, I just bit my tongue and carried on dicing the carrots, I closed my eyes and fought back the tears, everything I was doing was wrong. The door opened and in they walked, Bobby could see I was upset. I put the knife down and went to cuddle Jacqueline, wiping the tears discreetly as I walked.

"Dinner is going to be a short while yet, would you like a drink?"

"I'll do them," Bobby offered.

"Where is Jack?" Mrs Watson asked curiously.

"Oh, I think he is having a lie down," I lied. I walked back into the kitchen to finish cutting the carrots, Mr and Mrs Watson cooed over Jacqueline, and Bobby poured the drinks.

"Can I help at all?" he asked.

"Yes please, those spuds won't chop themselves," I

jested trying to make light of the situation and hiding the fact that Jack and I had argued twice in two days.

"Are you okay?" he mouthed. I wasn't but didn't want to get into it; I smiled.

"Of course." He knew I was lying; he threw potato peel at me; I laughed and threw a carrot back.

"Missed," he said ducking out of the way. He came closer to me, brushing my shoulder as he washed the potatoes, I looked up at him and he stared back at me. Oh no, am I leading him on again, I put my head down quickly to diffuse the situation.

"Jack," Mrs Watson exclaimed, "How long have you been standing there?" We both turned around to see Jack stood in the doorway, watching us. I felt guilty; we weren't doing anything so why did I feel that way.

"Hi bro," Bobby said coyly. Jack just looked at him, without saying a word. He looked at me in the same blank manner, the same as he had done the night he stood with Clara at the door of his parents, as if I meant nothing to him.

"There's a special someone here to see you tonight, Jack," Mrs Watson looked at me, as if to say come and get Jacqueline, I responded.

"No, you go, it's fine," she looked confused but held Jacqueline up to Jack. His eyes lit up, he smiled at her, the first time I had seen him properly beam. I realised in that moment that our love might be dead. He didn't look at me that way anymore; he seemed to look at me with nothing but emptiness. Before he went off to war whenever he looked at me, it was full of love and pride, and now nothing. I had mixed emotions, I was so happy that he loved her, but distraught that it could be over for him and me forever. Bobby distanced himself from me and went to sit on the settee, I watched Jack with Jacqueline some more and then got back to making dinner, daring not to look in Bobby's direction.

"She is your double mate, look at them eyes," Bobby made conversation.

"Yeah?" Jack seemed delighted with that news. I wanted to join in, but I felt uncomfortable, this was not right.

"What do you think Nina, him or you?" Thanks Bobby, I thought rolling my eyes, I turned round and put on a fake smile.

"Well, she is as pretty as her daddy is handsome, and she definitely has your eyes Jack," I concurred. Jack looked at me as if he was trying to analyse me.

"Are ye' sure she's mine?" I couldn't believe what he had just said.

"What?" I whispered disgusted.

"Just kidding," he laughed insincerely. Mr and Mrs Watson looked at one another, confused by the allegation, but no one responded. I didn't know what to say, who was this man, and what has he done with my Jack?

Dinner was an awkward affair, I barely ate, Jack spoke a little, mainly about Jacqueline, and Bobby kept looking at me throughout. I was glad when it was over. They said their goodbyes and I went to put Jacqueline to bed. I came back downstairs, half-expecting Jack to be in bed just to avoid me, but he stood washing the pots. He turned to look at me, as he dried his hands on the tea towel.

"Thanks for dinner," he said sweetly. He was like

Jekyll and Hyde, one minute he appeared to hate me and the next he was like the sweet, caring Jack that I knew and loved.

"You're welcome," I replied struggling to keep up with his moods, it was draining. I understand he was shell-shocked; I had done some reading up on it at the library when I was in school. People come back from the war and didn't act like themselves anymore; they're scarred and wounded in their minds from what they have been put through. I understood the concept, but I just wish I knew the remedy.

"Would you like a glass of wine?" he asked, and I accepted. He sat opposite me, his elbows rested on his thighs and his fists were clenched into a ball in front of his face, he looked at me gravely.

"Remember when we finally got rid of Harry, how happy we felt that we could finally be together with no drama, no other people getting in the way?"

"Yes," where was he going with this.

"It's happened again hasn't it," he had an indignant expression on his face.

"What do you mean?" I gulped my wine.

"What's happened between you and Bobby? I deserve to know Nina," he looked saddened. I couldn't tell him the truth, he couldn't handle it, but I had to be honest, we were man and wife, and I didn't want to lie to him, especially if we had any hope of moving forward. He had obviously spotted something between us, I felt rotten. I sighed.

"Do you promise not to get mad?" He shut his eyes tightly.

"I can't make those promises, Nina, it's not fair of ye'

to ask me." I carried on, my heart racing with worry.

"Since you've been gone, there have been a few moments between Bobby and I that neither of us could explain."

"Like what?" He wanted to know everything.

"The odd touch here, the long awkward stare there, we both put it down to grief. Well, I did anyway."

"What is that supposed to mean?"

"I am telling you this because I love you, Jack, and you deserve to know everything before you decide if you want to be with me anymore," he continued to listen. "A few weeks back Georgie came to visit, and I set her up on a date with Bobby, they both reluctantly agreed to go, but it ended with nothing happening between them. Georgie told me the following day that Bobby had got drunk and declared his love for me." Jack glanced sideways, not giving any emotion away. I continued, "The following day when everyone had gone, he told me himself that he had fallen in love with me," Jack exhaled deeply, shaking his head.

"So ye' slept with him?" He outright asked.

"No, of course not! I went into labour before we could even finish the conversation."

"He did it whilst ye' were pregnant?" He asked angrily.

"Yes, but we didn't talk about it again, until a few nights ago." The pain of the attack began to creep back, how scared I had been, how I had just forgiven him, so I had someone in my life, I was ashamed to tell him about it.

"Go on," he urged.

"Jackie stayed at your mum and dad's house, and he

cooked me a meal, and told me he wanted to talk," I hung my head. I kissed Bobby back; whatever I was going to say next was going to hurt him. He stared at me hanging on for my next word. "We kissed, and it did become heated," I looked at the living room floor sadly, Jack followed my gaze.

"So ye' fucked him?" He was raging now, his breath raced.

"No! Not exactly, you have to remember Jack that I had not long since had a baby. All I wanted was you, he was here, and I thought maybe that was what I wanted. He started to undress me and kiss me, and I feel sick thinking about this, but he reminded me of you." Jack stood up and walked towards the window, looking out on the garden so he didn't have to see me, his fists were clenched.

"I stopped it, Jack, as soon as I thought of you I stopped it there and then, only Bobby..."

"Only Bobby what?" He turned round, more curious now.

"Bobby didn't want it to stop." I put my head down, how do I tell him the next bit? He neared me, crouching down in front of me.

"What do ye' mean?" Tears crept into my eyes, the night was coming back to me, how afraid and helpless I had felt.

"He pushed me to the ground and continued to try taking my underwear off, he kept kissing me, and I was saying no, it was like he couldn't hear me, he just wanted me." I looked up at Jack, his eyes were wide with fury, he was grinding his back teeth with force. "I finally got him off me by biting him, but he realised straight away what he had done," Jack didn't say a word, he stood up and stormed out of the house, I knew where he was going. What could I do, Jackie was in bed? I couldn't follow him, so I telephoned through to Mrs Watson.

"Hello…" I cut her off.

"Mrs Watson it's Nina, please can you come and watch Jackie, it's urgent," I sounded panicked, what was Jack going to do.

"Of course, dear…" I cut her off again.

"Please rush!" I put the phone down. She will see Jack walking there, I needed her to hurry, I didn't have time to wait, I took Jackie from her crib, wrapped her in a blanket and set off to Mrs Watson's house. It was so cold outside, and I felt terrible for getting Jackie out of bed, but I needed to make sure Jack didn't do anything he would regret. As I walked in, I heard arguments, I entered the living room and saw Mr Watson in the corner holding a furious Jack back.

"Mrs Watson, please take Jackie," I shouted, she did as she was told and left the room.

"Go on then, deny it in front of, Nina," Jack screamed.

"She wanted it too!" Bobby bellowed, how dare he? My face was white with shock.

"Don't deny it, Nina, the looks you gave me, the hugs we shared, the nights we sat on the sofa and you put your legs up on me. You kissed me back that night, you let me undress you, you wanted more, you acted like my wife, and we weren't even married. Sex was the only thing missing," he had convinced himself. Jack stood taking it all in.

"What is going on here?" Mr Watson sounded stern.

"I'll be honest," Bobby continued.

"I have feelings for Nina, I can't lie to you, Jack, I am in love with her." Jack laughed.

"Love her? ye' don't know what love is, you've never had a proper girlfriend in your whole life."

"You fell in love with her quickly having never experienced real love before, so why can't I?" Bobby responded. I didn't know where to look. "She loves me too, but couldn't move past you, and now you are back to royally mess things up again. I would have made her mine, given the time," he was so cock sure of himself.

"That is enough, Bobby!" Mr Watson shouted.

"Do ye' love him, Nina?" Jack looked at me regretfully. I didn't hesitate.

"NO, I don't, I love you, Jack. I can't explain why I kissed him, I missed you, I was lonely, and he reminded me of you," I answered honestly. "It will always be you, Jack." Jack sat down on the sofa; he was a broken man, a former version of himself. We all stood with bated breath waiting for him to reply.

"Nina, I know I have been snappy, but I am trying to get my head around everything. I can't go into what happened over there, I don't even know where to start. I am not that man anymore; I can't even begin to explain it. I don't have the energy for this. I thought we had put all the drama behind us, but people can't leave us alone or let us be happy. I can't blame Bobby for falling in love with ye' but I can't be the Jack ye' fell in love with again." He sighed a deep exhale and walked towards me.

"This kills me to say, but you're better off without me," his words cut through me like a dagger. "I think we need some time apart; I think we should get a divorce," he finished and began to walk past me. I grabbed his arm.

"No, Jack, you don't mean it, you are just struggling, I will give you space, and you will come round. Whatever happened between Bobby and I, it meant nothing." He looked at me, he pulled the hair from my eyes as he did once before.

"I mean it, Nina, I need to be on my own, and ye' need to be with someone who can care for ye' both and can provide for ye' and give ye' the life ye' deserve. Ye' need to think about Jacqueline now." I was furious.

"You married me for richer or poorer, in sickness and in health, well this is sickness, you are not well up here Jack," I pointed to his head, "And I get why, but I am here for you. I am Nina Hughes remember," tears fell from his eyes once more. "We've been through so much shit in our short relationship. Since we've met, we've lost a baby, had a baby, been bombed, been married, you nearly died, I nearly died, and had two people try to steer us from one another. If we can get through any of that then this is a piece of cake!" I grabbed his face. "Go to that stream near the barn in your head, find that peace, I will be waiting for you." Somewhere in my mind, I knew I had lost him. Jack looked at Bobby and his dad, he was processing everything I had said, and then he uttered those fateful words.

"I don't love ye' anymore, Nina." I released his arm.

"But you said yesterday..." he cut me off.

"I lied. When I saw ye' I didn't feel anything... I knew it was what ye' wanted to hear. I'm sorry. I feel nothing about anything at the moment." I stared at him speechless for a minute, taking it all in.

"Well congratulations, Jack, you've managed to break my heart once more." I nudged past Bobby out of the door into the street, hot tears fell down my face, I needed to be alone.

Jack

I was never going to be good enough for that girl now, she needed to hear those words, it was the only way she would let me go. My dad looked at me pitifully, Bobby stared at me, both trying to work out what was going on in my head; even I didn't know. I couldn't relax anymore, every noise I heard made me jump, I was scared of my own shadow. My mind was a jungle, everything incoherent as though it had a dark cloud hovering above it. My thoughts kept going back to Collier burning in that plane, and the literal torture I had suffered, everywhere I turned, there was something to remind me of hell. I had taken the worst types of beatings from the Nazi's, they had whipped me, cut me, burned me, sliced me, made me watch innocent people be killed, starved me, and worked me to the bone; how was I ever going to function normally again? Normal life seemed pointless. I felt like I should be grateful to be here, but I felt lifeless, like I hadn't died physically in Calais, but I had died mentally.

"I know you hate me, Jack," Bobby muttered, "but why did you just do that to her?" I was filled with so much anger. How could my brother betray me like this? How could he hurt Nina in that way? He knew Nina was the love of my life, whether I was alive or dead, what right did he have to try and take her, and make her his own? She will always be my Nina, not his.

"Don't ye' fucking speak to me," I pointed at him, "ye' disgust me," I seethed.

"I can't help how I feel, Jack, you were gone, and we got to know one another…"

"NO, ye' fucking took advantage of her, knowing she was pregnant, and knowing she was grieving! Ye' forced her to try and have sex with ye' have ye' any idea how warped that is?!" He didn't even seem remorseful.

"What does it matter anyway, you've got rid of her now, she's fair game again." I saw red; I charged towards Bobby and punched him in his face, multiple times, I couldn't stop.

"Don't fucking speak about her that way, she won't touch ye'", I continued to punch him on the floor, my dad pulled me off him. I put my hands against the wall to catch my breath.

"Stop it, Jack!" My dad shouted at me.

"If he wasn't here, I would have killed ye', you're scum!" I walked past Bobby curled up on the floor bleeding and threw open the door storming out into the cold dusk. I had no feelings towards that man. He was not my brother anymore, not after today. I had nowhere to go, everything seemed unfamiliar to me now, I found myself walking towards the train station. I had no belongings and no money, all I thought was, I need to see Staines, and there was no one I would rather see than him right now. I arrived in Biggin Hill, managing to slope off the train without paying for my fare. I knew this place like the back of my hand, it was late, it must have been nine pm by now, and the chill in the air had followed me. I walked into the main camp, this place

215

was the last place I saw before Calais, I stopped to take a deep breath, this felt more like home to me, I felt more at peace here.

"Fuck me, am I seeing things, Watson is that you?" I turned around to see Megson approaching me. He walked towards me in disbelief.

"Mate I thought you were…how the hell are you?" and he hugged me, slapping my back.

"I've been better, I was hoping to see Staines, is he around?" I wasn't in the mood for chat, as much as I loved this guy, I needed to clear my head, I just wanted the Group Captain.

"Yeah, he's in his usual tent, listen when you are ready to catch up let me know, it's really good to see you," and he walked off. I bounded towards the tent and flung open the curtains.

"Jack, what are you doing here?" Group Captain Staines exclaimed surprised.

"I need help, sir," I sounded desperate.

"Okay, Okay, what's happened, sit yourself down," he did his usual thing and poured us both a glass of whisky, the pure gold liquid that makes life feel just that little bit better. He passed me the glass and I chugged it straight down. "Talk to me," he said gently.

"I'm lost. My marriage is over, I will probably never see my daughter again, I've just beaten my brother to a pulp and my mum and dad think that I am a psycho," I poured my heart out, like verbal vomit. Staines took it all in.

"Let's start with the first, most important thing, what happened with Nina?" Just hearing her name made me miserable, I had well and truly blown it with her.

"I told her I wanted a divorce and that I didn't love her anymore," I choked back the tears, a lump formed in my throat. I acted like a bastard, but I had done it for the right reasons, I knew I had, deep down. Staines patted me on the back.

"Why did you do that? You're a logical man, you don't do things for no reason," he understood me; he seemed to know me better than anyone at the moment.

"She was unhappy, and she wouldn't let me go. I know in her head me returning was the best thing ever to happen to her and Jacqueline, but how it actually played out was far from how she had imagined. But she loves me and would do anything for me, regardless. For that reason, I had no choice; I had to lie, so she would let me go. I can't be the husband or the man that she wants me to be," I poured myself another whisky and took a hefty swig. "I was pretty convincing, it was the hardest thing I've ever had to do, to bare face lie to the woman I adore more than anything in this world. She needs to start again, and find love, I just hope it's not Bobby, I will kill him."

"Bobby, as in your brother?" Staines asked confused.

"Aye, he announced that he is in love with her, after Nina told me that he tried to force himself on her," it made me feel sick saying it out loud, all I could picture was his hands all over her, kissing her, when all she wanted was for him to stop.

"I wanted to kill him then and I still do now."

"How does it make you feel?" he asked calmly.

"Disgusted, in him, not her. I understand she thought I was dead, she was grieving, pregnant and alone, but he took advantage of her!"

"Jack, I had to tell your family that you had gone down, Bobby was devastated," he spoke slowly.

"I don't believe a word that comes out of his mouth, what sort of sick bastard does that to a woman, not just any woman, my wife!" I was seething with him.

"How does Nina feel about him?"

"I don't know, she is upset and confused about everything. She said she loves me and that they would never be together, and I do believe her. What I don't get, is why she let him stick around when he had done that to her?"

"Grief does weird things to you, Jack, maybe she thought that it was Bobby's way of dealing with your loss, or maybe she just needed someone, anyone, to be there for her and the baby. She was in a desperate situation, and she is a good, honest person. You can't change what has happened since you have been away; you can only work to repair it. But in order to fix it, you need to fix yourself." He was right; I was in no fit state to be around people who I loved, because I was only going to do more damage.

"I know someone who specialises in a new concept, Jack; it's called Person Centred Therapy. Since the beginning of the war, I know a few soldiers who have utilised it; it might be worth a shot. Their base is in central London," he fumbled for a piece of paper on his desk.

"What is it?" I asked curiously.

"It's basically a talking therapy, where the person you speak to lets you vent, get everything off your chest and then offers some words of advice. They are professionally trained in matters of the mind, and it is all confidential," it sounded promising.

"Am I going to be prodded and poked and given medication? I don't want to end up in a loony bin," even though that is probably where I should be right now.

"I don't know the ins and out of it, Jack but it's worth making contact with this chap. It's a new concept, I am confident that the days of soldiers just having to plod on like nothing has happened to them, is changing. After World War 1, with the amount that were left shell-shocked or with extreme mental torment, something needed to change. There's nothing to be ashamed of in getting some help," he smiled reassuringly. I took the paper with an unknown man's name and address scrawled on it and put it in my pocket, I will go tomorrow. I looked around the tent reminiscing.

"It's weird being back here ye' know," I stared into my empty glass.

"I can imagine, it will get easier, Jack, time is a great healer," I hope he was right; because right now I felt like the walls were closing in on me.

"What's your plans after here?" he asked.

"I dunno if truth be told, I need to find some digs somewhere."

"Are you not going to go back home?"

"No, not right now, I can't face any of 'em," I sighed. They'd had months of getting used to me not being around, what difference would a few more months make? If I ever did go back, I wanted to be back to the man I once was, not this depleted shell. I knew where I was going to sleep tonight; I thanked Staines for his time and made my way outside.

"You know where I am, Jack, don't be a stranger!" he

called after me. I waved back towards him and went on my way.

I headed through the woods near to the camp and headed to the barn. It was still abandoned but it was how I remember it, and I was so thankful, I needed the familiarity and peace that it offered. I had taken a blanket from Staines tent, and I climbed up into our spot. I looked out onto the stream, it was just as beautiful in the moonlight, the sound was so soothing. I never thought I'd see this place again; tears pricked my eyes. I knew I was a damaged soul, I looked around the barn recollecting images of when Nina was here, and we made love, our body heat keeping us warm on that cold January day. I took out a picture from my pocket; it was Nina, the one I had kept in my tent at the camp. I had found it in a box of my belongings that she had kept in the wardrobe. I stared at it, admiring her beauty; I wish I could make her happy again. I eventually fell into a light sleep, listening to the babbling torrent, and watching over Nina's image, I will get there again, I will make it back to you, my love.

The birds tweeted in the morning sun, the stream was the first thing I saw; it looked even more beautiful on a summer's day, twisting and curling around the rockery. The smell of blossom and freshly cut grass awoke my nostrils. I was feeling refreshed and much more positive than I had felt yesterday; I was in my happy place. I was heading to London today to see, Albert Flack, the man who was apparently going to make my life better. Staines had given me some money to get myself settled whilst I was there, I was so thankful to have him as a friend.

The train ride to London was quick and before I knew it, I was in the big smoke, with no possessions except that photograph. I followed the directions and it led me to a stately home, it was huge, and a grand field surrounded it. Blushing buds scattered the grass, and the sound of a lawnmower hummed in the distance. It was luxurious, I was sure I had come to the wrong place. I pulled the great gold doorknocker that hung from the stained glassed, wooden doorframe, and a petite, elderly woman answered.

"Can I help you dear?"

"Erm, I aren't sure if I am at the right place actually, I am here to see a Mr Albert Flack, he's not expecting me, I was just given this address," she smiled warmly.

"Come and sit inside, son," and she gestured me in. I waited for five minutes while the lady walked off, I felt nervous and uneasy, was I doing the right thing? Before I had time to think about it further a dumpy, balding man approached me.

"Good morning, sir, how can I help you?"

"Are ye' Albert Flack?" I enquired.

"Indeed," he was a very posh English man; you could tell he had come from wealth. His suit was grey pinstripe, and he had a golden pocket watch fixed to his chest pocket. His thick-rimmed glasses were looped onto a chain that was tied around his neck.

"I've been given your name as someone who, erm, might be able to help me?" I said it how it was, I was amongst strangers, there was no point denying it, I needed help desperately and I trusted Staines' judgement.

"Who gave you my name?" he enquired.

"Group Captain Staines, I'm an RAF pilot…" he cut me off.

"Absolutely, what an honour to meet you, sir, what is your name?

"My name is Jack Watson," I replied.

"Come this way," he ushered me to follow him, and I did so blindly. "I was actually aware you might visit, sir." I was surprised.

"Oh how?"

"Group Captain Staines himself, he has forwarded many young, troubled soldiers onto me since the war began," he shepherded me into an office and closed the door behind me. "Please take a seat, sir." He pointed to the chair in front of the desk, he sat down on a majestic, mahogany, leather chair and put on his glasses. He was a funny looking man, he had a big black moustache, and not much hair on his head, it was as if his hair had fallen down onto his upper lip. He was plump around the middle but quite slim everywhere else. A pipe lay dormant on his desk, and a glass of water was perched next to a globe. The room itself had high ceilings, and so many books, all packed into tall bookcases that were squashed like sardines into the room. It was a magnificent looking office, something I could envisage myself in if I was ever lucky enough to rise through the ranks. I admired the view, looking around at all of his certificates, framed proudly on the wall.

"What can I do for you then, Jack?" he began to light his pipe whilst eyeing me. I didn't know what to say at first, the words 'fix me' seemed a bit desperate.

"I've been advised to speak to ye' about some form of person-centred therapy," I read from the paper Staines had provided me.

"Of course, let me introduce myself," he put his pipe down. "I am Albert Flack, I am a trained Psychologist, specialising in this new talking therapy and I have been a psychologist for eighteen years. This method is about you talking to me, opening up, and us working together to try change how you see yourself, and the issues you talk to me about. It is about getting all the horror and trauma off your chest, a problem shared is a problem halved. I can then give my expert opinion on what I think you can do to help yourself; some coping mechanisms if you like." He stopped to take a toot on his pipe. "The plan would be to live under this roof whilst we undertake the therapy, so you can be at peace, with no distractions from the real world until you're ready. Are you with me so far?" he paused for breath.

"Yes sir," I replied taking it all in.

"I don't expect much from you today, but what is your main concern, Jack? In a nutshell," he looked at me over the tops of his glasses.

"It's hard to explain, I just aren't myself anymore and I feel there is no way to get back to the normal me, it is as though there's a constant doom looming over me. I have so many vivid flashbacks of death and torture, like I am re living them all over again," it felt easier saying it aloud in front of a total stranger.

"Normal you?" he quizzed. I took a deep breath.

"The me before I was captured by the Nazis and held in a prisoner of war camp. The me that had a beautiful wife and a baby on the way," I said directly. He took his glasses off and put them down on the table.

"You poor man, this is a common case for a soldier,

it's shellshock," he empathised, "you are in the right hands. Are you ready to get a session started today? No time like the present," he insisted. What did I have to lose?

"Yes, let's go," and I began to tell him my story. After the first session I felt drained and emotional, I walked into the grounds of the estate, just feeling the breeze in my hair; I had gone back to places in my mind that I never wanted to visit again. The dark areas I had sealed up and thrown away the key for. I felt like a small weight had been lifted from my shoulders. All Albert had done was listen to me, I hadn't gone into great detail as that was going to take some time, but I had told him the gist about what I endured in camp. I touched upon Nina, Bobby and Jacqueline – he took it all in, and said nothing, he just made notes as I spoke. It was definitely therapeutic to vent to a stranger, knowing I wouldn't be judged, he wouldn't feel sorry for me or try to comfort me. The old woman from the door was called Joan, she was lovely, and had offered to go buy me some clothes, as all I had was the shirt on my back, quite literally. She showed me to my room, a small, plain yet bright room but it was all I needed, my view overlooked the blossom trees, I was more than happy with that. I sat on my bed feeling very weary after speaking for two hours about my afflictions. I'll close my eyes for a short while, I thought, and I was gone.

The next few sessions with Flack were harder. I had to talk about what I had seen and physically had to deal with in Calais in more detail. I had seen women and children beaten, and sent into gas chambers to die, they had tied me to a pole so I couldn't sleep for twenty-four hours at a time, they had beat me black and blue with whatever they could find, mainly the ends of their metal guns, and they had sliced me with knives. I have no idea why they kept me and ten other soldiers alive, some days all I had wanted to do was die, I felt like it was a pleasure or hobby to them, beating the hell out of British soldiers, I bet it gave them great satisfaction. On the day the British Army stormed the camp, I had been out in the blistering heat digging the foundations to a building, probably another barracks or gas chamber. My face had started to burn in the sun, we had had no water and the heat felt as though it was fifty degrees Celsius. I had made pals with another soldier named Dennis; he was from Newcastle and had been part of the Grenadiers. I saw his demise from start to finish; he began a burly, cocky man, and ended up a scrawny wreck, who died that very day from dehydration. If I thought how I felt losing Collier was bad, that place was no match. Some days I didn't even know how I made it through, constantly being in fear of what they were going to do next, was I going to die today, or just take a beating, would I be given water today or made to drink my own piss just to stay alive.

I have only been back from there three weeks now, and I was dealing with it better than I thought I would, maybe I was mentally stronger than I anticipated. After Collier, I realised how weak-minded a man I actually could be, every little thing seemed to get to me, but I felt stronger now, I don't know if it was the therapy or what, but the old Jack appeared to be coming back fighting. Aside from the failed marriage, beating up my brother and seeing my baby girl just once in her tiny life, I was getting there, slowly but surely. Nina would have no idea where I was, but I couldn't think about that now, I needed to get sorted, I would let her know in time.

Staines visited me often and we would sit and hark back to the good old days, about stories where Collier was involved, it felt like another lifetime. I had knocked drinking alcohol on the head, that only made me feel gloomier, and I didn't need any more misery. The therapy seemed to be working, when I caught myself thinking about the bad, I spoke with Flack, he was my very own agony aunt, and he never grew tiresome of hearing me vent. I would enter a session thinking my life is terrible, I have nothing to live for, and I would come out thinking, I am grateful to be alive, and blessed to have time on this earth to rectify any mistakes and make some new, happy memories. The man was truly a genius.

As the week went on, I was excited to wake up in a morning and see how the day went rather than turn over and wallow in my pit. I even envisaged life back in the RAF – I felt stronger, and what had happened to me, only made me more determined to make sure it didn't happen to someone else. As for my relationships, I had come to the realisation that although I loved Nina with every fibre of my being, we were bad for each other. From day one, it had been nothing but stress for both of us. Some things are worth fighting for, but not if around every corner, there was a hurdle that killed a small piece of us every single time. I was still of the mind-set that she needed someone else who could make her happier, and although I felt much more like me again, I wasn't ready for that commitment or pressure. I would love

Jacqueline with every part of me, because she was my flesh and blood, and I was hopeful Nina would still give me that chance, despite my absence. I had no feelings towards Bobby anymore, the hate and anger had diminished. I didn't want to speak to him again, he had hurt me but worse still, he had hurt Nina. I would never forgive him, because I could never trust him again. He was the worst sort of human to me. I would be amicable for my mum and dad's sake; I couldn't put that burden on them, I loved them and after all the anguish I had caused I wanted them to be happy.

Three months had passed, today was my final session with Flack, I felt ready to take on the next hurdle, I was going to go back home. I felt more like the Jack Watson that started in the RAF - no wife, no sorrow, no hurt or upset, just plain old me, who was happy go lucky and wanted to fly a plane. It was the middle of December; Christmas was coming, and I decided it was the right time to go and face home. I knew there would be some obstacles along the way, but I felt I was mentally prepared for them now. Staines had brought me my uniform, I checked myself in the mirror, I felt proud to put it back on, it had been a long slog, but I was nearly through the other side. Let battle commence, I thought. I thanked Flack for everything he had done for me.

"You've done it yourself, Jack, take credit for how head strong you really are," he smiled. Group Captain Staines stood by waiting to give me a lift to Ruislip.

"I am looking forward to being a brand ambassador for your cause Albert, more soldiers need to know about ye', and the good ye' do, I cannot thank ye' enough," and I shook his hand tightly. I put on my cap and bid farewell to Joan.

"Right, let's do this," I walked off towards Staines'
vehicle about to embark on reality.

Chapter 11

Nina

"Who's a beautiful girl?" I shrieked and blew a raspberry on Jacqueline's tummy, she giggled, what a delightful sound. It was nearing her first Christmas and I couldn't wait to make it magical. Mr and Mrs Watson were having Jacqueline tonight so I could put the decorations up in the house; I was so excited for it. There had been a light layer of snow and she really didn't know how to take it, her reactions made me squeal with laughter, and she pulled the funniest faces. I don't know what I would do without that girl. Bobby had moved out, and taken some time away from Ruislip in general, he kept in touch with Mr and Mrs Watson, but I didn't miss him one bit. I was glad he had left, because it was all too complicated, and I put myself into a compromising position just to keep him around, I needed to start being the old Nina again now. No man would walk all over me again; I wanted to set the right example for my daughter. I had not seen Jack in three months, and none of us had any idea where he was. Of course, I had been worried, but he didn't want to be found and we needed to respect that. Mr Watson had been to visit Staines who had been cagey with him on his whereabouts, he said that Jack was okay, but he needed to be alone. That was enough to suggest he was at least still alive, so we tried to get on with our lives the best we could. What Jack had said that night had cut me deep, but I couldn't force him to love me anymore. I still loved him, and thought about him daily, I was my own worst enemy really. I was enjoying maternity leave with my girl, and she was coming on in leaps and bounds; whatever I had failed at in life, I was doing okay at being a mum.

Georgie had announced to everyone that she was getting married in July of next year and I was delighted for her. She had been worried after me and Jack had ended the way we had, but I had come to terms with the fact that Jack and me were probably broken before we even started, as sad as it sounded. Faye had moved out of dad's, just for some independence, it was only round the corner, but it was a start for her, and I was happy. I had contemplated moving back home. I hadn't mentioned this to Mr and Mrs Watson because they doted on Jackie, but aside from them, there was nothing here for me anymore. I wasn't going to go back to work in the bakery, I wanted a real career, I loved being a mum, but I had always wanted something for me that made me feel like I was making a difference. Policing hadn't worked out, so I contemplated charity work that related to mental health, especially that of soldiers. I had seen how severely affected Jack had been, and I wished I had understood him better, so maybe I could have saved us. I had made a decision to study psychology once my maternity leave was over and my goal was to train to be a counsellor.

It was two pm and the snow was beginning to settle, I made the decision to take Jackie to Mr and Mrs Watson's now before it laid thicker. I got her belongings together and headed over. The flakes settled on my hair, the smell of ice laden the air, the village had put its Christmas lights up and it felt magical. Christmas was one of my favourite times of the year and to share it with Jackie was going to be wonderful.

"Helllloooooo little one," Mrs Watson took Jackie from my arms immediately and snuggled her. "Are we going to have a sleepover tonight?" I loved how she was with Jackie; she needed that stability and love from someone other than me. Jackie flashed her a big, gummy smile and Mrs Watson cooed.

"It's coming down thick out there, do you want a lift back, Nina?" Mr Watson offered, he had not been one hundred percent with me since the whole Bobby and Jack debacle, especially after I was the reason why Jack nearly left Bobby for dead. But in time, he was coming round. Mrs Watson was more familiar with matters of the heart and said she understood where we were all coming from. Even though she was Jack and Bobby's mum she continued to treat me like her daughter, it was something I had been missing for so long, I treasured her.

"No, I will walk thanks, I love the snow, it's so peaceful," I followed Mrs Watson into the living room, and all of us gathered round Jackie who lay on the rug in the middle of the floor. "She's been giggling like a trooper today!" I announced. I heard the door bang.

"Oh, shoot I must have left it open," I stood up to go close it and in he walked, it was Jack, with Group Captain Staines.

"Hi," he smiled at me. Mr and Mrs Watson jumped up upon hearing his voice, leaving Jackie laid down on the rug.

"Son, oh my god where have you been?" Mrs Watson hugged him, and he hugged her back.

"I'm sorry, mum," and he squeezed her tight, "I've been getting my life back on track." Mrs Watson rubbed his cheek with her palm and squeezed his hand.

"You look really well." And he did, he was back to his normal weight, he stood tall and muscular, his scars had faded, his hair was thick and thrown into his side parting, and he was back in his RAF blues – he was a welcome sight. My heart hurt that he was no longer mine. All I wanted to do was run over to him, kiss him and never let him go. I collected Jacqueline from the floor and hugged her standing out of the way so Mr and Mrs Watson could have a moment with him and say their hellos to Staines. I felt like a stranger that should not be there, as if I was a fly on the wall watching a family behind closed doors. I spoke quietly.

"Mrs Watson, we can forget tonight if you like and I'll take Jackie back with me," I smiled.

"No dear, I want her!" She approached me and took Jackie from my arms. Without Jackie close by, I felt even more of an outsider. Mrs Watson took Jackie over to see Jack, he seemed nervous but beamed when she got close. "…and Nina said she's just started giggling," Mrs Watson explained.

"She's perfect," he beamed at her and reached out to grab her hand, that's the most contact he'd had with her since she was born. Staines noticed me stood alone with my arms folded, watching on, he approached me.

"How are you, Nina?"

"Oh, fine," I nervously laughed, "actually I was just heading off, so I will leave you all to it." Jack looked at me, why did his gaze always make me feel exposed, like his eyes were looking straight through me. I still loved him more than I'd care to admit, even to myself. I thought I was over him, but this confirmed I wasn't.

"Don't go on my account," he said politely.

"I was going anyway, the Christmas decorations await me," I laughed nervously, "nice to see you, you look well, h-have a good night." I kissed Jackie on the head and made for the exit. I heard footsteps behind me.

"Nina, wait a second," it was Jack.

"I was hoping to speak to ye', are ye' free right now?" he continued.

"Sure," I felt uncomfortable yet hopeful.

"Shall we go in there?" and he pointed to the dining room, and walked through, I followed.

"How have ye' been?" he asked, genuinely interested.

"Oh, you know, so so," I wasn't going to lie, what was the point. "And you?"

"I am great…now," he seemed so positive, like a version of Jack I had never seen before, it was endearing, it made me love him even more.

"Nina, I am going to be frank with ye', I've been in therapy, completely re-evaluating my life, working through my demons, as it were, and I have come out a stronger, better man. I like where I am at the moment," he rubbed his forehead, gearing himself up to say the next sentence. "I wish it was different but my feelings towards ye' still haven't changed," he placed some paperwork on the table. "I'm sorry." it was the divorce papers, my heart broke again, why did he keep doing this to me? What did I expect though, I nearly slept with his brother, and was the least understanding wife I could have been when he returned, I made it about me, it was what I deserved, he was always too good for me. He continued not giving me chance to respond, "I was hoping ye' would let me be a part of Jacqueline's life still. I want to be the best dad I can be, and I've got some making up to do!" he half smiled. I choked back tears, I was not going to cry, I didn't want him to know I was bothered.

"That's fine," I smiled falsely. I could barely speak due to the lump in my throat, he saw tears in my eyes and observed me, I could see he felt sorry for me, I didn't want his pity. I collected the divorce papers from the table. "I would never stop you seeing your daughter, and I will get these back to you straight away," I held them up. "Please excuse me," I walked past him out of the dining room and out of the house, into the freezing snow, I could finally let the tears out, and they did not stop on the walk home.

I entered the house, I wasn't in the mood to put up the decorations anymore, instead I got out some wine from the fridge and poured myself a giant glass, just watching the papers. I had stared at them a good hour, before I located a pen and just signed, leaving them out on the table. I went up to bed; I was done with today, if he wanted a divorce, he could have one, I had no fight left in me anymore.

Knock knock knock – that was a loud bang, *knock knock knock,* it banged again, oh, it was the door. I lifted my head from the pillow, ouch; I had such a terrible headache. I looked around my room and noticed two empty bottles of wine, oh yes that will explain it. I clambered out of bed and brushed my teeth, washed my face, and clinked the bottles downstairs, quickly disposing of them in the bin. The knocking had stopped but I saw silhouettes outside through the glass panel in the door, there looked to be a large group of people; I was not in the mood for company. I opened the door, and there stood Mr and Mrs Watson, Jack, Staines and Jacqueline in the pram, I didn't want to see *him* today.

"Dear, it's 1pm is everything okay? I was expecting you for 11am!" Mrs Watson sounded panicked. I looked at the clock, oh shit I had well and truly slept in.

"I thought you were doing the decorations?" she pushed herself in with the pram, as I stood aside.

"I got side-tracked," I didn't look at Jack; he probably thought I looked a state, oh well, he doesn't care anymore. Mrs Watson got Jackie out of the pram and put her on the rug.

"She's been as good as gold for daddy," she smiled at Jack, "hasn't she Jack?" He smiled at me awkwardly.

"Fabulous," I feigned a smile. Mrs Watson approached the table and saw the papers opened up, on the table.

"Are you two getting a divorce?" she shrieked. Mrs Watson looked at Jack.

"Mum," he tried to speak but she cut him off, "Jack, what about that little girl? She needs a loving family." I wanted this to end.

"She's got one, Delilah, it just doesn't involve me and Jack being together," I rarely called her that, but she wasn't just Mrs Watson now, she was no longer my mother-in-law, she was Jackie's grandmother and that was all. I walked over to collect the papers, folded them up and passed them to Jack, with force.

"All signed for you. Now if you don't mind, I want to be with alone with Jackie, I will ensure that I drop her off at your mum and dad's so you can collect her from there when you want to see her," I looked at Jack with no emotion. He nodded.

"Thanks, I am sorry, Nina," and he left the house, followed quietly by the rest of them.

Christmas was a quiet one this year, there didn't feel like much to celebrate, but I made it as special for Jacqueline as I could. We went back to Lincolnshire to celebrate with dad and Faye, and I made my way back home on Boxing Day so the Watsons could spend the day with Jackie.

I needed to get used to being alone again. The coming months were strange, I saw less and less of Mr and Mrs Watson due to the agreement myself and Jack had made where we would drop Jackie off with them for the other to collect her. We were trying to avoid all contact, or at least I was, it was too difficult seeing him. It had been six months since I signed the papers, and I had not seen him since and I had heard nothing about the divorce, I had never been divorced before so wasn't sure what I was meant to hear in all honesty.

It was coming up to Jackie's first birthday, and Mrs Watson had asked if she could throw an elaborate party for her at her house. The day was about Jackie, so I agreed, I was not sure if I was even invited. Mrs Watson did parties properly, this was going to be a grand affair, I had overheard her hiring white doves, it would make the Royal parties look dull. The invites had stated, *'Wear your best evening wear to celebrate my Granddaughter's first birthday in style'*; I was actually looking forward to getting dressed up. I had started my first attachment with a mental health charity for my degree, and I had met someone. It was early days, and I was biding my time, there would be no leaps of faith with this one. He was called Jude and was a fellow counsellor, he was kind and not like a man I had dated before. He was so happy with life, not a single thing seemed to get him down and I needed that energy. He had not met Jackie yet, and I had no intentions of him doing so anytime soon.

The day of the party arrived. I dressed Jackie up in a beautiful lilac, frilly dress with a matching bow, she looked like a princess. I approached the house, feeling extremely nervous, there were many cars parked on the drive and the road, I couldn't believe that this many people had come for her first birthday; I felt so happy for her. I had picked the most striking crimson dress to wear, it flowed at the back like a waterfall, and it had a gorgeous diamanté clasp across the bosom - I felt like a model wearing it. My scarlet lipstick matched, and my hair was loosely curled, I wore some expensive perfume that Jude had bought me for my birthday and some beautiful diamanté earrings; I hadn't dressed up in what felt like forever. I knocked at the door, no one answered, Jackie was walking now so I held her hand as we strolled through the doors to the house.

"SURPRISE," the room erupted. Jackie didn't know what to do; she looked on wide-eyed at all the people gathered in the room, dressed in their prettiest frocks and suits. She clapped her hands in excitement; she was such a happy child. I looked around the room and didn't recognise many people. I saw Group Captain Staines, a few RAF soldiers, some local couples and their children from the village. Bobby stood at the back hiding himself, and stood at the front was dad, Georgie and Faye.

"OH MY GOD!" I squealed picking Jackie up and running to them, I had no idea they were coming. I threw my arms around Faye; I had never been happier to see her.

"What are you doing here?" I shouted ecstatically.

"Well, it's my niece's first birthday," she replied sarcastically.

"Mrs Watson, you sneaky thing," I said playfully.

"Actually dear, it was Jack who sorted it," he appeared from behind Mr Watson, my heart skipped a beat, after all this time he still had the ability to make me lose my breath.

"Hi Nina," he looked me up and down, "ye' look wonderful, ye' both do," he smiled.

"H-hi," I didn't know what else to say. "Thanks for bringing them down, Jackie will love it," I smiled sheepishly.

"Can I have a cuddle, and he held his arms out for Jackie," she reached forward for him immediately, it made my heart buzz with happiness, I had never really seen their bond before. The rest of the party was spent catching up with dad, Georgie and Faye and keeping an eye out on Jackie who was in her element. She was eating cake and ice cream, playing with the other children, and was amongst everyone who loved her; my heart could have burst with joy. Every so often my eye caught Jack's, I looked away immediately as it did, I was struggling with his presence, despite starting to court Jude, I couldn't believe I was still not over him. I was beginning to think I never would be. There was a tap at the door, everyone's spirits were so high, and today was just what I envisaged her first birthday to be when I was pregnant. Mrs Watson answered the door.

"Hi dear, what are you doing here?" Her voice seemed slightly high pitched, as though she was panicked.

"I thought I would swing by and say hello to the birthday girl," the voice replied, she sounded American. I looked over to the door where a skinny, Mediterranean looking woman stood. Her hair fell long to her bottom and was as black as ebony, her skin was tanned like well brewed tea, her lips as nude as my skin. She was heavily made up, and was attractive, in a cabaret girl sort of way. I wonder who she was. She walked into the packed room; she looked like a celebrity, with her eyes hidden behind black sunglasses.

"Who is that?" Georgie murmured, I followed this mystery woman's eye line, she was looking at Jack, of course she was, which red-blooded woman wasn't. He looked at me sheepishly but approached the anonymous woman. I continued to watch on, my heart broke as he leaned forward and kissed her, I shouldn't be looking but I couldn't process it, he had moved on already – how?

"What a wanker," Georgie muttered angrily - hers, Faye's and my eyes were fixated on them. Jack looked my way apologetically. They began to approach me; I wanted the ground to swallow me whole.

"You've got this sweetie," Faye whispered to me.

"Nina, this is Ivy, she is…" Jack tapered off. Bobby interjected.

"Ah you got my invite, Ivy…this is Jack's new girlfriend, Nina, that was quick wasn't it," Bobby got great delight in finishing that sentence. I nodded at her civilly.

"Hi," she replied back uninterested.

239

"Ivy, this is Nina, the mother of Jackie," Bobby said, loving every second. He was trying to punish me for how things were left.

"Oh," she seemed shocked, she looked me up and down, how dare she. She looked the complete opposite of me, what did he see in her?

"Come on let's go find Jackie," Jack began to move her away from where I stood.

"She's met Jackie?" I was furious.

"Yes, is that a problem?" he replied calmly.

"Well, I don't know her from the next girl, the decent thing you could have done would be to inform me that you've picked up a new woman."

"'Scuse me, picked me up," she punched back in her Yankee accent.

"What happened to 'I need to be alone, I need to sort my head out'? instead you just find some woman dressed like a burlesque dancer and introduce her to our daughter. I bet you were shagging her all along," the room fell silent.

"Nina, that is enough," Jack shouted.

"You're right it is enough, where is Jackie we are leaving?" The stare coming from Ivy could have cut me in half, but I didn't care, the whole day was now a wash out thanks to Jack, once again.

"Let's calm down, it's Jackie's birthday, Nina, why don't we get you a drink," Mrs Watson tried to be nice.

"You knew about her didn't you, both of you" I snapped back at her and Mr Watson. They both hung their heads and looked away guiltily. I shook my head, looking around at the room; all eyes were on me, how do I always play the fool. I bet he always had his sights on another woman, which is why he didn't try to make our relationship work. All the effort and heartache that I had put into the relationship was for nothing. He never even wanted me. Bobby looked on, pleased with himself, he had managed to take my heart and shatter it into smithereens. I had humiliated myself once again.

"I need to go," I whispered, I began to head for the door.

"Good riddance," I heard Ivy mutter. Why had he picked such a bitch, the old Nina wouldn't have stood for that, the new Nina won't either. I turned around and approached her quickly, she did not have time to react. I grabbed her long mane and dragged it down to the ground with force, her body came crashing down with it.

"Go on, Nina," I heard Georgie shout. She was the sort of friend you would want around you in a fight, not that I had ever done this sort of thing before. I approached the table of drinks, eyeing a chalice of red wine, I poured it with great pleasure, onto ivy's brilliant white, frilly dress.

"You are welcome to each other," I eyed Jack, with rage in my eyes, he had pushed me too far now. I collected Jackie, and with my family by my side, I walked towards the exit. Bobby found it hilarious, he laughed manically, and people around the room were whispering to one another, all eyes glared at me as I departed. Ivy stood up.

"You bitch, you really are a piece of work, thank God you got rid of that first baby because two spawns of you would be too much for this world," Georgie and Faye gasped. I stopped in my tracks, I turned back to face her, and began to walk towards her; a look of pure evil filled

241

my eyes. Jack walked towards me to block us both.

"Nina, please don't. Ivy, that is disgusting, how dare ye' say something like that," he was shocked with her; too little too late *Jack*.

"You are lucky that there is someone in the way of me and you right now, because you'd be fucking dead if there wasn't," and I walked off, mortified.

I had never acted that way in my life, now my dad knew the whole story about the abortion. I had humiliated myself in front of everyone I knew and cared about, I had ruined Jackie's birthday, and Jack had punched me in the heart…again. There was only one thing I could do now, and that was go back to Lincolnshire, where I should have gone long ago.

I heard nothing from Mr and Mrs Watson the following week, they knew they had upset me, but I think they were even more affronted that I had embarrassed them in front of all their friends and family; Mrs Watson was such a proud woman. I had to tell them about my plans for the future; they deserved an explanation as to why I was taking their granddaughter and Jack's daughter away and never coming back. I plucked up the courage, and approached the house, the memories came flooding back from the previous week, I wonder if that bitch will be here. I didn't care; my feelings towards Jack had shifted. I never thought he could be the man who would hurt me the way he had. I felt like our whole past was a lie, all the things he had said were deceits. I knocked timidly. Mrs Watson answered, she was surprised to see me.

"Nina, I didn't expect it to be you."

"I need to speak with you, is Jack here?" She looked

back into the house.

"Nina, please don't start with him again." I interrupted.

"I don't want to start anything, but I need to talk to you all, can I come in?" there was no sentiment in my tone; I just wanted to get the whole thing out of the way. The log fire burned, I was going to miss the peacefulness of Ruislip, back to the busy life of Lincoln, where the smell wouldn't be burning wood, it would be burning rubber. It was for the right reasons though; I needed to be with family, away from all the negativity. I entered the living room – Bobby and Mr Watson were sat at the table, they looked astounded to see me. Bobby had clearly wormed his way back in. I saw Jack sat on the window seat, to look at him hurt, I felt utterly betrayed, I needed to make this quick and as painless as possible.

"Would you like a drink, dear?" Mrs Watson asked, she was clearly not as mad at me as I had anticipated.

"No thanks, I just thought I would come and let you all know out of courtesy more than anything, that me and Jackie are moving back to Lincolnshire," I was blunt.

"What?" Jack stood up, "ye' can't take her away from me," he sounded in despair.

"I can, I am her mum, and although it upsets me to do it, there is nothing round here for me anymore. It is unfair of you to ask me to stay in a place where I don't belong," I looked around the room; their expressions were of pain.

"Nina, if this is because of Ivy…" I didn't want to talk about *her.*

"You aren't the man I thought you were, Jack, everything I have ever done has been for you. I can't do it anymore, I need to think of me and Jackie, and being round here is not working anymore. It is turning me into this miserable woman, and I aren't that girl." Mrs Watson began to sob, I didn't want to break her heart, she had been so kind to me, like the mother I never had. I sighed and looked to the floor continuing. "We are leaving tomorrow, I don't want the house, Jack so do with it as you please, move in with Ivy and have some more kids for all I care," I was being petty, but I wanted him to know how much he had hurt me.

"Me and Ivy aren't together anymore," my stomach fluttered; I wanted to know why but dare not ask.

"I don't care," I looked at him with no emotion, the way he had looked at me when he told me he no longer loved me. He looked out of the window, thinking to himself.

"Feel free to take Jackie tonight, bring her back by dinner tomorrow, and then we are going," I left the house. I felt like such an awful human being, but I was protecting myself, and it was about time I did. I walked home, taking in the view and the smell of the wonderful summer's day. My mind went back to the day in the barn, the peaceful serenity we had felt, where we told each other we loved one another. My eyes pricked with tears, who was I kidding, I was not over him; he will always be the love of my life. I had to pack and leave this all behind, now. I headed home and Mr Watson came and collected Jackie, neither of us spoke a word to one another. Faye and dad had made a start on the packing.

"Are you sure this is what you really wanna do sis?" Faye asked.

"I have no choice, I am going to be forever reminded

of what awfulness has happened since I moved here, if I stay. Me and Jack have been over since that day he walked out to war, I need to start again," I walked off to continue packing in another room, I needed some space.

Moving day arrived, it was nearing dinnertime, and I saw three figures walking towards the house through the kitchen door. There was a faint tap, and I opened it slowly. It was Bobby, Mr and Mrs Watson and Jackie, I looked for Jack, but he wasn't there.

"Can we wave you off?" Mrs Watson teared up, handing Jackie over to me.

"Sure," I replied and let them step inside the house.

"Jack couldn't come, he said goodbye," I rolled my eyes.

"I expected nothing less," I retorted.

"As much as I wish my brother hell after he came back and beat me to a pulp, he doesn't deserve this Nina, you are being unreasonable," Bobby defended.

"No, what is unreasonable is him walking out on me and his daughter, him asking for a divorce knowing full well I was irrevocably in love with him, him brandishing some harlot in my face and introducing her to my daughter without so much as a mention to me, her mother. I have sat back and always been the bad guy, I got rid of a baby, I took shit from Harry and was the whore. I let Jack walk away when I was pregnant with his child. When he didn't come home, you developed feelings for me, and you tried forcing yourself on me yet, I was the one who was served divorce papers and was left broken-hearted again. I caused a scene at my daughter's party because of his actions. I forever have to justify myself and I have had enough! It stops now." I put Jackie's coat on and loaded her into Faye's car; dad was following behind with my life possessions in a moving van. Mr and Mrs Watson kissed Jackie on the head and squeezed her hand.

"Bye bye," Jackie uttered. That was her first word, Mrs Watson squealed with delight.

"What a clever girl!" She began to sob and looked at me. I approached her.

"I am sorry it has ended this way, Mrs Watson, you have been so good to me, both of you have, but I need to go, I hope you can understand," I hugged her tightly, it was not her fault. They both stepped away from the vehicle and I got into the passenger seat, looking at the house, filled with so many mixed emotions. This was it, the end of an era.

Jack

I sat in the dark living room alone, with only my thoughts for company. Mum and dad had just taken Jackie back to Nina's. How had my life got back to being this complicated again, I thought I had turned a corner, but I felt myself slipping back into despair. When would I see my daughter again? Did I deserve to? I hadn't anticipated the effect Ivy would have had on Nina. In my mind she was over me, I know she had been courting someone, I thought that was what she wanted. I never really cared about Ivy, she was just a distraction from what I really wanted, and that was Nina. Nina and I seemed to have this way of not being able to communicate how we were really feeling, and now it was too late. Was it too late? I could maybe change her mind; tell her how I still feel about her. I had made up my mind. I ran to the door and flung it open and sprinted so fast I could barely breathe, I had to get there; I might still have time. I approached the house, panting, I was too late, the car was moving, I ran as fast as I could.

"NINA!" I screamed, but she did not hear me, my mum turned to face me, tears ran down her face.

"It's too late son." I crouched on the floor my head in my hands and took a minute to compose myself. I walked towards the house, creaking open the door.

"I want to be alone," I shouted to them. I walked in and closed the door behind me, sniffing the familiar scent of lilies and mahogany. All the memories came flooding back, sat on the veranda watching her gold wedding band sparkle in the sun, her little pot belly when she was first pregnant with Jackie, the last time we made love in our bed, I had so many plans for how our future would be. I crept up to the bedroom and pushed open the door. I hadn't been in this room in over a year, it was still the same as it was the last night I slept in that bed. She hadn't taken the furniture, but all her belongings, her clothes and perfumes were gone. The house felt ghostly, it was quiet and still. On the bed, I noticed an envelope. I approached it, and upon reading it I began to sob, it was the letter entitled, '*To my wonderful Wife Nina.*' The letter I had written before I died, the one she would have read knowing my fate. I opened it up, reading each line, over and over, why had I left it this long to realise what was right for us.

I sat alone, this time it felt like I was the one who had lost a spouse; I was now the widow.

Chapter 12

1945

Nina

"Our dear Channel Islands will be free tomorrow. Hostilities will end officially at one minute after midnight tonight, Tuesday 8th May…The war with Germany is therefore at an end…Long live the cause of freedom. God save the king!" A rapturous round of applause sounded throughout our living room; Churchill had announced over the wireless that the war was finally over. The war had become a reality for us in Lincoln since moving back, we had been hit numerous times and even had the great tragedy of a Lancaster Bomber crashing into a row of houses about fifteen minutes from where we lived. The world was no place for Jackie to grow up in, until today. We could all breathe a sigh of relief; the boys would be coming home, back to their families.

Georgie was overjoyed, she had given birth to a baby boy called Theo three months ago, he was the cutest bundle of joy and Jackie adored him. Georgie just wanted Sid home, and now she would get her wish. He was moving to Lincoln to be with her upon his return, he still hadn't met Theo so it would be the best welcome home gift ever. Faye had settled down with a man named Peter, he was a polite, quiet musician, just Faye's type. They had set up home close by and were planning to get married. Dad was happy; he had finally retired from his job in the mill and loved playing the doting granddad to Jackie. I was much happier here; everyone had moved on. One of my worries coming back was that I would see Harry and I did see him, just the once, but he blanked me after noticing Jackie, he obviously knew she was Jack's - that will do for me, I wanted to leave behind all that. Mr and Mrs Watson had Jackie every third weekend in the month, and she stayed Friday to Monday, but soon she would be starting school. Where had my little girl gone? Jack saw Jackie when she went to his parents; at least I think he did. Jackie told me tales of what she had done that weekend, but she rarely mentioned daddy. I had no idea what he was up to now. The day I left Ruislip I had seen him running towards the car, I nearly stopped, but for once I let my head rule my heart, and I have been happy ever since. I had heard that he'd met someone new and they were living together near Ashton, but it was on the grapevine through a friend of Sid's who was an RAF pilot. Once again, it hadn't taken him long, not that I was bitter. I had stayed single since leaving, I had no time for matters of the heart anymore, and my main focus was Jackie. Every relationship I had encountered brought me nothing but misery so I decided being alone would be wise. Jackie was due to go to Ruislip this weekend but Mr Watson had fallen and broken his ankle so could not drive. I had offered to take her and have a weekend to myself nearby. I deserved a little minibreak and what better way to celebrate the war ending.

We woke at 7am and set off on our journey, it was a warm summer's day, everyone who we passed seemed jovial, spirits were high and there was a buzz in the air, we were free, no longer would we have to fear bombs dropping on our homes and heads. I took in a deep breath, and started singing to Jackie.

"Pack up your troubles in your old kit bag and smile, smile, smile, while you've a Lucifer to light your fag, smile boys that's the style…" Jackie took over.

"What's the use in worrying, it never was worthwhile, SO!" we laughed, she loved that shouting bit. Never a truer song written. We arrived at the Watson household, and I unpacked her belongings, it had been a long time since I had been here, at least four years, the place had not changed at all. I knocked at the door and waited.

"Hello." Mrs Watson answered looking well, she had aged gracefully.

"Grandmaaaaa," Jackie shouted with glee. They embraced; Mrs Watson still doted on her.

"Come in dear, I have just brewed the tea," I entered, looking around the house, they had decorated the kitchen, but nothing more had altered. Mr Watson sat at the dining table, his leg in plaster.

"Oh dear," I winced, "how are you?"

"Fantastic, what is a broken leg when the war is over and we can all finally be at peace?" He shouted overjoyed. I laughed; it was as if everyone was drunk on elation. I sipped my tea, whilst Jackie ran around like a maniac.

"What are your plans then, dear?" Mrs Watson enquired.

"I don't actually know. Check into a B&B, maybe find a quiet pub, have a nice summer's walk, read a book, there's lots to do, just having some alone time will be greatly welcomed," I chortled.

"Where will you be staying?"

"I aren't sure, any recommendations?" Mrs Watson looked at Mr Watson, she was up to something, I could see it in her eyes.

"Well I aren't sure whether you know but that old barn near the RAF base has been converted into a B&B. I know it meant so much to you," that was thoughtful of her, but do I want to go back to a place from my past.

"I'll see," I sipped my tea. I was going to go, of course I was, she had planted the seed now, I was down here for the first time in four years, I wanted to see what it was like. We never talked about Jack when we saw one another; it was like this forbidden topic of conversation for both of us.

"I am leaving, Jackie," I stood and gave her a cuddle, "be good for gran and granddad and I shall see you on Monday." She kissed me and ran off without giving me another moment's thought. I laughed and bid farewell to the Watsons.

Right, to Biggin Hill it is, and I set off on my way. The fragrance of lavender pouring through my open window was exhilarating, the wind blew through my hair, I felt on cloud nine. I neared closer to Biggin Hill, I could see the planes circling the sky above the air base, they were obviously in mass celebration about our imminent liberty. I bet there was a huge buzz on camp. I took the sights in, briefly remembering what had occurred in those grounds, but I whizzed past it, today was about relaxation. I turned right just before the air base where I saw a cobbled road had been constructed; I drove down it, taking in all the familiar sights. I approached the dilapidated barn, it wasn't so decrepit anymore, it looked magnificent. The building was white brick with a thatched roof it looked quaint and had character. There was a beer garden in the rear, surrounded by baskets of rainbow-coloured geraniums and posies and the tall trees from the woods hung over it, making it enclosed, like it was in its own bubble. Pink roses lined the path towards the entrance, and I could still hear the gentle bubble of the babbling stream, it was beautiful - I would be lucky to get a room here tonight. I approached the entrance and walked into a small but bright, carpeted room, with a roaring log fire. I approached the reception desk and waited to be seen.

"Hello," a man with white hair greeted me.

"Hi, I know I am probably too late, but do you have any rooms available for a few nights please?"

"Are you Nina?" He asked, surprising me.

"Why yes, do I know you?"

"No, your room has already been booked in advance, by a Mr and Mrs Watson," he read off the sheet of paper in front of him. That is why she looked so sheepish, bless her heart.

"That is so sweet of her, yes that is me," I confirmed.

"It was the accent! Allow me to take your bags and show you to your room," I followed him, taking in the sights from each vast window on the staircase, I was going to be at ease here for a few days, I might never leave. The room was perfect; it was bright and airy, with lilies in the vase on the dressing table. A four-poster double bed was located in the middle of the room, and the view from my window was the stream, this will have been where Jack and I sat talking, where we made love, it had to be. I looked around, envisaging it as it once was. I felt a pang of sadness; I wonder how he is doing. I was so close yet so far.

"Your table is booked for 8pm, ma'am," the white-haired man said.

"What? What table?" I enquired.

"Your dinner for tonight, ready for 8pm, feel free to come down earlier and have a drink in the bar, courtesy of us," he smiled and left. I felt like I was being treat as though I was royalty, I could get used to this. I had a snooze to recharge my batteries and began to get myself ready for the evening meal. I wonder if people might think it sad to be dining alone, but I was overjoyed at having some me time and I did not care in the slightest. The bar was heaving, military personnel were stood waiting to be served, all were celebrating, waiting for midnight so they could shout hurray, no doubt. I made my way to the front and asked for a glass of white wine.

"Are you Nina?" How did these strangers seem to know who I was?

"Yes, how do you know?" Two soldiers stood next to me and stared on, they nodded their heads, when I caught them looking.

"You're famous here," the barmaid laughed.

"What do you mean?" she looked behind her and on the wall above the bar I saw the sign, carved in wood, it was the name of the establishment, 'Nina's Retreat'.

"Ohhh, Nina is quite a common name," I laughed.

"Nina Hughes?" she commented back, what was going on?

"I don't meant to sound rude but how do you know who I am, you are the second person today," she passed me my wine glass. The soldier next to me laughed.

"You are the woman from the photographs."

"What photographs?" I was beginning to feel as though I was in some alternate universe now; they were talking gibberish.

"That one, there's a few of them," and he pointed to the

wall, where sure enough an image of me on my wedding day, was placed in a glass frame. What the hell? I walked to inspect it further, gawping at it.

"You know who owns this place don't ya?" The soldier continued. I had no idea.

"No who?"

"Group Captain Jack Watson," my heart fluttered, I felt like I was going to have a heart attack, had Mr and Mrs Watson set me up.

"I didn't know that, no," I mumbled.

"It's nice to finally meet ya', we have been coming here for a year, such a beautiful place, Jack speaks fondly of the woman who this was built for."

"H-he comes in here?"

"Yes, he is only based at the air base, he will be along soon I would have thought, drinks are on him tonight he said, so we are expecting a shin dig. We need to celebrate being free!" He roared. "Do you not know him?" He continued.

"Not anymore," I replied sadly, downing my wine. "Can I have another one please?" The barmaid smiled and filled my glass. I didn't know if I was furious or curious, it sounded like he had been promoted. He had really made a go at things, I knew me leaving him behind was what he needed, more's the pity. I sat down in the corner, each passer by scrutinised me as they walked in, the bar was full now. I looked at my watch, 8pm – I didn't want to eat. I contemplated going to my room, but the inquisitiveness got the better of me, was he going to come in? What did he look like now? Why had he made this place in my memory? I approached the soldiers at the bar again.

"What happened to Group Captain Staines?" I asked

making idle chat.

"He got promoted," the soldier offered me a cigarette, I didn't even smoke, but took one, I needed something to take the edge off. "He'll probably be here soon too."

"Is Jack with anyone, do you know?"

"I thought he was with you?" He looked at me confused. I laughed.

"No not anymore, we were married but we got divorced," I had no idea why I was pouring my heart out to this stranger.

"He still wears a wedding ring," he replied.

"It's probably not for me, I signed those papers five years ago, haven't heard anything since."

"Then you are probably still married sweetheart, you would have had to go through the courts to divide up any assets, my cousin is a solicitor," he took a swig of his beer. Surely not! Married still, after all this time. That cannot be right.

"Why don't ya' ask him yourself," and he nodded towards the door. I turned round, and as clear as day there he was, stood magnificently at the door, decorated in more medals and a smarter uniform, he took my breath away as he had done all those years ago. His hair was lighter, his skin was more tanned, he looked youthful and so good-looking. I noticed the girls swoon for him as he entered; I felt a pang of jealousy. He noticed me immediately, his expression changed from beaming joy to shock, he had no idea I would be here, I could tell. His mum and dad had done this on purpose. We just gazed at one another, I felt like the whole room stared at us, they seemed to know our story, how could they not, it was draped all over this building. He lifted his stare from me briefly and addressed the room.

"Right, everyone. Tonight is about letting ye' hair down and celebrating our victory over the Nazi wankers!" The room erupted in a loud cheer. "Drink, eat and be merry, and at one minute past midnight, we can go outside and look up at the skies and thank our lucky stars that we made it, well done boys!" He looked at me, smiling "and ladies." A huge round of applause raptured through the room. He nodded for me to follow him; I did as was asked of me. He took me to an office down the corridor, and closed the door behind him; we were alone, for the first time in four years.

"I cannae believe it's you," he grinned, his dimply smile.

"Yep, it's me alright. Just so you know I had no idea when I came that this was yours. Your mum and dad booked me a room here as they have Jackie for the weekend, and it looked beautiful, so I stayed. I can leave if you want me to."

"I don't mind that ye' are here, what could be more fitting than ye' being here today of all days? It's the day of victory," he grinned.

"I hear you got a promotion!" I smiled back.

"Aye, I'm Group Captain now," he looked at his insignia.

"You deserve it, you gave everything to this job," and I meant everything.

"How are ye' keeping? Mum and dad keep me in the loop," he sat down at a desk and clinked two glasses out of a cabinet. He filled them with whisky and passed one to me, I accepted. He did not take his eyes from me for one second. He seemed different; he was more confident;

more sure of himself and assured in what he wanted.

"I am good. I continued my Psychology course and passed, I am a trained counsellor now, probably four years too late," I joked. He gave a small laugh.

"I am proud of ye', I bet ye' are an asset to them in that role." I smiled.

"I never ask Jackie, or your mum and dad but have you seen her much?"

"Of course, every time they have her, so long as I aren't working, obviously war stops for no one. I love seeing what she has grown into, she looks more and more like you every time I see her," he looked deep in thought as if he was remembering her.

"What is this place about?" I had to ask. He laughed.

"Well, this was our happy place, and ye' were my motivation to pick myself up and make a better life for Jackie. I wanted to remember ye'. Ye' have and always will hold a special place in my heart," he smiled sincerely.

"I can't believe this was the dilapidated barn where we made…" I tapered off.

"Aye, I remember it well," he grinned at me cheekily. "Ye' left that letter behind, and the last thing I read was I will meet ye' again at the barn with the babbling stream, and it stuck in my head. This has always been our place," he looked around at the walls. "I want to apologise for all the hurt I put ye' through, Nina. I'm sorry. I reacted terribly to the Bobby thing, and although I was struggling, I shouldn't have walked out on ye'. And Ivy, well I don't know what I was thinking there, except that I probably wasn't," he looked at me his eyes filled with sorrow.

"It is fine, it's all in the past now, we appear to both be in a better place," I raised my glass. "To freedom." He raised his glass back and we chinked them.

"Are ye' with someone then?" I knew that topic was going to crop up.

"No, I have given men a wide birth!" I laughed.

"Me too, plus I don't think I could have ever replaced ye' if I'd tried," his words hit me like a warm cloud, there was love there still, on both parts. There was a knock at the door.

"Come in," Jack called and in walked Staines.

"Oh, sorry I just wanted to...Nina?" He was surprised to see me.

"Hi sir," I smiled back familiarly.

"Well don't you look a sight for sore eyes," he complimented me. Jack looked at me.

"Yes, I never commented on how beautiful she looks tonight," his gaze made my stomach flutter, I felt shy, and began to blush. He looked away happy with himself.

"Can I help ye,' sir?"

"Nope just came to check everything was okay, but I shall leave you to it, catch you later," and he walked away closing the door gently behind him. Jack put his glass down and walked towards me, slowly.

"I have no right to do this, Nina, and I don't blame ye' if ye' retreat..." he moved the hair from my eyes, I inhaled deeply. He had me all over again, like the first time. I loved this man and no matter what I did or how much time I spent away from him, I would never stop loving him. He would always make me weak at the knees and capture me under his spell. He moved his face towards me, bringing his lips closer to mine, I felt like I should run, but I didn't want to, I had longed for the day he wanted me again, his lips met mine slowly and tenderly. He tasted of whisky; he smelled the same as before. His hands brushed through my hair, mine stroked the back of his neck, I was lost in the lust. The kiss ended, I felt flustered, but I wanted more. I didn't hesitate or say a word; I just took his hand and guided him to my bedroom.

"What does this mean?" I whispered sitting down on my bed.

"It means I love ye', I always have, and I always will," and he kissed me once more. We made passionate love in the same place we did those four years ago, each touch and kiss as wonderful as it first was. I had missed him with my whole being. We lay there in a sweaty heap cuddling, he held my hand tightly and stroked my arm, we gazed at one another, just drinking it all in. How after all this time was I back here, with my Jack.

"We are meant to be together, Nina, our future was mapped out for us, it's what ye' said back in that kitchen isn't it," he smiled. He was right, and deep down I had always hoped I was right. "I have a confession too, I never did anything with those divorce papers, so we are technically still married," he looked guilty, "I am sorry, I couldn't bring myself to complete it, I didn't want it to be the end."

"I don't care, Jack, all I care about is if we do this again that we make it work properly, for Jackie and for us, I love you, and have never stopped."

"It's a promise." He kissed me once more, a huge eruption of applause sounded downstairs.

"It must be midnight," the fireworks began to explode outside, "let's go join them," I smiled, stroking his face.

"No, I am right where I want to be, I have all I need right

here," and he embraced me tightly. Our love might have been war, but we had our victory at last. As the saying goes, 'Per Ardua Ad Astra' – through adversity to the stars.

Follow me on Instagram:

 ngnovels_

Printed in Great Britain
by Amazon

70111669R00156